SADLIER
VOCABULARY WORKSHOP
ENRICHED EDITION

NEW!
FOR
LEVELS D–H

2005

Level E

SADLIER
VOCABULARY WORKSHOP
ENRICHED EDITION

JEROME SHOSTAK

90's

SADLIER-OXFORD
Vocabulary Workshop
New Edition
With Online Audio Program

80's

2012

70's

60's

Powerful **NEW** features
enhance a 50-year tradition
of success.

WHAT'S STILL TRUE?

The new *Vocabulary Workshop: Enriched Edition* for Grades 9–12 maintains a high level of academic rigor, focusing on vocabulary development for high-achieving, college-bound students.

Time-proven list of 300 words found on standardized tests— organized in 15 units with 20 words each.

---

vocabularyworkshop.com: iWords) audio program 🖳 interactive word games

Definitions

Note the spelling, pronunciation, part(s) of speech, and definition(s) of each of the following words. Then write the word in the blank spaces in the illustrative sentence(s) following. Finally, study the lists of synonyms and antonyms.

1. abridge
(ə brij')

(v.) to make shorter
Travel by air _____ the time needed to reach far-distant places.
SYNONYMS: shorten, condense, abbreviate
ANTONYMS: expand, enlarge, augment

2. adherent
(ad hēr' ənt)

(n.) a follower, supporter; (adj.) attached, sticking to
The senator's loyal _____ campaigned long and hard for her reelection.
Before we c[...]
to remove a[...]
SYNONYM: (n.) dis[...]
ANTONYMS: (n.) o[...]

3

Antonyms

*Choose the word from this unit that is most nearly opposite in meaning to the **boldface** word or expression in the phrase. Write that word on the line. Use a dictionary if necessary.*

1. a **demonic** expression on the gargoyle's face _____

2. the social position of a **wealthy person** _____

3. showed laudable **temperance** at the buffet table _____

4. **initiated** talks between the warring parties _____

5. a **novel** approach to a familiar subject _____

Completing the Sentence

From the words in this unit, choose the one that best completes each of the following sentences. Write the word in the space provided.

1. Bands of _____ broke through the frontier defenses of the province and began to plunder the rich farmlands of the interior.

Words reviewed in several contexts and exercises lead to mastery.

> I've used *Vocabulary Workshop* for years. My college-bound students have great scores on the SAT!

WHAT'S NEW?

At Sadlier, we're listening to you and your students. We've studied the latest research and the Common Core State Standards. We've considered the latest technology. This valuable information culminated in this enriched edition of the leading vocabulary development program.

1 Aligns to Common Core State Standards for Vocabulary

2 Expands Vocabulary in Context

3 Deepens Vocabulary Understanding

4 Blends Print with Powerful Online Components

I can check out vocabulary words on my smartphone—anytime!

1 Aligns to Common Core State Standards for Vocabulary

C **Word Study**, a new five-page section, aligns to Common Core State Standards for Vocabulary Acquisition and Use and expands students' knowledge of vocabulary words with instruction and practice.

Learn and write with Idioms/Proverbs/Adages.

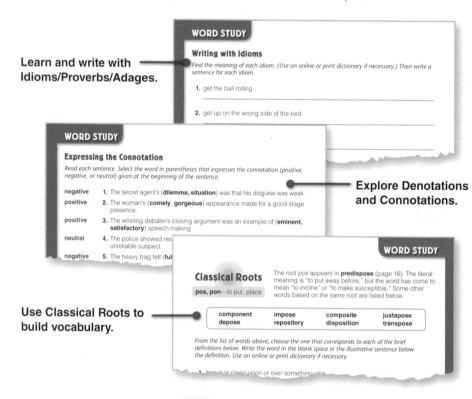

WORD STUDY

Writing with Idioms
Find the meaning of each idiom. (Use an online or print dictionary if necessary.) Then write a sentence for each idiom.

1. get the ball rolling

2. get up on the wrong side of the bed

WORD STUDY

Expressing the Connotation
Read each sentence. Select the word in parentheses that expresses the connotation (positive, negative, or neutral) given at the beginning of the sentence.

negative | 1. The secret agent's (**dilemma, situation**) was that his disguise was weak.
positive | 2. The woman's (**comely, gorgeous**) appearance made for a good stage presence.
positive | 3. The winning debater's closing argument was an example of (**eminent, satisfactory**) speech making
neutral | 4. The police showed res... unreliable suspect.
negative | 5. The heavy bag felt (**ful...**

Explore Denotations and Connotations.

WORD STUDY

Classical Roots

pos, pon—to put, place

The root *pos* appears in **predispose** (page 16). The literal meaning is "to put away before," but the word has come to mean "to incline" or "to make susceptible." Some other words based on the same root are listed below.

component	impose	composite	juxtapose
depose	repository	disposition	transpose

From the list of words above, choose the one that corresponds to each of the brief definitions below. Write the word in the blank space in the illustrative sentence below the definition. Use an online or print dictionary if necessary.

1. to put or place upon or over something else

Use Classical Roots to build vocabulary.

Vocabulary Workshop uses literary contexts and increasingly complex texts—just what the Common Core calls for.

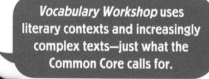

C **Aligns with Common Core State Standards.**

Expands Vocabulary in Context

NEW!

Reading Passages and Vocabulary in Context support Common Core State Standards for Reading Literature and Informational Texts.

UNIT 1

*Read the following selection, taking note of the **boldface** words and their contexts. These words are among those you will be studying in Unit 1. As you complete the exercises in this unit, it may help to refer to the way the words are used below.*

I'll Wait for the Movie
<Compare-and-Contrast Essay>

Cue scene: Middle-Earth characters Aragorn, Legolas, and Gimli leap off a ship, swords in hand, to **breach** archenemy Sauron's lines in the epic Battle of Pelennor Fields. This is a crucial moment in the movie version of *The Lord of the Rings: Return of the King*. Alas, the haunting showdown with the ghostly **brigands** does not actually occur in author J.R.R. Tolkien's books.

Film fans do not have to speak Elvish to enjoy director Peter Jackson's blockbuster *Lord of the Rings* (LOTR) trilogy. But do the movies do justice to Tolkien's enduring and popular novels? And is it possible for the LOTR purist to watch the films without cringing at every discrepancy? Readers are often disappointed with movie adaptations of their favorite novels. In fact, they might be **predisposed** to dislike any movie version. This is a perennial problem

for film directors, scriptwriters, readers, and moviegoers alike.

Filmmakers often **commandeer** the story and make it their own. Their motivation might be this cliché: "a picture paints a thousand words." They eliminate characters or events, or they add new ones. And authors can't complain: When they sell the rights to their work, they usually **relinquish** control. Filmmakers understand that their audience is **opinionated**, as evinced by LOTR fans posting online comments about Jackson's adaptation. Some claim that Jackson made a **muddle** of the books, that his tinkering is **spurious**, or that the films show only **spasmodic** flashes of greatness. Other fans show **unbridled** enthusiasm, saying that Tolkien's **perennial** classics are too long and **diffuse** and that the director's snipping

was essential. And some fans are more **circumspect** in their criticism, realizing that it is impossible to please everyone.

The **dilemma** facing filmmakers is that reading a book is a more interactive experience than watching a movie. A reader visualizes every scene in the book and decides what the characters look and sound like, what they wear, how their environs appear. For those who read the LOTR books first, the movie's Frodo may not resemble the Frodo they imagined. How can Peter Jackson's vision of Middle-Earth reflect the ones created in the mind's eye of millions of readers?

It is easy to imagine that moviegoers and readers are always **deadlocked** over which medium is better. Those who have read the book may come away from the multiplex disappointed: *The movie left out so much! Why was that memorable scene transposed to the beginning?* On the other hand, those who see the movie first may be awed by the director's imaginative retelling or by the stirring music and special effects. Most movies based on books retain key characters, scenes, and themes. Directors and scriptwriters strive to tell the same story and evoke the same emotions as the author of the original book. Both share an audience yet address one that is exclusively their own.

In the end, directors must rely on fans to accept the limitations of the movie. How is it possible for a two-hour movie (or even a sprawling movie trilogy) to include all of the details woven throughout a long novel? A movie that attempted to do this would end up unwieldy and **cumbersome**—a surefire way to disappoint moviegoers and book lovers alike.

Snap the code, or go to vocabularyworkshop.com

A poster for the first movie in director Peter Jackson's Lord of the Rings trilogy.

J.R.R. Tolkien's epic fantasy is one of the most popular novels of all time.

12 • Unit 1

Unit 1 • 13

Introduce vocabulary in context of informational text to activate students' prior knowledge.

Vocabulary in Context

Literary Text

*The following excerpts are from Sir Arthur Conan Doyle's novel The Hound of the Baskervilles, featuring the famous detective Sherlock Holmes. Some of the words you have studied in this unit appear in **boldface** type. Complete each statement below the excerpt by circling the letter of the correct answer.*

6

1. All day today the rain poured down, rustling on the ivy and dripping from the eaves. I thought of the convict out upon the bleak, cold, shelterless moor. Poor devil! Whatever his crimes, he has suffered something to **atone** for them.

To **atone** for something means to
   a. make up for it   c. repeat it
   b. be punished for it   d. be very hurt by it

2. Our conversation was **hampered** by the presence of the driver of the hired wagonette, so that we were forced to talk of trivial matters when our nerves were tense with emotion and anticipation. It was a relief to me, after that unnatural restraint, when we at last ~~passed~~ Frankland's house and knew that we were

Promote understanding of words with excerpts from canonical literature.

3 Deepens Vocabulary Understanding

Writing: Words in Action has students use the vocabulary words in an extended context. Two writing prompts allow students to demonstrate their understanding of new vocabulary.

The first prompt asks students to use the Unit words to respond to a question about the Reading Passage.

Writing: Words in Action

1. Look back at "I'll Wait for the Movie" (pages 12–13). How do the challenges of a filmmaker differ from those of an author? Write a short expository essay in which you explore how some of the major artistic decisions a filmmaker has to make differ from those a novelist has to make. Use at least two details from the passage and three unit words to support your understanding.

2. Do you prefer reading a book to seeing a movie, or do you think that movies tell a story in a more interesting way? In a brief essay, support your opinion with specific examples from your observations, studies, reading (refer to pages 12–13), or personal experience. Write at least three paragraphs, and use three or more words from this unit.

The second prompt is modeled after writing tasks found on standardized tests such as the SAT.

Students continue to deepen their understanding of vocabulary through **Vocabulary in Context** and **Word Study** sections.

> With *Words in Action*, my students are writing and using new vocabulary in context just like they do on standardized tests.

4 Blends Print with Powerful Online Components

Online Components reinforce print content and make the program more accessible for students. Extend learning beyond the classroom at vocabularyworkshop.com with:

- iWords Audio Program
- Interactive quizzes
- Interactive flashcards
- Interactive word games
- Additional practice

QR Codes (or Quick Response) are bar codes at point-of-use on student pages that link to selected online components when snapped with a smartphone.

I can snap QR Codes to listen to the *iWords* and take my quizzes.

iWords Audio Program

- Word pronunciations
- Definitions
- Examples

Interactive Quizzes

- Unit Reviews
- Immediate feedback

CREATING THE RIGHT BLEND
FOR YOU

Vocabulary Workshop seamlessly combines print and online resources, personalizing a blended approach for students and teachers.

Student Edition

Interactive Student Edition

Annotated Teacher's Edition

Professional Development

Test Prep: Blackline Masters

Online Components

20 online resources available for students and teachers

Assessment

Track students' progress with the Online Student Assessment System or printed Test Booklets.

vocabularyworkshop.com

ANNOTATED TEACHER'S EDITION

SADLIER

VOCABULARY WORKSHOP

ENRICHED EDITION

Level D

Jerome Shostak

Senior Series Consultant

Vicki A. Jacobs, Ed.D.
Associate Director, Teacher Education Program
Lecturer on Education
Harvard Graduate School of Education
Cambridge, Massachusetts

Series Consultants

Louis P. De Angelo, Ed.D.
Associate Superintendent
Diocese of Wilmington
Wilmington, Delaware

John Heath, Ph.D.
Professor of Classics
Santa Clara University
Santa Clara, California

Sarah Ressler Wright, NBCT
English Department Chair
Rutherford B. Hayes High School
Delaware City Schools, Ohio

Carolyn E. Waters, JD, Ed.S.
ELA/Literacy 6–12 Supervisor
Cobb County School District
Marietta, Georgia

Reviewers

The publisher wishes to thank for their comments and suggestions the following teachers and administrators, who read portions of the series prior to publication.

Rivkie Eisen
English Teacher
Ateret Torah High School
Brooklyn, New York

Jennifer Etter
English Dept. Chair
Shorecrest High School
Shoreline, Washington

Eileen Ghastin
English Teacher
John F. Kennedy High School
Bronx, New York

Sheri Goldstein
English Dept. Chair
Ida Crown Jewish Academy
Chicago, Illinois

Claudia Lefkowitz
English Teacher
Central Florida Preparatory
Gotha, Florida

Scott Leventhal
English Teacher, Dept. Chair
Council Rock H. S. South
Holland, Pennsylvania

Jeanne Pellegrino
English Teacher, Dept. Chair
Plantation High School
Plantation, Florida

Jennifer Portilla
English Teacher
Pace Brantley School
Longwood, Florida

Kausam R. Salam, Ph.D.
English Teacher-Dual Credit
Cypress Falls High School
Houston, Texas

Linda Schwartz
English Dept. Chair
Seaford School District
Seaford, New York

Patricia Stack
English Teacher
South Park High School
South Park, Pennsylvania

Barbara Swander Miller
Language Arts Dept. Chair
Cowan Jr/Sr High School
Muncie, Indiana

Stephanie K. Turner
English and French Teacher
St. Ursula Academy
Cincinnati, Ohio

Robert Viarengo
English Dept. Chair
Palma School
Salinas, California

Cover: Concept/Art and Design: MK Advertising and William H. Sadlier, Inc.; Cover pencil: Shutterstock/VikaSuh. **Photo Credits:** Blend/Jose Luis Pelaez Inc: T7 *right*. Corbis/Ian Lishman/Juice Images: T30. iStockphoto/alexsl: T7 *left*; Neustockimages: T1, T8 *center*; shapecharge: T3; sjlocke: T4. Ken Karp: T2, T6. Shutterstock/RTimages: T8 *right background*; vgstudio: T8 *right front*.

For additional online resources, go to vocabularyworkshop.com **and enter the Teacher Access Code: VW12TDJPK67P**

CONTENTS

ENRICHED EDITION: NEW FEATURES

Vocabulary Workshop has for more than five decades been the leading program for systematic vocabulary development for grades 6–12. It has been proven a highly successful tool in helping students expand their vocabularies, improve their vocabulary skills, and prepare for the vocabulary strands of standardized tests.

This Enriched Edition of Vocabulary Workshop preserves and improves key elements of the program that have made it so effective, *and* it introduces important new features that make the series more comprehensive in scope and more current in its approach to vocabulary instruction, especially with respect to standardized testing and the **Common Core State Standards** for English Language Arts.

QR Codes

QR Code

Snap the code, or go to
vocabularyworkshop.com

New QR (Quick Response) codes appear on the **Reading Passage** and **Vocabulary in Context** pages. The code can be read with a smartphone camera. To read the QR code, users may download any free QR code application to a smartphone. Snapping this code links students directly to the relevant Vocabulary Workshop Web site, where they can listen to iWords or take an interactive vocabulary quiz.

Use a smartphone camera and a QR code application to snap this code to link to the Vocabulary Workshop home page.

Reading Passages

New Reading Passages open each Unit of Vocabulary Workshop. At least 15 of the 20 Unit vocabulary words appear in each Passage. Students read the words in context in informational texts to activate prior knowledge and then apply what they learn throughout the Unit and the review, providing practice in critical-reading skills. Idioms, adages, and proverbs used in articles provide exposure to figurative language. Passage topics are high-interest and represent a variety of genres, including simulated interviews, blogs, diary entries, and newspaper articles, as well as expository texts, informational essays, historical nonfiction, and biographies. Snap the code or go to the Vocabulary Workshop home page to listen to iWords.

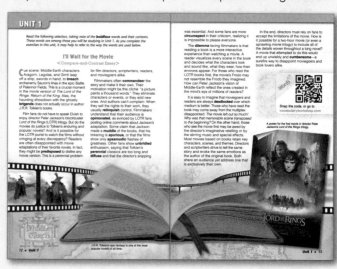

Writing Prompts

Students practice writing responses to two types of prompts. The first prompt refers to the Passage that introduced the Unit and encourages close reading of the text. The second prompt is modeled on those that appear on standardized tests, such as the SAT and ACT.

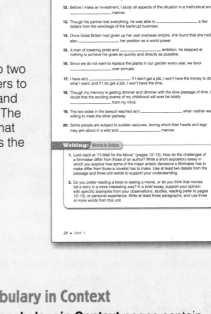

Vocabulary in Context

The **Vocabulary in Context** pages contain excerpts from classic literature. Each excerpt uses one of the vocabulary words from the Unit and provides students with exposures to the vocabulary in the context of authentic literature. Multiple choice questions give practice in standardized-test format. An interactive quiz using the Unit words is accessible by snapping the QR code on the page or by visiting **vocabularyworkshop.com**.

Word Study

In accordance with the Common Core State Standards, the **Word Study** pages address figurative language with instruction and practice using idioms, adages, and proverbs, as well as provide instruction on determining and applying denotation and connotation. This new section appears every three Units, after the Review.

VOCABULARY WORKSHOP
AND THE COMMON CORE STATE STANDARDS

The Enriched Edition of VOCABULARY WORKSHOP is aligned with and supports relevant and applicable standards contained in the Common Core State Standards for English Language Arts. The program is fully aligned with the Vocabulary Acquisition and Use standards and supports them with the kind of instruction, modeling, and practice that promote and cultivate corresponding vocabulary skills. Additionally, the Enriched Edition of VOCABULARY WORKSHOP addresses several Common Core Reading and Writing standards—in particular those associated with the role of vocabulary both in determining meaning and nuance within the broader context of reading, and in refining usage and expression in written and oral communication. (A full listing of the Common Core State Standards for English Language Arts is available at **commoncore.org**.)

In this Teacher's Edition, the Common Core State Standards addressed in the form of instruction and/or practice in any given section of the Student Edition are indicated at the bottom of the corresponding page or pages. The standards are identified in an abbreviated notation. For example, "CCSS Vocabulary 4.c, 4.d" indicates that the vocabulary skill or skills represented on that page support Vocabulary Acquisition and Use standards 4.c and 4.d. Similarly, "CCSS Reading (Informational Text) 4.6" is shorthand for Reading Standards for Informational Text 4.6, and "CCSS Writing 1.2, 2.d" stands for Writing Standards 1.2 and 2.d.

The full language of the corresponding Vocabulary, Reading (both Informational Text and Literature), and Writing standards for grades 9 and 10 is provided below. Note that in some instances, text is highlighted to show specific correlations between a particular skill and a more general standard. (A full correlation of the VOCABULARY WORKSHOP program to the Common Core State Standards is available at **vocabularyworkshop.com**.)

Common Core State Standards for English Language Arts

Language Standards
(Grades 9–10)

Vocabulary Acquisition and Use

4. Determine or clarify the meaning of unknown and multiple-meaning words and phrases based on *grades 9–10 reading and content*, choosing flexibly from a range of strategies.

   a. Use context (e.g., the overall meaning of a sentence, paragraph, or text; a word's position or function in a sentence) as a clue to the meaning of a word or phrase.

   b. Identify and correctly use patterns of word changes that indicate different meanings or parts of speech (e.g., *analyze, analysis, analytical; advocate, advocacy*).

   c. Consult general and specialized reference materials (e.g., dictionaries, glossaries, thesaureses), both print and digital, to find the pronunciation of a word or determine or clarify its precise meaning, its part of speech, or its etymology.

   d. Verify the preliminary determination of the meaning of a word or phrase (e.g., by checking the inferred meaning in context or in a dictionary).

5. Demonstrate understanding of figurative language, word relationships, and nuances in word meanings.

   a. Interpret figures of speech (e.g., euphemism, oxymoron) in context and analyze their role in the text.

   b. Analyze nuances in the meaning of words with similar denotations.

6. Acquire and use accurately general academic and domain-specific words and phrases, sufficient for reading, writing, speaking, and listening at the college and career readiness level; demonstrate independence in gathering vocabulary knowledge when considering a word or phrase important to comprehension or expression.

Reading Standards for Literature
(Grades 9–10)
Craft and Structure
4. Determine the meaning of words and phrases as they are used in the text, including figurative and connotative meanings; analyze the cumulative impact of specific word choices on meaning and tone (e.g., how the language evokes a sense of time and place; how it sets a formal or informal tone).

Reading Standards for Informational Text
(Grades 9–10)
Key Ideas and Details
2. Determine a central idea of a text and analyze its development over the course of the text, including how it emerges and is shaped and refined by specific details; provide an objective summary of the text.

Craft and Structure
4. Determine the meaning of words and phrases as they are used in a text, including figurative, connotative, and technical meanings; analyze the cumulative impact of specific word choices on meaning and tone (e.g., how the language of a court opinion differs from that of a newspaper).

6. Determine an author's point of view or purpose in a text and analyze how an author uses rhetoric to advance that point of view or purpose.

Writing Standards
(Grades 9–10)
Text Type and Purposes
1. Write arguments to support claims in an analysis of substantive topics or texts, using valid reasoning and relevant and sufficient evidence.

   c. Use words, phrases, and clauses to link the major sections of the text, create cohesion, and clarify the relationships between claim(s) and reasons, between reasons and evidence, and between claim(s) and counterclaims.

ENRICHED VOCABULARY APPROACH:
Systematic Vocabulary Instruction

The VOCABULARY WORKSHOP program focuses on the words, their meanings, their ranges of application, and their uses in context. The approach is systematic because it begins with and builds upon a word list drawn from vocabulary that students will encounter in their reading. It provides students with the vocabulary skills they will need to achieve higher-level reading proficiency and to succeed at standardized tests.

With the introduction of reading passages and literary text, the Enriched Edition goes further than previous editions in integrating vocabulary instruction in the context of reading. (For a discussion of the importance of vocabulary in reading comprehension, see pages T31–T32. For more on how VOCABULARY WORKSHOP can be used to complement a literature program, see pages T33–T35.)

A cornerstone of the VOCABULARY WORKSHOP approach is intensive practice through varied and abundant "hands-on" exercises. This method provides both exposure to different meanings of the key words studied and coverage of the range of each key word through its appearance in many different contexts. The aim of the pattern of intensive practice is to embed the words in the students' active, daily-use vocabulary.

Grade-Level Placements

The chart below shows suggested grade placement for each Level of VOCABULARY WORKSHOP. In determining proper placement of a particular Level, consider the following:

- Grade placements are based on teacher experience and recommendations.
- Differences in grade are reflected in the difficulty of the words presented, the maturity of the sentences, and other contexts in which those words are used.

Grade Placements			
Average Students		**Above-Average Students**	
Level	Grade	Level	Grade
D	9	D	8
E	10	E	9
F	11	F	10
G	12	G	11
		H	12

- Grade levels should not be taken too literally. Experimentation and the use of the program's diagnostic materials will establish the correct placement of a particular Level in a given situation.
- The use of Level H with above-average students is designed to enhance preparation for the SAT and other college entrance examinations.

Word Lists

Each Student Level presents 300 vocabulary words organized into 15 Units. Mastering these words will help students understand academic texts and increase their everyday language abilities.

For a discussion by Vicki A. Jacobs of the importance of academic vocabulary to reading comprehension, see pages T31–T32.

Criteria for Selection: The selection of **VOCABULARY WORKSHOP** words is based on four criteria: currency in and usefulness for present-day American oral or written communication; frequency on recognized high-utility and academic vocabulary lists; applicability to standardized tests; current grade-placement research.

General Sources: The lists of key words were developed from many sources: traditional, classic, and contemporary literature, including novels, short stories, essays, newspaper and magazine articles, plays, and films. Spelling and vocabulary lists recognized as valid bases for teaching language skills at the middle and secondary levels are used, as well as current subject-area textbooks, glossaries, and ancillary materials (especially for general, nontechnical terms).

Dictionary and Reference Sources: The following were the primary dictionary resources used for word (and definition) selection:

- *Webster's Third International Dictionary of the English Language* (unabridged)
- *Merriam-Webster's Collegiate Dictionary* (Ninth, Tenth, and online editions)
- *The American Heritage Dictionary of the English Language* (editions 1–4)
- *The Random House Dictionary of the English Language* (unabridged editions)
- *The Compact Edition of the Oxford English Dictionary*

Standard Word-Frequency Sources: Standard word-frequency studies were conducted to evaluate and revise the word list.

- *Primary* Dale-O'Rourke: *The Living Word Vocabulary*, Carroll-Davies-Richman: *The American Heritage Word Frequency Book*
- *Supplementary* Harris-Jacobsen: *Basic Reading Vocabularies*, Thorndike-Lorge: *The Teacher's Word Book of 30,000 Words*, Zeno-Ivens-Millard-Duvvuri: *The Educator's Word Frequency Guide*

"Sliding-Scale" Placement

Each word list works on a sliding scale based on the following principles: Any word that according to Dale-O'Rourke is known in a given grade is not presented in that grade. It is presented two or three grades earlier. Each grade level contains mostly words not known (according to Dale-O'Rourke) two or three grades later, with an admixture (in decreasing numbers) of words not known four or more grades later. The higher the grade, the larger the percentage of more difficult words contained in the word list. This ambitious approach accommodates as many "SAT-type" words as possible in the key word lists for Grades 10–12.

Professional development papers discussing the research supporting the instructional approach of **VOCABULARY WORKSHOP** may be found in the Teacher Center of **vocabularyworkshop.com**.

PRINT COMPONENTS

This Enriched Edition of VOCABULARY WORKSHOP, Levels D–H, consists of an integrated array of print and digital components. Print materials for each Level include:

- Student Texts
- Teacher's Annotated Editions
- Test Booklets with Combined Answer Keys (Forms A and B)
- SAT-Type TEST PREP Blackline Masters (answers included)

Student Texts/Teacher's Annotated Editions

Each of the five Student Texts (Levels D–H) presents 300 key words and is organized in the same way: 15 Units of 20 words each and 5 Reviews following Units 3, 6, 9, 12, and 15. Preceding the first Unit is a section on types of questions students will find throughout the program. Concluding each Student Text is a Final Mastery Test.

In the Teacher's Annotated Editions, answers are shown for each student page. Correlations to CCSS are also noted on page.

Reading Passages

New nonfiction Reading Passages open each Unit of VOCABULARY WORKSHOP. At least 15 of the Unit vocabulary words, as well as examples of figurative language such as idioms, adages, or proverbs, are used in each Passage. Students read the words in context to activate prior knowledge, and then they apply what they learn throughout the Unit and the Review.

Definitions

DEFINITIONS The definitions provided are clear, useful, and informal. The intent is to give students a reasonably good core idea of what each word means without extensive detail or secondary connotations. Generally, only a single meaning of maximum usefulness is given.

PART OF SPEECH Simple abbreviations give the part of speech with each definition. When a word functions as several parts of speech, the appropriate abbreviation appears before the corresponding definition.

PRONUNCIATION A simple set of diacritical marks presented at the beginning of every Student Text (inside front cover) indicates the pronunciation. Only one pronunciation is given for each word, except when a word changes its pronunciation in accordance with its use as different parts of speech (*ob´ject* and *ob ject´*).

Students may utilize the **Online** iWords **Audio Program** for each Unit. Available at **vocabularyworkshop.com**, this program provides nearly four hours of spoken material per Student Text, including pronunciation and examples of usage.

ILLUSTRATIVE SENTENCE Concluding each key entry is an illustrative sentence. These sentences provide a context that clarifies the meaning of each word. By writing the word in such contextual settings, students begin to see how the word can be used effectively in their own writing.

SYNONYMS AND ANTONYMS Each word has a list of synonyms and/or antonyms if there is one or more of either for the word. By studying the given synonyms and antonyms, students will better understand the denotational family of words of which each key word is part; and by comparing specific usages of key words and their synonyms, students can better appreciate appropriate contexts for these words. Note that the lists of synonyms and antonyms are not exhaustive.

Choosing the Right Word

In this activity, students choose one of a pair of words that most satisfactorily completes the sentence. Completing this activity requires a thorough understanding of a range of a word's definitions.

Synonyms and Antonyms

In this section, students read phrases that include synonyms or antonyms for the Unit words. Students must choose the Unit word that matches the given synonym or antonym. Besides reinforcing meanings, this exercise provides students with further examples of usage and context.

Completing the Sentence

This activity provides a simple completion exercise in which students choose and write the word that logically and meaningfully fits into a blank in a given sentence.

When using this activity in the classroom, the teacher should bear in mind the following considerations:

- The sentences in this activity call for the literal or direct (as opposed to the metaphorical or extended) meaning of the words involved.
- The sentences are designed so that only one of the words fits in the given blank. Context clues have been placed in each sentence.
- The words are to be used as the part of speech given in Definitions. The only exceptions are: Nouns given in the singular in Definitions may be plural in the sentences; verbs given in the base form in Definitions may be used in any tense or form (including participial) required by the sentence.

Writing: Words in Action

New prompts provide practice with writing responses to two modes of writing. The first prompt is in the form of a text-dependent question that asks students to respond to the Reading Passage at the beginning of the Unit. The second prompt is modeled on those that appear on standardized tests. Students write their responses on a separate sheet of paper. Teachers should grade the responses using a rubric of their choice.

Vocabulary in Context/Literary Text

This activity provides Unit vocabulary words used in classic literature, which:

- gives examples of usage for the selected words,
- offers an opportunity to derive meaning from context, and
- provides practice in the sort of vocabulary exercises found on standardized tests.

Refer students to Student Text page 7 for an introduction to the strategies involved in studying vocabulary in context.

Review

A Review follows every three Units.

- Vocabulary for Comprehension: This section is designed to help students prepare for the critical-reading sections of standardized tests. Students read a Passage and then answer vocabulary-in-context and comprehension questions related to the texts.
- Two-Word Completions: Students practice with word-omission (cloze) exercises that appear on typical standardized tests, including the SAT.

Word Study

A Word Study section follows every Review. Exercises include instruction and practice with figurative language and relationships in meaning:

- Choosing the Right Idiom/Adage/Proverb
- Writing with Idioms/Adages/Proverbs
- Denotation and Connotation/Shades of Meaning
- Building with Classical Roots

The Final Mastery Test

The Final Mastery Test in the Student Text is a practice test of 70 items that gives students and teachers fair insight into how much progress has been made during the year and what kind of additional work is in order.

The purpose of the Final Mastery Test is threefold.

- It can serve as a dry run in preparation for the more formal (and secure) tests available as optional components of this program.
- It can serve as an informal evaluation of achievement to date.
- It can serve as a reinforcement activity.

Test Booklets (Optional)

Two Test Booklets (Form A and Form B) may be used to reduce the risk of answers being passed on. Though the formats of the Test Booklets are the same, the items tested in any given section are completely different. The contents are: a list of the 300 tested vocabulary words; a Warm-Up Test; 15 Unit Tests, each consisting of 25 items focusing on pronunciations, parts of speech, spelling, definitions, synonyms, antonyms, and sentence completions; and 5 Cumulative Tests of 52–110 items each.

TEST PREP Blackline Masters (Optional)

The TEST PREP component provides practice with SAT-type test questions and formats and also with review tests covering the corresponding Student Text. Prep Tests approximate the word-omission sections of the SAT and provide practice in the vocabulary-in-context strand with brief reading passages as well. Answer sheets in SAT-type test format develop student ease and familiarity with standardized testing materials. Mastery Tests are used when students have completed the corresponding group of three Units in the Student Text. Each test covers basic meanings, synonyms, antonyms, and sentence completions. Answer keys, including selected answer rationales, are provided for all tests.

DIGITAL COMPONENTS

Digital resources for each Level are available at **vocabularyworkshop.com** and include:

- iWords Audio Program
- Online Interactive Games
- Vocabulary in Context: Informational Text
- Diagnostic Tests and Cumulative Reviews
- Professional Development Videos
- Interactive Quizzes

The components have been designed for use in an integrated year-long vocabulary program, as suggested in the chart on pages T24–T26.

PDFs of the following materials may be found online for each level and include:

- Correlations to the Common Core State Standards
- Vocabulary in Context: Informational Text
- SAT and ACT Practice Worksheets
- Additional Practice and Quiz pages for each lesson
- Greek and Latin Roots Reference Guide
- Diagnostic Tests and Cumulative Reviews
- Pacing Guides

DIGITAL COMPONENTS *cont.*

iWords Audio Program

The VOCABULARY WORKSHOP iWords Audio Program provides students with pronunciations, definitions, and examples of usage for all program vocabulary words and word meanings. Students can visit **vocabularyworkshop.com** to listen to each word or download MP3 files of the words.

- The audio program is ideal for English Language Learners (ELL) and ELL classrooms.
- Students hear the recommended pronunciation of each word at least six times and are given two opportunities to pronounce each word themselves.
- Pronunciations are followed by brief definitions and examples of the word used in complete sentences.
- For recommendations on when to use iWords program, see pages T24–T30.

Online Interactive Vocabulary Games

For each Level, students are provided interactive word games using the vocabulary presented in the Units. These activities include flashcards, crossword puzzles, word searches, "hangman," and Test Your Vocabulary questions. Additional Practice and Quiz pages including Interactive Quizzes provide more possibilities for academic assessment.

Vocabulary in Context: Informational Text

A Reading Passage that uses key Unit words provides another opportunity to read vocabulary in context. Each Passage is followed by multiple-choice questions for extra practice with nonfiction texts, the Unit vocabulary words, and question types found on standardized tests.

Diagnostic Test and Cumulative Reviews

- A **Beginning-of-Year Diagnostic Test** contains a sampling of words from the program to assess students' prior knowledge.
- After Units 3, 6, 9, 12, and 15, students can complete **Cumulative Review Tests**. Questions on Choosing the Right Meaning and Two-Word Completions provide practice on SAT-style questions. Activities on analogies and vocabulary enrichment are also included.

SAT and ACT Practice Worksheets

For teachers who wish to offer their students extra practice for the SAT or ACT, 45 standardized-test worksheets are available online for each Level. These practice worksheets are accessible only to teachers.

For each Level, there are 15 worksheets in standardized-test format for each of the following:

- comprehension and vocabulary skills assessed on the SAT and ACT,
- multiple-choice grammar and usage items included in the Writing section of the SAT and in the ACT, and
- step-by-step guidance in crafting a timed essay of the kind that is required on the SAT (and is optional on the ACT).

Teacher Resources

Available in PDF format:

- Correlations to the Common Core State Standards
- Pacing Guides
- Greek and Latin Roots Reference Guide
- Graphic Organizers

Online Student Assessment System (Optional)

The Web-based VOCABULARY WORKSHOP Online Student Assessment System allows teachers to quickly and easily create secure, interactive Unit practice and assessment pages that are automatically scored and provide students with immediate, prescriptive feedback. With a database of nearly 4,000 test items per Level, teachers have the option to individualize tests.

The Online Student Assessment System provides:

- the ability to create and edit question sets and tests,
- the ability to scramble answer choices and/or questions so that multiple versions of the same test can be administered securely,
- a wide assortment of question types: pronunciation, part of speech, spelling, definitions, synonyms, antonyms, sentence completions, sentence framing,
- preformatted Unit tests, ready for immediate use,
- a secure portal to assign practice/test pages, with the option to print these pages,
- immediate feedback on each question,
- a detailed end-of-assignment report to help you know exactly how students are progressing,
- the ability to track student progress through a comprehensive reporting system,
- a way to create detailed reports on class and individual student results, and
- the option to send practice/test pages and student results to learning management systems.

The VOCABULARY WORKSHOP Online Student Assessment System is a convenient and secure source of assessment and/or extra practice. The Online Student Assessment System is easy to use, either as needed or more systematically, as an integral part of the VOCABULARY WORKSHOP series. See pages T24–26 for recommendations on how it may be used in conjunction with the Student Text and other components.

IMPLEMENTING THE PROGRAM

VOCABULARY WORKSHOP not only provides vocabulary instruction but also teaches students a variety of other essential Language Arts skills. Teachers have many options for pacing VOCABULARY WORKSHOP'S activities to best meet the needs of their students and classes.

Overview of Weekly Vocabulary Instruction

The charts on pages 24–26 offer multiple ways to provide consistent vocabulary instruction to high-school students. Both the weekly schedule charts and the daily activity charts offer specific methods to integrate VOCABULARY WORKSHOP into the Language Arts classroom. Schedules among districts vary greatly, however, so the program methods suggested provide ideas that each teacher can tailor to ensure success within his or her own classroom.

Weekly Schedule

Week	Student Text	Suggestions for Implementing the Program
1	**Beginning-of-Year Diagnostic Test**	When reviewing the Beginning-of-Year Diagnostic Test, available at vocabularyworkshop.com, encourage students to use the words in their writing and speaking, not just to recognize meaning.
2	**Unit 1**	Start by reviewing the Unit 1 words through the Reading Passage. Implement a focused study of four words each day with students (see "Suggestion for Studying Four Words a Day" on page 27). Complete VOCABULARY WORKSHOP activities in the book and online (see the "How to Use VOCABULARY WORKSHOP Exercises" charts on the following pages). Examine Best Practices on pages 28–30 for further vocabulary activities. Testing Options: Assign Unit 1 Test from test booklets or from the Online Student Assessment System.
3	**Unit 2**	Follow procedure for Unit 2 as shown in Unit 1. Testing Options: Assign Unit 2 Test from test booklets or from the Online Student Assessment System, and review Unit 1 Test to encourage deeper recall of all words.
4	**Unit 3**	Follow procedure for Unit 3 as shown in Unit 1. Testing Options: Assign Unit 3 Test from test booklets or from the Online Student Assessment System, and review Units 1–2 Tests to encourage deeper recall of all words.
5	**Review Units 1–3**	Complete Review Units 1–3 activities, and ensure knowledge of all 60 vocabulary words as well as the mastery of other essential English skills. Mastery Test Units 1–3 available as Test Prep Blackline Masters.

Continue with the above pattern for weeks 2–5 for the rest of the year, having students complete the Final Mastery Test for Units 1–15 at the end of the year.

For Each Unit

How to use VOCABULARY WORKSHOP Exercises & Online Activities with Three Sessions/Periods

Assignment	Day 1	Day 2	Day 3
Class work	**1.** Review previous Unit's test results. **2.** Review word meaning and usage in context in the Unit's Reading Passage. **3.** Present any words not used in the Reading Passage.	**1.** Review Choosing the Right Word, Synonyms, and Antonyms. **2.** Assign Writing: Words in Action Prompt 1 and/or 2. **3.** Assign SAT/ACT Practice Worksheets at **vocabularyworkshop.com**.	**1.** Review Vocabulary in Context: Literary Text. **2.** Assign the Unit Test (Test Booklet or Online Student Assessment System).
Homework	**1.** Have students download and listen to iWords. **2.** Assign Choosing the Right Word, Synonyms, and Antonyms. **3.** Have students play online Unit games.	**1.** Assign Vocabulary in Context: Literary Text. **2.** Have students play online Unit games. **3.** Assign Interactive Quiz.	Have students read the next Unit's Reading Passage.

How to use VOCABULARY WORKSHOP Exercises & Online Activities with Five Sessions/Periods

Assignment	Day 1	Day 2	Day 3	Day 4	Day 5
Class work	**1.** Review previous Unit's test results. **2.** Review word meaning and usage in context in the Unit's Reading Passage. **3.** Present any words not used in the Reading Passage.	**1.** Review Choosing the Right Word. **2.** Assign online SAT/ACT Practice Worksheets.	**1.** Review Synonyms and Antonyms and also Completing the Sentence. **2.** Assign the first prompt for Writing: Words in Action.	**1.** Share excerpts (with vocabulary usage) from Writing: Words in Action. **2.** Assign Vocabulary in Context: Literary Text.	Assign Unit Test (Test Booklet or Online Student Assessment System).
Homework	**1.** Download and listen to iWords. **2.** Assign Choosing the Right Word.	**1.** Assign Synonyms and Antonyms, and also Completing the Sentence. **2.** Have students play online Unit games.	**1.** Assign the second prompt of Writing: Words in Action.	Assign online interactive quiz.	Have students read the next Unit's Reading Passage.

For Review Units

How to use VOCABULARY WORKSHOP Review Exercises & Online Activities with 3 Sessions/Periods

Assignment	Day 1	Day 2	Day 3
Class work	**1.** Review previous Unit's test results. **2.** Complete Vocabulary for Comprehension. **3.** Present Word Study Idioms/Adages/Proverbs.	**1.** Review Two-Word Completions and Word Study Idioms/Adages/Proverbs. **2.** Present Word Study Denotation/Connotation.	**1.** Assign Mastery Test (Test Prep Blackline Masters). **2.** Review Word Study Denotation/Connotation. **3.** Present Building with Classical Roots.
Homework	**1.** Assign Two-Word Completions. **2.** Assign Word Study Idioms/Adages/Proverbs.	**1.** Have students finish Word Study Denotation/Connotation. **2.** Have students play online Unit games.	Have students read the next Unit's Reading Passage.

How to use VOCABULARY WORKSHOP Review Exercises & Online Activities with 5 Sessions/Periods

Assignment	Day 1	Day 2	Day 3	Day 4	Day 5
Class work	**1.** Review previous Unit's test results. **2.** Assign Vocabulary for Comprehension.	**1.** Review SAT/ACT Worksheets and Two-Word Completions. **2.** Present Idioms/Adages/Proverbs.	**1.** Review Idioms/Adages/Proverbs. **2.** Present Denotation/Connotation.	**1.** Review Denotation/Connotation. **2.** Present Building with Classical Roots.	Assign Mastery Test (Test Prep Blackline Masters).
Homework	**1.** Assign online SAT/ACT Practice Worksheets. **2.** Assign Two-Word Completions.	**1.** Assign Idioms/Adages/Proverbs. **2.** Play online Unit games.	**1.** Assign Denotation/Connotation. **2.** Have students play online Unit games.	Review Building with Classical Roots.	Assign the next Unit's Reading Passage.

Implementing the Weekly and Daily Schedules

The following may prove helpful when adapting the foregoing schedules to specific situations.

- Students need to recognize the value of learning vocabulary and completing the vocabulary exercises. Simply assigning words and the exercises for class work or homework does not provide intrinsic value for those who are learning new vocabulary. Teachers should model vocabulary usage and encourage students to learn the words to improve their speaking, writing, reading comprehension, and test scores (see "Best Practices" T28–T30 for suggestions).

- The teacher may adapt the models shown to the situation at hand.
- Activity order and timings are to some extent hypothetical. Teachers may switch items around and adjust timings as needed. Similarly, items may be modified or deleted.
- VOCABULARY WORKSHOP Units may also be adapted so that only 10 words are studied each week. The Online Student Assessment System allows teachers to easily create quizzes for the first or second 10 words of a Unit, if desired. Students completing the exercises in VOCABULARY WORKSHOP can either wait until the second week to work on the activities, or they can identify the words they know and complete only those blanks that relate to the week's words being studied.

Suggestion for Studying Four Words a Day

Each day, teachers may project or write the four vocabulary words of the day in contextual sentences. Students should identify each word's meaning and part of speech through context clues; students can then create their own flashcards or charts that can be used as a study aid. By focusing each day's study on specific words, students can break down their learning into manageable chunks of information.

Student Study Guides

When students employ a review system for their vocabularies, they tend to learn the words and their meanings more thoroughly. Students may create flashcards or a vocabulary chart as two simple review methods. However, what students write down on their flashcards or charts may vary among learning styles.

For Basic Vocabulary Learners: Students should write the vocabulary word on one side of a flashcard (or in the first chart box), then a mnemonic device, synonym/brief definition of the word, and a short, student-created phrase incorporating the word on the back of the flashcard (or in chart boxes two, three, and four). Students then review by looking only at the word side of the flashcard or the first column of the chart (folding the paper so the other information is behind the first column) and seeing if they can remember the mnemonic device or phrase that enables them to recall the word's meaning.

For Kinesthetic Learners: Students may create a motion that goes with a vocabulary word definition when possible. Students then write the word on one side of a flashcard (or in the first chart box), then the motion and a synonym/brief definition on the back of the flashcard (or in the second and third chart boxes). Students may review by looking only at the word side of the flashcard or first column of the chart (folding the paper so the other information is behind the first column) and seeing if they can recall first the motion, then the word's meaning.

For Visual/Artistic Learners: Students draw a picture that goes with each vocabulary word definition. Students may write the word on one side of a flashcard (or in the first chart box) and then draw the associated picture and write the synonym/brief definition on the back of the flashcard (or in the second and third chart boxes). Students then review by looking only at the word side of the flashcard or first column of the chart (folding the paper so the other information is behind the first column) and seeing if they can recall first the drawing, then the word's meaning.

For Auditory Learners: In addition to the Basic Vocabulary Learner review sheet, teachers may strongly encourage these learners to review iWords on a daily basis to recall definitions.

BEST PRACTICES FOR USING VOCABULARY WORKSHOP IN THE CLASSROOM

Classroom experience and research have shown that repeated exposure to and application of vocabulary words embed meaning in students' minds. The more teachers and students utilize vocabulary in the Language Arts class period, the more likely students are to understand and use new vocabulary themselves.

Classroom Environment

Depending on the reading proficiencies of their students, teachers may differentiate and/or scaffold instruction to accommodate varying learning styles and backgrounds—for example, by reading aloud or having students read aloud the passages that introduce the Units.

To encourage students' use of vocabulary, teachers may post vocabulary words in the classroom—on bulletin boards, walls, or chalkboards/whiteboards.

Students and teachers may bring in examples of vocabulary from print sources to be displayed in the classroom. Additionally, students may create visual representations or drawings of vocabulary words that can be posted in the classroom.

Recognition of Vocabulary Discovery and Usage

Students may share experiences in which they hear or use vocabulary outside of the classroom. Whether it is another teacher who said a vocabulary word, a television show or movie that incorporated vocabulary, or the student him- or herself who embedded a word in an assignment, it is important to recognize the use of academic vocabulary.

For students who repeatedly find or use vocabulary outside of the classroom, recognize their achievements with points toward a class competition goal or other acknowledgment of their efforts.

Daily Discussion and Review

Teachers may model vocabulary usage by including vocabulary words in their instructions or conversations with students. The more frequently the teacher uses a word, the easier it becomes for students to understand the word's meaning and how to use it properly.

Teachers can have "Words of the Day" that students must incorporate into classroom activities. Whoever correctly uses the words the most might receive a reward.

During debates, discussions, or other times when students are conversing, teachers should require them to use the learned vocabulary words. A set minimum number of words can be established, and students who go above the minimum should be recognized for their efforts.

When there is extra time, the class may review vocabulary words. This activity can be teacher-directed or student-led. If student-directed, begin with one student saying a vocabulary word, then select another student to define it. Once he or she defines the word, that student can then select a new word that another student defines, and so on.

Categorizing Vocabulary

When reviewing vocabulary words, students may categorize words as they relate to current events. By creating meaningful associations with each word, students more easily recall word meaning.

Students can also learn vocabulary by creating more general categories. These categories can be as simple as "praise" or "insult" or as elaborate as students want (travel words, food words, etc.). When students learn new words, they can place them in the categories they have created.

Writing with Vocabulary

Students should incorporate at least one or two vocabulary words into their daily writing prompts, reading journals, or other forms of informal communication.

Whenever students write formally for class (essays, stories, etc.), teachers may require a set minimum number of vocabulary words to be used, check to make sure that the usage is appropriate, and provide feedback.

Teachers may also:

- Have students create puns that incorporate vocabulary. Example: "I have no fear," Tom said **unflinchingly**.
- Ask students to write poems for individual words. Example: "There once was a word called ____."
- Suggest that students write an acrostic poem that defines a word from the Unit.
- Ask students to write a "Where I'm From" poem that explains both a word's origins and use, and that also traces its genealogy to related words.
- Have students write myths about the origins of individual words or groups of words.

Vocabulary Projects

Students may create advertisements for a word to "sell" its uses. Example: "Race to your local dictionary and pick up the word ____. Whether frustrated with your social life or unhappy with a school assignment, this word can be used in a variety of ways…" Alternatively, teachers may have students sell a product, but have them use as many vocabulary words as possible to describe the attributes of the item.

Students often learn words best when setting them to music. Students may write lyrics incorporating all (or most) of a Unit's vocabulary words/definitions and then perform or record their finished products.

Vocabulary Games

Groups of students can act in skits or pantomimes that demonstrate a word's meaning; the rest of the class must guess the word being enacted.

Student groups may tell stories using vocabulary words. Groups should be created according to the ability and level of students.

Alternative Assessment

The following types of assessment may be used in addition to or in lieu of the objective-scoring materials provided in VOCABULARY WORKSHOP, Levels D–H.

- Teachers may have students write a story or essay incorporating vocabulary words (word list provided by the teacher).

- Teachers can write a series of true/false statements, each concerning a vocabulary word, and then have students decide whether the statements are true or false based on their understanding of the words.

- Students can use vocabulary words in conversations throughout the week. Students may either write down their statements or collect signatures from peers or adults who heard the student using each word. Students turn in their sheets at the end of the week for an assessment grade.

- Teachers should consider using a suggestion from "Writing with Vocabulary" or "Vocabulary Projects" as a final assessment.

ACADEMIC VOCABULARY AND READING COMPREHENSION

by Vicki A. Jacobs
Senior Series Consultant

As students advance into the high-school grades and reading becomes more and more a matter of comprehending the concepts that represent relationships among facts and information, learning the academic vocabulary that represents those concepts becomes more critical to comprehension.

For example, to understand the vocabulary of literature—plot, characterization, imagery, theme—students must read to understand more than a narrative's simple sequence of events. They need to apply their understanding of the concepts that such vocabulary words represent. They need to know how to inquire about why an author chooses particular events and how an author uses characterization, imagery, and plot to develop a thematic statement.

Similarly, comprehension of content-area text requires more than the location of specific information; it also requires an understanding of the concepts that represent relationships among facts. Successful readers make conceptual connections among facts by activating and organizing relevant background knowledge and experience that they have gained from real-word experience and previous reading (the "given") and then use this foundation as the context for the "new" information and concepts that the text offers.

Comprehension then becomes a complex matter of confirming the relationship between the "given" and "new" and of resolving the differences. Successful readers skillfully identify the relationships among facts and information, analyze and synthesize often conflicting facts and points of view, and test the validity of what they have comprehended and thus learned.

To comprehend increasingly sophisticated content-specific texts, high-school students need to be able to draw upon their knowledge of three kinds of vocabulary.

The first is the language of their everyday experience, often called the "given" of what students bring to a text. The second is the academic language that content areas share (e.g., argument, persuasion, analysis, synthesis, comparison, and contrast). The third kind of vocabulary includes the specialized meanings that content areas assign to more general academic language (e.g., *conflict* and *resolution* represent different concepts in the study of literature and in the study of history), and it also includes discipline-specific concepts (e.g., *allegory, mitosis, sine, colonialism*).

Vocabulary also plays an integral role in the cognitive processes that are characteristic of inquiry-based learning and reading comprehension. Such processes involve three instructional stages: preparation, strategic guidance, and consolidation of learning, as described on the following page.

Stage I:

Preparation for Learning/Reading

Teachers:

- provide the means by which students can activate, extend, and organize their background knowledge and experiences that will be relevant to learning new concepts and the vocabulary that represents those concepts; and
- explain how students' background knowledge and experience will be relevant to understanding a lesson or a text's central concepts and vocabulary.

Stage II:

Strategic Guidance of Learning/Reading

Teachers facilitate students' inquiry/comprehension by providing the means by which students can:

- investigate, enrich, deepen, and revise their understanding of a reading's central concepts and key vocabulary; and
- practice new skills, including vocabulary.

Stage III:

Consolidation of Learning/Reading

Teachers provide students with the means to consolidate their learning and comprehension by:

- providing the means by which they can test the validity of their understanding (comprehension) of new concepts and vocabulary; and
- preparing students to demonstrate their understanding (comprehension) through the application of new concepts and vocabulary to novel contexts.

Above all, the comprehension and vocabulary strategies teachers use must explicitly support their teaching goals, which can span from memorization of facts and information to deep understanding and skilled application of abstract concepts. Strategies for memorizing vocabulary or reading-for-facts are different from strategies designed to support students' deep comprehension and understanding.

Further, students need to understand how to use various strategies as ways to achieve particular learning goals—as well as *why* such strategies are important. One of the biggest differences between successful and struggling adolescent readers is their different approaches to learning. Skilled students monitor their progress in their attempts to achieve learning goals, recognize when learning or comprehension has broken down, and choose the most expedient strategy to correct their course. To become skilled in this way, students need not only instruction in reading strategies but also in direct instruction about how to employ those strategies as well as why and when those strategies are most useful. In other words, students need to be taught explicitly how to learn independently if they are to become ongoing students of an academic discipline and to graduate from high school—or, to adopt the language of the Common Core State Standards, to be "college and career ready."

CLASSIC LITERATURE TO USE WITH THE PROGRAM

Levels D and E

Louisa May Alcott *Little Women*

Maya Angelou *I Know Why the Caged Bird Sings*

Ray Bradbury *Fahrenheit 451*

Charlotte Brontë *Jane Eyre*

Emily Brontë *Wuthering Heights*

Pearl S. Buck *The Good Earth*

Lewis Carroll *Alice's Adventures in Wonderland*

Willa Cather *My Antonia*

Sandra Cisneros *The House on Mango Street*

Daniel Defoe *Robinson Crusoe*

Charles Dickens *A Tale of Two Cities*

Sir Arthur Conan Doyle *The Hound of the Baskervilles*

George Eliot *Silas Marner*

William Golding *Lord of the Flies*

Frank Herbert *Dune*

Harper Lee *To Kill a Mockingbird*

Carson McCullers *Member of the Wedding*

Nicholasa Mohr *El Bronx Remembered*

Walter Dean Myers *Fallen Angels*

George Orwell *Animal Farm*

Alan Paton *Cry, the Beloved Country*

John Steinbeck *The Pearl*

Level F

Sherwood Anderson *Winesburg, Ohio*

James Baldwin *Go Tell It on the Mountain*

Stephen Crane *The Red Badge of Courage*

Kate Chopin *The Awakening*

Ralph Ellison *Invisible Man*

Louise Erdrich *Love Medicine*

Jack Finney *Time and Again*

F. Scott Fitzgerald *The Great Gatsby*

Nathaniel Hawthorne *The Scarlet Letter*

Joseph Heller *Catch-22*

Ernest Hemingway *A Farewell to Arms*

Zora Neale Hurston *Their Eyes Were Watching God*

Henry James *Washington Square*

Maxine Hong Kingston *Woman Warrior*

N. Scott Momaday *The Way to Rainy Mountain*

Toni Morrison *Beloved*

John Steinbeck *The Grapes of Wrath*

Amy Tan *The Joy Luck Club*

Mark Twain *The Adventures of Huckleberry Finn*

Kurt Vonnegut, Jr. *Slaughterhouse Five*

Alice Walker *The Color Purple*

Edith Wharton *The House of Mirth* and *The Age of Innocence*

Richard Wright *Black Boy*

Levels G and H

Chinua Achebe *Things Fall Apart*

Margaret Atwood
The Handmaid's Tale

Jane Austen *Pride and Prejudice*

Joseph Conrad *Lord Jim* and *Heart of Darkness*

Charles Dickens *David Copperfield*

Isak Dinesen *Out of Africa*

George Eliot *The Mill on the Floss*

Thomas Hardy *The Return of the Native*

Aldous Huxley *Brave New World*

James Joyce *A Portrait of the Artist as a Young Man*

Gabriel Garcia Marquez
One Hundred Years of Solitude

Mark Mathabane *Kaffir Boy*

V.S. Naipaul *A House for Mr. Biswas*

Mary Wollstonecraft Shelley
Frankenstein

Muriel Spark *The Prime of Miss Jean Brodie*

Jonathan Swift *Gulliver's Travels*

Virginia Woolf *A Room of One's Own* and *To the Lighthouse*

To coordinate reading and vocabulary study, the following may prove helpful:

• Students may devote a notebook to vocabulary. As they encounter key words in their reading, they should head a page of the notebook with the word; copy the title of the work; and then indicate (a) the definition used in that sentence, (b) its part of speech, and (c) whether it is used in a literal or figurative sense.

• Students may then be instructed to check *Bartlett's Familiar Quotations* for other famous examples of the use of the key word in question. These quotations may be copied into the notebook and shared with others in the class.

Vocabulary in Context

VOCABULARY WORKSHOP uses excerpts from classic literature to show how a Unit's vocabulary words are used in context.

Level D Vocabulary in Context Literary Selections

Unit 1	Louisa May Alcott	*Little Women* and *Little Men*
Unit 2	Charlotte Brontë	*Jane Eyre*
Unit 3	Charles Dickens	*Great Expectations*
Unit 4	Daniel Defoe	*The Life and Adventures of Robinson Crusoe* and *A Journal of the Plague Year*
Unit 5	Henry James	*Washington Square* and *The Portrait of a Lady*
Unit 6	Sir Arthur Conan Doyle	*The Hound of the Baskervilles*
Unit 7	Jules Verne	*Around the World in 80 Days*

Unit 8	H.G. Wells	*The Time Machine* and *War of the Worlds*
Unit 9	Jane Austen	*Pride and Prejudice*
Unit 10	Wilkie Collins	*The Woman in White*
Unit 11	Nathaniel Hawthorne	*The House of the Seven Gables* and *The Scarlet Letter*
Unit 12	Henry Fielding	*Joseph Andrews*
Unit 13	Thomas Hardy	*The Woodlanders*
Unit 14	Stephen Crane	*The Red Badge of Courage,* "The Blue Hotel," and *The Monster*
Unit 15	Mary Wollstonecraft Shelley	*Frankenstein*

Level E Vocabulary in Context Literary Selections

Unit 1	Charles Dickens	*A Tale of Two Cities*
Unit 2	Edgar Allan Poe	*The Works of Edgar Allan Poe, Vols. 1 and 2*
Unit 3	Anne Brontë	*The Tenant of Wildfell Hall*
Unit 4	Louisa May Alcott	*Little Women* and *Little Men*
Unit 5	Willa Cather	*My Antonia*
Unit 6	Emily Brontë	*Wuthering Heights*
Unit 7	Charles Dickens	*Oliver Twist*
Unit 8	Alexandre Dumas	*The Three Musketeers*
Unit 9	James Fenimore Cooper	*The Last of the Mohicans*
Unit 10	Charlotte Brontë	*Jane Eyre*
Unit 11	Sir Arthur Conan Doyle	*The Adventures of Sherlock Holmes*
Unit 12	Charles Dickens	*Great Expectations*
Unit 13	George Eliot	*The Mill on the Floss* and *Silas Marner*
Unit 14	Nathaniel Hawthorne	*The House of the Seven Gables*
Unit 15	Jane Austen	*Emma*

VOCABULARY STRATEGY: Word Structure

One important way students build vocabulary is to learn the meaning of word parts that make up many English words. These word parts consist of **prefixes**, **suffixes**, and **roots**, or **bases**. A useful strategy for determining the meaning of an unknown word is to "take apart" the word and think about the parts.

Following is a list of common prefixes. Knowing the meaning of a prefix can help students determine the meaning of a word in which the prefix appears.

Prefix	Meaning	Sample Words
bi-	two	bicycle
com-, con-	together, with	compatriot, contact
de-, dis-	lower, opposite	devalue, disloyal
fore-, pre-	before, ahead of time	forewarn, preplan
il-, im-, in-, ir, non-, un–	not	illegal, impossible, inactive, irregular, nonsense, unable
in-, im-	in, into	inhale, import
mid-	middle	midway
mis-	wrongly, badly	mistake, misbehave
re-	again, back	redo, repay
sub-	under, less than	submarine, subzero
super-	above, greater than	superimpose, superstar
tri-	three	triangle

Following is a list of common suffixes. Knowing the meaning and grammatical function of a suffix can help students determine the meaning of a word.

Noun Suffix	Meaning	Sample Nouns
-acy, -ance, -ence, -hood, -ity, -ment, -ness, -ship	state, quality, or condition of, act or process of	adequacy, attendance, persistence, neighborhood, activity, judgment, brightness, friendship
-ant, -eer, -ent, -er, -ian, -ier, -ist, -or	one who does or makes something	contestant, auctioneer, resident, banker, comedian, financier, dentist, doctor
-ation, -ition, -ion	act or result of	organization, imposition, election

Verb Suffix	Meaning	Sample Verbs
-ate	to become, produce, or treat	validate, salivate, chlorinate
-en	to make, cause to be	weaken
-fy, -ify, -ize	to cause, make	liquefy, glorify, legalize

Adjective Suffix	Meaning	Sample Adjectives
-able, -ible	able, capable of	believable, incredible
-al, -ic,	relating to, characteristic of	natural, romantic
-ful, -ive, -ous	full of, given to, marked by	beautiful, protective, poisonous
-ish, -like	like, resembling	foolish, childlike
-less	lacking, without	careless

A base or root is the main part of a word to which prefixes and suffixes may be added. Many roots come to English from Latin. Knowing Greek and Latin roots can help students determine the meaning of a word.

In the Building with Classical Roots sections of this book students will learn more about some of these Latin and Greek roots and about the English words that derive from them.

Greek Root	Meaning	Sample Words
-astr-, -aster-, -astro-	star	astral, asteroid, astronaut
-auto-	self	autograph
-bio-	life	biography
-chron-, chrono-	time	chronic, chronological
-cosm-, -cosmo-	universe, order	microcosm, cosmopolitan
-cryph-, -crypt-	hidden, secret	apocryphal, cryptographer
-dem-, -demo-	people	epidemic, democracy
-dia-	through, across, between	diameter
-dog-, -dox-	opinion, teaching	dogmatic, orthodox
-gen-	race, kind, origin, birth	generation
-gnos-	know	diagnostic
-graph-, -graphy-, -gram-	write	graphite, autobiography, telegram
-log-, -logue-	speech, word, reasoning	logic, dialogue
-lys-	break down	analysis
-metr-, -meter-	measure	metric, kilometer
-micro-	small	microchip
-morph-	form, shape	amorphous
-naut-	sailor	nautical
-phon-, -phone-, -phono-	sound, voice	phonics, telephone, phonograph

-pol-, -polis-	city, state	police, metropolis
-scop-, -scope-	watch, look at	microscopic, telescope
-tele-	far off, distant	television
-the-	put or place	parentheses

Latin Root	Meaning	Sample Words
-cap-, -capt-, -cept-, -cip-	take	capitulate, captive, concept, recipient
-cede-, -ceed-, -ceas-, -cess-	happen, yield, go	precede, proceed, decease, cessation
-cred-	believe	incredible
-dic-, -dict-	speak, say, tell	indicate, diction
-duc-, -duct-, -duit-	lead, conduct, draw	educate, conduct, conduit
-fac-, -fact-, -fect-, -fic-, -fy-	make	faculty, artifact, defect, beneficial, clarify
-ject-	throw	eject
-mis-, -miss-, -mit-, -mitt-	send	promise, missile, transmit, intermittent
-note-, -not-	know, recognize	denote, notion
-pel-, -puls-	drive	expel, compulsive
-pend-, -pens-	hang, weight, set aside	pendulum, pension
-pon-, -pos-	put, place	component, position
-port-	carry	portable
-rupt-	break	bankrupt
-scrib-, -scribe-, -script-	write	scribble, describe, inscription
-spec-, -spic-	look, see	spectator, conspicuous
-tac-, -tag-, -tang-, -teg-	touch	contact, contagious, tangible, integral
-tain-, -ten-, -tin-	hold, keep	contain, tenure, retinue
-temp-	time	tempo
-ven-, -vent-	come	intervene, convention
-vers-, -vert-	turn	reverse, invert
-voc-, -vok-	call	vocal, invoke

DENOTATION, CONNOTATION, AND SHADES OF MEANING

The **denotation** of a word is its specific dictionary meaning.
Here are a few examples:

Word	Denotation
scholarly	learned
grasping	overly eager for material gain
travel	make a journey

The **connotation** of a word is its **tone**—that is, the emotions or associations it normally arouses in people using, hearing, or reading it. Depending on what these feelings are, the connotation of a word may be *favorable* (*positive*) or *unfavorable* (*negative, pejorative*). A word that does not normally arouse strong feelings of any kind has a *neutral* connotation. Here are some examples of words with different connotations:

Word	Connotation
scholarly	favorable
grasping	unfavorable
travel	neutral

Every Word Study section of VOCABULARY WORKSHOP has two pages of instruction on and practice with the denotation and connotation of words. The exercises in this section will prepare students to meet the Craft and Structure requirements of the Common Core State Standards.

FIGURATIVE LANGUAGE

After every three Units of Vocabulary Workshop, there is a Review that also contains a Word Study section, for a total of five Word Study sections per book. Each Word Study section contains a two-page lesson on idioms, proverbs, or adages. These three types of figurative language, especially problematic for ELL students, are important in light of the Common Core State Standards, which require students in grades 9–12 to demonstrate an understanding of figurative language by interpreting figures of speech in context and analyzing their role in the text. The Common Core directive that students read texts (both literary and informational) of increasing complexity means that students are more likely to encounter figurative expressions in their reading. Furthermore, these three types of figurative language frequently appear in standardized test items.

- An **idiom** is an informal expression whose literal meaning does not help the reader or listener figure out what the expression means. English is particularly rich in idioms and idiomatic expressions, such as "raining cats and dogs," "the apple of my eye," "a dark horse."

- An **adage** expresses a common experience, often in the form of a sentence, such as "Time flies when you're having fun."

- A **proverb** is a statement that provides a lesson or a moral, such as "A stitch in time saves nine" and "A rolling stone gathers no moss."

Teachers may note with students that every language has its own idioms, proverbs, and adages. Students may find or think of examples from other cultures, especially if another language is spoken at home. Understanding the meaning of common English idioms, adages, and proverbs will improve reading ability and enrich students' writing.

How to Use the Word Study Lessons

The first page of each lesson refers to one of the introductory Reading Passages in the three preceding Units. An idiom, adage, or proverb is embedded in the Passage, where it is used in context. Students next encounter the idiom (or adage or proverb) on the first page of the Word Study section. Following instruction and examples of these figures of speech, students are given ten sentences containing different idioms (or adages or proverbs) in context and are asked to match each with its definition. The second page is a **writing exercise** in which students are required to write original sentences using ten additional idioms (or adages or proverbs).

Enriching the Word Study Lessons

Teachers may suggest that students draw a cartoon that uses a proverb or an adage as a caption, or they might write brief narratives or fables with a proverb or adage as the moral. Standardized tests, such as the SAT, might use a proverb as a writing prompt; students are then asked to discuss the proverb, drawing from their personal experiences, observations, and reading. Students will practice writing such essays in the **Writing: Words in Action** activities during the course of the school year.

SADLIER

VOCABULARY WORKSHOP

ENRICHED EDITION

Level D

Jerome Shostak

Senior Series Consultant

Vicki A. Jacobs, Ed.D.
Associate Director, Teacher Education Program
Lecturer on Education
Harvard Graduate School of Education
Cambridge, Massachusetts

Series Consultants

Louis P. De Angelo, Ed.D.
Associate Superintendent
Diocese of Wilmington
Wilmington, Delaware

Sarah Ressler Wright, NBCT
English Department Chair
Rutherford B. Hayes High School
Delaware City Schools, Ohio

John Heath, Ph.D.
Professor of Classics
Santa Clara University
Santa Clara, California

Carolyn E. Waters, JD, Ed.S.
ELA/Literacy 6–12 Supervisor
Cobb County School District
Marietta, Georgia

Sadlier

Reviewers

The publisher wishes to thank for their comments and suggestions the following teachers and administrators, who read portions of the series prior to publication.

Cover: Concept/Art and Design: MK Advertising and William H. Sadlier, Inc.; Cover pencil: Shutterstock/VikaSuh. **Photo Credits:** Interior: age Fotostock/Topicphotoagency: 71 *top right*, 99 *top left*. Akademie der Künste, Berlin/Bild-Kunst: 109 *center*. akg-images/RIA Nowosti: 65. Alamy/24BY36: 164; Alexey Zarubin: 99 *top left*; Boaz Rottem: 127 *right*; Christiaan May: 184 *background*; Classic Image: 155; ClassicStock: 93; Dave Stamboulis: 50 *left*; David R. Frazier Photolibrary, Inc.: 55; Gerry Reynolds: 23 *inset*; Interfoto: 97; Manfred Grebler: 127 *left*; Mary Evans Picture Library: 59; Moviestore collection Ltd: 31 *center right*; Moviestore collection Ltd : 117; Photos 12: 21 *center right*; Ville Palonen: 61 *right*. Animals/Mark Boulton/ Ardea: 126. Animals Animals/Roger De La Harpe: 61 *left*. Art Resource, NY/The Jewish Museum, New York / Robert Mann Gallery: 109 *bottom right*. Artville: 50 *frame*, 51 *left*. Associated Press/Brandi Jade Thomas: 136 *right*; Jerome Delay: 137. The Bridgeman Art Library: 109 *bottom left*; Bibliotheque de l'Institut de France, Paris, France: 169; Look and Learn: 131; Philip Mould Ltd, London: 141. Corbis/Bettmann: 22 *inset*, 27, 32 *bottom left*, 33 *bottom right*, 98 *bottom left*, 98 *bottom right*, 145, 189; Hein van den Heuvel: 165 *bottom*; John Springer Collection: 41; Tony Korody/Sygma: 103. DigitalVision/Michael Cleary: 98 *background*. Everett Collection: 193. Geovision, Inc./Nils Fonstad: 108 *bottom*. Getty Images/Archive Photos: 184 *right*; Brand X Pictures: 99 *top right*; Hulton Archive/Stringer: 17; Jonathan And Angela/Taxi: 51 *top left*; Natalie Fobes/Science Faction: 164; Popperfoto: 184 *left*; Sports Illustrated: 184 *right*; SuperStock: 179; William A. Allard/National Geographic: 23 *background*. The Granger Collection, New York: 32 *background*, 70 *bottom*, 71 *top right*, 75. The Image Works/ArenaPal/Topham: 99 *top center*. The Kobal Collection/20TH Century Fox: 79; Channel 4/Pathe: 173; Dreamworks/Paramount: 107; Hollywood/Caravan/Ron Batzdorff: 69; MGM: 183; New Line/Saul Zaentz/Wing Nut: 12 *inset*, 12 *background*, 13 *bottom right*; Warner Brothers: 135. Library of Congress/Alexander Gardner/M.P.Rice: 37. Myrleen Pearson: 146 *inset*, 147 *inset*. New Mexico State Planning Office Photograph Collection, courtesy New Mexico State Records Center and Archives, image no. 11209: 22 *inset*. Photo Researchers, Inc./Mark Burnett: 165 *top*. Photodisc: 22 *frame*, 23 *frame*, 136 *left*. Photolibrary/Gerard Lacz/Peter Arnold: 60 *left*; Imagesource: 51 *background*; J-L. Klein & M-L. Hubert: 151; Rob Van Petten/Monsoon Images: 113. Shutterstock: Antonio Jorge Nunes: 60 *background*; cofkocof: 146 *background*; Falconia: 12 *center*; Leigh Prather: 12 *center*; Login: 146 spot, 147 spot; Melissa King: 184 *frame*; Risto Viita: 22 *frame*; Sergey Furtaev: 35; theromb: 108 *background*.

Illustration Credits: Tim Haggerty: 46, 84, 122, 160, 198. Andrea Orani: 174–175. Sholto Walker: 88.

For additional online resources, go to vocabularyworkshop.com and enter the Student Access Code: VW12SDUJY5RW

ENRICHED EDITION: New Features

For more than five decades, VOCABULARY WORKSHOP has proven to be a highly successful tool for guiding systematic vocabulary growth and developing vocabulary skills. It has also been shown to help students prepare for standardized tests.

New in this edition are the **Reading Passages, Writing, Vocabulary in Context,** and **Word Study** activities. Nonfiction, high-interest passages use 15 or more of the Unit vocabulary words in context. Two writing prompts require a response to the reading and provide practice in writing for standardized tests. New Vocabulary in Context activities present words from the Unit as they are used in classic works of literature. After every three units, Word Study activities, developed in conjunction with Common Core State Standards requirements, provide practice with idioms, adages, and proverbs, as well as denotation and connotation and classical roots.

Look for the new **QR** (Quick Response) codes on the **Reading Passage** and **Vocabulary in Context** pages. The code can be read with a smartphone camera. To read the QR code, download any free QR code application to a smartphone. Snap the code with a smartphone camera to go directly to iWords for the Unit or an interactive quiz. With iWords you can listen to one word at a time or download all of the words in a Unit to listen to them at your convenience.

The new structure of VOCABULARY WORKSHOP is made up of 15 Units. Each Unit consists of the following sections: a **Reading Passage, Definitions, Choosing the Right Word, Synonyms and Antonyms, Completing the Sentence, Writing,** and **Vocabulary in Context**. Together, these exercises provide multiple and varied exposures to the taught words—an approach consistent with and supportive of research-based findings in vocabulary instruction.

Five **Reviews** cover Vocabulary for Comprehension and Two-Word Completions. Vocabulary for Comprehension is modeled on the reading sections of standardized tests, and as in those tests, it presents reading comprehension questions, including specific vocabulary-related ones, that are based on a reading passage.

A **Final Mastery Test** assesses a selection of words from the year with activities on Synonyms, Antonyms, Analogies, Two-Word Completions, Supplying Words in Context, Word Associations, and Choosing the Right Meaning.

In each level of VOCABULARY WORKSHOP, 300 key words are taught. The words have been selected according to the following criteria: currency and general usefulness; frequency of appearance on recognized vocabulary lists; applicability to, and appearance on, standardized tests; and current grade-level research.

ONLINE COMPONENTS
vocabularyworkshop.com

At **vocabularyworkshop.com** you will find iWords, an audio program that provides pronunciations, definitions, and examples of usage for all of the key words presented in this level of VOCABULARY WORKSHOP. You can listen to one word at a time or, if you wish, download to an MP3 player all of the words of any given Unit. You will then be able to listen to the audio program for that Unit at your convenience.

At **vocabularyworkshop.com** you will also find **interactive vocabulary quizzes, flashcards, games and puzzles** that will help reinforce and enrich your understanding of the key words in this level of VOCABULARY WORKSHOP.

CONTENTS

iWords Audio Program available at **vocabularyworkshop.com**.

VOCABULARY STRATEGY: Using Context

The **context** of a word is the printed text of which that word is part. By studying the word's context, we may find **clues** to its meaning. We might find a clue in the immediate or adjoining sentence or phrase in which the word appears; in the topic or subject matter of the passage; or in the physical features—such as photographs, illustrations, charts, graphs, captions and headings—of a page itself.

The **Vocabulary in Context, Vocabulary for Comprehension**, and **Choosing the Right Meaning** exercises that appear in the Units, the Reviews, and Final Mastery Test provide practice in using context to decode unfamiliar words.

Three types of context clues appear in the exercises in this book.

A **restatement clue** consists of a *synonym* for or a *definition* of the missing word. For example:

Faithfully reading a weekly newsmagazine not only broadens my knowledge of current events and world or national affairs but also _____ my vocabulary.

a. decreases **b.** fragments **c.** increases **d.** contains

In this sentence, *broadens* is a synonym of the missing word, *increases*, and acts as a restatement clue for it.

A **contrast clue** consists of an *antonym* for or a phrase that means the opposite of the missing word. For example:

"My view of the situation may be far too rosy," I admitted.
"On the other hand, yours may be a bit (**optimistic, bleak**)."

In this sentence, *rosy* is an antonym of the missing word, *bleak*. This is confirmed by the presence of the phrase *on the other hand*, which indicates that the answer must be the opposite of *rosy*.

An **inference clue** implies but does not directly state the meaning of the missing word or words. For example:

"A treat for all ages," the review read, "this wonderful novel combines the _____ of a scholar with the skill and artistry of an expert _____."

a. ignorance . . . painter   **c.** wealth . . . surgeon
b. wisdom . . . beginner   **d.** knowledge . . . storyteller

In this sentence, there are several inference clues: (a) the word *scholar* suggests *knowledge*; (b) the words *novel*, *artistry*, and *skill* suggest the word *storyteller*. These words are inference clues because they suggest or imply, but do not directly state, the missing word or words.

VOCABULARY STRATEGY: Word Structure

Prefixes, **suffixes**, and **roots**, or **bases**, are word parts. One strategy for determining an unknown word's meaning is to "take apart" the word and think about the parts. Study the prefixes and suffixes below to help you find out the meanings of words in which they appear

Prefix	Meaning	Sample Words
com-, con-	together, with	compatriot, contact
de-, dis-	lower, opposite	devalue, disloyal
il-, im-, in-, ir, non-, un-	not	illegal, impossible, inactive, irregular, nonsense, unable
super-	above, greater than	superimpose, superstar

Noun Suffix	Meaning	Sample Nouns
-acy, -ance, -ence, -hood, -ity, -ment, -ness, -ship	state, quality, or condition of, act or process of	adequacy, attendance, persistence, neighborhood, activity, judgment, brightness, friendship
-ant, -eer, -ent, -er, -ian, -ier, -ist, -or	one who does or makes something	contestant, auctioneer, resident, banker, comedian, financier, dentist, doctor
-ation, -ition, -ion	act or result of	organization, imposition, election

Verb Suffix	Meaning	Sample Verbs
-ate	to become, produce, or treat	validate, salivate, chlorinate
-fy, -ify, -ize	to cause, make	liquefy, glorify, legalize

Adjective Suffix	Meaning	Sample Adjectives
-al, -ic,	relating to, characteristic of	natural, romantic
-ful, -ive, -ous	full of, given to, marked by	beautiful, protective, poisonous

A **base** or **root** is the main part of a word to which prefixes and suffixes may be added. On the Classical Roots page of the Word Study section, you will learn more about Latin and Greek roots and the English words that derive from them. The following lists may help you figure out the meaning of new or unfamiliar words.

Greek Root	Meaning	Sample Words
-cryph-, -crypt-	hidden, secret	apocryphal, cryptographer
-dem-, -demo-	people	epidemic, democracy
-gen-	race, kind, origin, birth	generation
-gnos-	know	diagnostic
-lys-	break down	analysis

Latin Root	Meaning	Sample Words
-cap-, -capt-, -cept-, -cip-	take	capitulate, captive, concept, recipient
-cede-, -ceed-, -ceas-, -cess-	happen, yield, go	precede, proceed, decease, cessation
-fac-, -fact-, -fect-, -fic-, -fy-	make	faculty, artifact, defect, beneficial, clarify
-tac-, -tag-, -tang-, -teg-	touch	contact, contagious, tangible, integral
-tain-, -ten-, -tin-	hold, keep	contain, tenure, retinue

For more prefixes, suffixes, and roots, visit **vocabularyworkshop.com**.

VOCABULARY AND READING

Word knowledge is essential to reading comprehension. Your knowledge of word meanings and ability to think carefully about what you read will help you succeed in school and on standardized tests, including the SAT, the ACT, and the PSAT.

New **Reading Passages** provide extra practice with vocabulary words. Vocabulary words are boldfaced to draw students' attention to their uses and contexts. Context clues embedded in the passages encourage students to figure out the meanings of words before they read the definitions provided on the pages directly following the passages.

Students read excerpts from classic literature in the **Vocabulary in Context** exercises. Each excerpt includes one of the Unit vocabulary words as it is used in the original work. Students can use what they learn about the word from its use in context to answer questions on the definition.

The **Vocabulary for Comprehension** exercises in each review consist of a nonfiction reading passage followed by comprehension questions. The passages and questions are similar to those that you are likely to find on standardized tests.

Kinds of Questions

Main Idea Questions generally ask what the passage as a whole is about. Often, but not always, the main idea is stated in the first paragraph of the passage. You may also be asked the main idea of a specific paragraph. Questions about the main idea may begin like this:

- The primary or main purpose of the passage is. . .
- The passage is best described as. . .
- The title that best describes the content of the passage is. . .

Detail Questions focus on important information that is explicitly stated in the passage. Often, however, the correct answer choices do not use the exact language of the passage. They are instead restatements, or paraphrases, of the text.

Vocabulary-in-Context Questions check your ability to use context to identify a word's meaning. Use line references to see how and in what context the word is used. For example:

- **Eminent** (line 8) is best defined as. . .
- The meaning of **diffuse** (line 30) is. . .

Use context to check your answer choices, particularly when the vocabulary word has more than one meaning. Among the choices may be two (or more) correct meanings of the word in question. Choose the meaning that best fits the context.

Inference Questions ask you to make inferences or draw conclusions from the passage. These questions often begin like this:

- It can be inferred from the passage that. . .
- The author implies that. . .
- Evidently the author feels that. . .

The inferences you make and the conclusions you draw must be based on the information in the passage. Your own knowledge and reasoning come into play in understanding what is implied and in reaching conclusions that are logical.

Questions About Tone show your understanding of the author's attitude toward the subject of the passage. Words that describe tone, or attitude, are "feeling" words, such as *indifferent*, *ambivalent*, *scornful*, *astonished*, *respectful*. These are typical questions:

- The author's attitude toward . . . is best described as. . .
- Which word best describes the author's tone?

To determine the tone, pay attention to the author's word choice. The author's attitude may be positive (respectful), negative (scornful), or neutral (ambivalent).

Questions About Author's Technique focus on the way a text is organized and the language the author uses. These questions ask you to think about structure and function. For example:

- The final paragraph serves to. . .
- The author cites . . . in order to . . . .

To answer the questions, you must demonstrate an understanding of the way the author presents information and develops ideas.

Strategies

Here are some general strategies to help you as you read each passage and answer the questions.

- Read the introduction first. The introduction will provide a focus for the selection.

- Be an active reader. As you read, ask yourself questions about the passage—for example: What is this paragraph about? What does the writer mean here? Why does the writer include this information?

- Refer to the passage when you answer the questions. In general, the order of the questions mirrors the organization of the passage, and many of the questions include paragraph or line references. It is often helpful to go back and reread before choosing an answer.

- Read carefully, and be sure to base your answer choices on the passage. There are answer choices that make sense but are not based on the information in the passage. These are true statements, but they are incorrect answers. The correct answers are either restatements of ideas in the text or inferences that can be drawn from the text.

- Consider each exercise a learning experience. Keep in mind that your ability to answer the questions correctly shows as much about your understanding of the questions as about your understanding of the passage.

WORKING WITH ANALOGIES

A verbal analogy expresses a relationship or comparison between sets of words. Normally, an analogy contains two pairs of words linked by a word or symbol that stands for an equals (=) sign. A complete analogy compares the two pairs of words and makes a statement about them. It asserts that the relationship between the first—or key—pair of words is the same as the relationship between the second pair.

In the **Analogies** exercises in the Final Mastery Test, you will be asked to complete analogies—that is, to choose the pair of words that best matches or parallels the relationship of the key, or given, pair of words. Here are two examples:

1. maple is to **tree** as
   a. acorn is to oak
   b. hen is to rooster
   c. rose is to flower
   d. shrub is to lilac

2. joyful is to **gloomy** as
   a. cheerful is to happy
   b. strong is to weak
   c. quick is to famous
   d. hungry is to starving

In order to find the correct answer to exercise 1, you must first determine the relationship between the two key words, **maple** and **tree**. In this case, that relationship might be expressed as "a maple is a kind (or type) of tree." The next step is to select from choices a, b, c, and d the pair of words that best reflects the same relationship. The correct answer is (c); it is the only pair whose relationship parallels the one in the key words: A rose is a kind (or type) of flower, just as a maple is a kind (or type) of tree. The other choices do not express the same relationship.

In exercise 2, the relationship between the key words can be expressed as "joyful means the opposite of gloomy." Which of the choices best represents the same relationship? The answer is (b): "strong means the opposite of weak."

Here are examples of some other common analogy relationships:

Analogy	Key Relationship
big is to **large** as **little** is to **small**	**Big** means the same thing as **large**, just as **little** means the same thing as **small**.
brave is to **favorable** as **cowardly** is to **unfavorable**	The tone of **brave** is **favorable**, just as the tone of **cowardly** is **unfavorable**.
busybody is to **nosy** as **klutz** is to **clumsy**	A **busybody** is by definition someone who is **nosy**, just as a **klutz** is by definition someone who is **clumsy**.
cowardly is to **courage** as **awkward** is to **grace**	Someone who is **cowardly** lacks **courage**, just as someone who is **awkward** lacks **grace**.
visible is to **see** as **audible** is to **hear**	If something is **visible**, you can by definition **see** it, just as if something is **audible**, you can by definition **hear** it.
liar is to **truthful** as **bigot** is to **fair-minded**	A **liar** is by definition not likely to be **truthful**, just as a **bigot** is by definition not likely to be **fair-minded**.
eyes are to **see** as **ears** are to **hear**	You use your **eyes** to **see** with, just as you use your **ears** to **hear** with.

There are many different kinds of relationships represented in the analogy questions you will find in the Final Mastery Test, but the key to solving any analogy is to find and express the relationship between the two key words.

UNIT 1

Note that not all of the 20 unit words are used in this passage. *Admonish*, *debris*, *efface*, and *salvage* are not included in the passage.

*Read the following selection, taking note of the **boldface** words and their contexts. These words are among those you will be studying in Unit 1. As you complete the exercises in this unit, it may help to refer to the way the words are used below.*

C CCSS Vocabulary: 4; Reading (Informational Text): 4, 6. (See pp. T14–15.)

I'll Wait for the Movie

<Compare-and-Contrast Essay>

Cue scene: Middle-Earth characters Aragorn, Legolas, and Gimli leap off a ship, swords in hand, to **breach** archenemy Sauron's lines in the epic Battle of Pelennor Fields. This is a crucial moment in the movie version of *The Lord of the Rings: Return of the King*. Alas, the haunting showdown with the ghostly **brigands** does not actually occur in author J.R.R. Tolkien's books.

Film fans do not have to speak Elvish to enjoy director Peter Jackson's blockbuster *Lord of the Rings* (LOTR) trilogy. But do the movies do justice to Tolkien's enduring and popular novels? And is it possible for the LOTR purist to watch the films without cringing at every discrepancy? Readers are often disappointed with movie adaptations of their favorite novels. In fact, they might be **predisposed** to dislike any movie version. This is a perennial problem for film directors, scriptwriters, readers, and moviegoers alike.

Filmmakers often **commandeer** the story and make it their own. Their motivation might be this cliché: "a picture paints a thousand words." They eliminate characters or events, or they add new ones. And authors can't complain: When they sell the rights to their work, they usually **relinquish** control. Filmmakers understand that their audience is **opinionated**, as evinced by LOTR fans posting online comments about Jackson's adaptation. Some claim that Jackson made a **muddle** of the books, that his tinkering is **spurious**, or that the films show only **spasmodic** flashes of greatness. Other fans show **unbridled** enthusiasm, saying that Tolkien's **perennial** classics are too long and **diffuse** and that the director's snipping

J.R.R. Tolkien's epic fantasy is one of the most popular novels of all time.

was essential. And some fans are more **circumspect** in their criticism, realizing it is impossible to please everyone.

The **dilemma** facing filmmakers is that reading a book is a more interactive experience than watching a movie. A reader visualizes every scene in the book and decides what the characters look and sound like, what they wear, how their environs appear. For those who read the LOTR books first, the movie's Frodo may not resemble the Frodo they imagined. How can Peter Jackson's vision of Middle-Earth reflect the ones created in the mind's eye of millions of readers?

It is easy to imagine that moviegoers and readers are always **deadlocked** over which medium is better. Those who have read the book may come away from the multiplex disappointed: *The movie left out so much! Why was that memorable scene transposed to the beginning?* On the other hand, those who see the movie first may be awed by the director's imaginative retelling or by the stirring music and special effects. Most movies based on books retain key characters, scenes, and themes. Directors and scriptwriters strive to tell the same story and evoke the same emotions as the author of the original book. Both share an audience yet address one that is exclusively their own.

In the end, directors must rely on fans to accept the limitations of the movie. How is it possible for a two-hour movie (or even a sprawling movie trilogy) to include all of the details woven throughout a long novel? A movie that attempted to do this would end up unwieldy and **cumbersome**—a surefire way to disappoint moviegoers and book lovers alike.

Snap the code, or go to
vocabularyworkshop.com

A poster for the first movie in director Peter Jackson's *Lord of the Rings* trilogy.

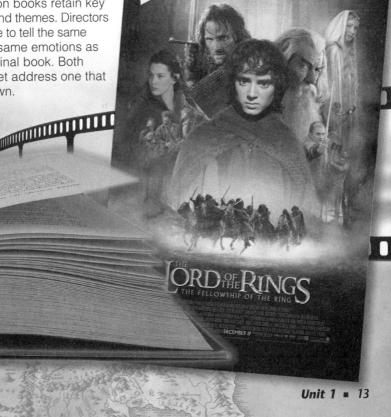

Definitions

Note the spelling, pronunciation, part(s) of speech, and definition(s) of each of the following words. Then write the word in the blank spaces in the illustrative sentence(s) following. Finally, study the lists of synonyms and antonyms.

1. admonish
(ad män' ish)

(*v.*) to caution or advise against something; to scold mildly; to remind of a duty

The librarian had to _____**admonish**_____ the noisy students several times before they settled down.

SYNONYMS: reprimand, call on the carpet
ANTONYMS: praise, pat on the back

2. breach
(brēch)

(*n.*) an opening, gap, rupture, rift; a violation or infraction; (*v.*) to create an opening, break through

Because of a serious _____**breach**_____ of the rules, two players were ejected from the game.

Our troops were unable to _____**breach**_____ the enemy's lines during the battle.

ANTONYMS: (*v.*) close, seal

3. brigand
(brig' ənd)

(*n.*) a bandit, robber, outlaw, highwayman

Ancient caravans passing through desolate areas were sometimes attacked by _____**brigands**_____.

4. circumspect
(sər' kəm spekt)

(*adj.*) careful, cautious

It is important for a diplomat to behave in a manner that is both discreet and _____**circumspect**_____.

SYNONYMS: wary, prudent, guarded
ANTONYMS: incautious, rash, reckless, heedless

5. commandeer
(käm ən dēr')

(*v.*) to seize for military or official use

Under certain circumstances the U.S. government has the right to _____**commandeer**_____ private property.

SYNONYMS: take over, requisition, expropriate

6. cumbersome
(kəm' bər səm)

(*adj.*) clumsy, hard to handle; slow-moving

The bus was filled to capacity with holiday shoppers carrying large and _____**cumbersome**_____ packages.

SYNONYMS: ponderous, difficult, uncomfortable
ANTONYMS: manageable, easy to handle

7. deadlock
(ded' läk)

(*n.*) a standstill resulting from the opposition of two equal forces or factions; (*v.*) to bring to such a standstill

After fifteen innings, the score remained a frustrating 3-to-3 _____**deadlock**_____.

ℂ CCSS Vocabulary: 4.c., 4.d. (See pp. T14–T15.)

The refusal of labor and management to modify their demands _____deadlocked_____ the contract negotiations.

SYNONYMS: (*n.*) standoff, impasse
ANTONYMS: (*n.*) agreement, accord, breakthrough

8. debris
(də brē')

(*n.*) scattered fragments, wreckage

After the storm, the beach was littered with driftwood and other _____debris_____.

SYNONYMS: remains, detritus, flotsam and jetsam

9. diffuse
(*v.,* dif yüz';
adj., dif yüs')

(*v.*) to spread or scatter freely or widely; (*adj.*) wordy, long-winded, or unfocused; scattered or widely spread

The scent of lilacs slowly _____diffused_____ through the open window.

The speech was so long and _____diffuse_____ that most audience members were thoroughly confused by it.

SYNONYMS: (*v.*) disperse; (*adj.*) verbose, prolix
ANTONYMS: (*v.*) concentrate; (*adj.*) brief, concise, succinct

10. dilemma
(di lem' ə)

(*n.*) a difficult or perplexing situation or problem

During the crisis the President found himself caught in a painful _____dilemma_____.

SYNONYMS: predicament, quandary, pickle, bind
ANTONYM: cinch

11. efface
(e fās')

(*v.*) to wipe out; to keep oneself from being noticed

Time had _____effaced_____ almost all signs of the struggle that took place on that famous battlefield.

SYNONYMS: blot out, erase, expunge

12. muddle
(məd' əl)

(*v.*) to make a mess of; muddle through: to get by; (*n.*) a hopeless mess

Too much stress and too little sleep will almost certainly _____muddle_____ a person's ability to concentrate.

The _____muddle_____ was principally caused by their failure to carry out the general's orders properly.

SYNONYMS: (*v.*) jumble, mess up; (*n.*) confusion, disorder
ANTONYMS: (*n.*) orderliness, neatness

13. opinionated
(ə pin' yən āt id)

(*adj.*) stubborn and often unreasonable in holding to one's own ideas, having a closed mind

My friend is so _____opinionated_____ that sometimes she will not listen to a reasonable proposal.

SYNONYMS: obstinate, pigheaded, inflexible
ANTONYMS: open-minded, reasonable

14. perennial
(pə ren′ ē əl)

(*adj.*) lasting for a long time, persistent; (*n.*) a plant that lives for many years

Pizza is a _____**perennial**_____ favorite of young and old alike in the United States.

A garden of _____**perennials**_____ is relatively easy to maintain.

SYNONYMS: (*adj.*) enduring, recurring
ANTONYMS: (*adj.*) brief, short-lived, fleeting, ephemeral

15. predispose
(prē dis pōz′)

(*v.*) to incline to beforehand

My genetic makeup seems to _____**predispose**_____ me to colds and sore throats.

SYNONYMS: tending to, liable to
ANTONYMS: immunize against, shield from

16. relinquish
(rē liŋ′ kwish)

(*v.*) to let go, give up

Severe illness forced me to _____**relinquish**_____ my role in the school play.

SYNONYM: surrender; ANTONYMS: hold on to, keep, cling to

17. salvage
(sal′ vij)

(*v.*) to save from fire or shipwreck; (*n.*) property thus saved

Fortunately, we were able to _____**salvage**_____ a few things from the fire.

_____**Salvage**_____ from sunken ships can be of great value to archaeologists and historians.

SYNONYMS: (*v.*) recover, retrieve, reclaim
ANTONYMS: (*v.*) abandon, scrap, junk

18. spasmodic
(spaz mäd′ ik)

(*adj.*) sudden and violent but brief; fitful; intermittent

_____**Spasmodic**_____ flashes of lightning and booming thunderclaps were accompanied by torrential rain.

SYNONYMS: irregular, occasional
ANTONYMS: steady, continuous, chronic

19. spurious
(spyü′ rē əs)

(*adj.*) not genuine, not true, not valid

Manufacturers who make _____**spurious**_____ claims for their products may face fines or lawsuits.

SYNONYMS: false, counterfeit, fraudulent, bogus
ANTONYMS: genuine, authentic, bona fide, valid

20. unbridled
(ən brīd′ əld)

(*adj.*) lacking in restraint

Sometimes the _____**unbridled**_____ enthusiasm of sports fans can get a little out of hand.

SYNONYMS: unrestrained, unchecked
ANTONYMS: restrained, held in check, muted

CCSS Vocabulary: 4.c. (See pp. T14–15.)

Choosing the Right Word

Select the **boldface** word that better completes each sentence. You might refer to the essay on pages 12–13 to see how most of these words are used in context.

1. Like the rings a pebble makes when tossed in a pool of water, the good feelings generated by the speech (**diffused, relinquished**) through the crowd.

2. To ensure they are not resented, the most powerful nations in the world must be extremely (**circumspect, opinionated**) in their foreign policy.

3. Instead of trying to (**admonish, commandeer**) the support of the student body, we must earn it by showing our sincerity and ability.

4. An economy in which the marketplace is considered "open" is one in which competition is more or less (**muddled, unbridled**).

Martin Luther King, Jr., delivering his "I Have a Dream" speech, August 28, 1963.

5. Our city government seems to have (**breached, muddled**) into a first-rate financial crisis.

6. The robber barons were a group of nineteenth-century captains of industry who amassed wealth by means that a (**brigand, salvager**) might use.

7. The evidence intended to show that some races or nationalities are superior to others proved to be completely (**spurious, cumbersome**).

8. The dean (**effaced, admonished**) the members of the team for neglecting their homework assignments.

9. In general, she is a confident person, so I'm sure she will be able to (**commandeer, salvage**) a few shreds of self-respect from her humiliating failure.

10. His attempts to rid his administration of inefficiency were so (**unbridled, spasmodic**) that he came to be called the "reformer by fits and starts."

11. After the fire, investigators searched through the (**debris, dilemma**) for clues that might reveal the cause.

12. Since she is so convinced that there is only one right way—her way—I find her too (**circumspect, opinionated**) for my liking.

13. My mother broke the (**debris, deadlock**) in the quarrel between my brother and me by saying that neither of us could use the car.

14. Developing nations in all parts of the world face the (**perennial, spurious**) problem of gaining a higher level of economic growth.

15. The senator refused to (**efface, relinquish**) the floor to any other speaker before he had finished his statement.

CCSS Vocabulary: 4.d. (See pp. T14–15.)

16. If only I could (**predispose, efface**) the memory of the look of shock and disappointment on my mother's face!

17. Even her refusal to dance with him did not seem to make a (**deadlock, breach**) in his gigantic conceit.

18. The nation was faced with a (**dilemma, brigand**) in which either to advance or to retreat might endanger its vital interests.

19. The organization of some government agencies is so (**cumbersome, perennial**) that it is all but impossible to know who is responsible for various activities.

20. How can you expect to succeed at your new job when you are (**diffused, predisposed**) to believe that it is "not right" for you?

21. After we agreed on the lineup of songs, we then (**salvaged, deadlocked**) over the choice of a name for our band.

22. When his precious collection of (**perennials, debris**) was torn up and trampled, the gardener was first heartbroken, then angry.

23. Although he was the world's expert on the subject, his lectures were so (**unbridled, diffuse**) that even his greatest fans grew bored.

24. When we discovered that she had never completed college, we knew that her claims of having once been a lawyer were (**spurious, opinionated**).

25. In spite of weeks of practice, he made a (**breach, muddle**) of his performance.

Synonyms

*Choose the word from this unit that is the same or most nearly the same in meaning as the **boldface** word or expression in the phrase. Write that word on the line. Use a dictionary if necessary.*

1. warn a child   admonish

2. a **rambling** and confusing letter   diffuse

3. make susceptible to infection   predispose

4. worn away by erosion   effaced

5. an **uncontrolled** appetite for luxury   unbridled

6. frustrated by **awkward** procedures   cumbersome

7. captured by **thieves**   brigands

8. a **stalemate** in the peace talks   deadlock

9. able to **rescue** cherished mementos   salvage

10. cleared the **rubble**   debris

CCSS Vocabulary: 5. (See pp. T14–15.)

Antonyms

*Choose the word from this unit that is most nearly opposite in meaning to the **boldface** word or expression in the phrase. Write that word on the line. Use a dictionary if necessary.*

1. the **tidiness** of her argument — **muddle**
2. **jettison** the project — **salvage**
3. **preserve** our cultural heritage — **efface**
4. **retained** title to the plot of land — **relinquished**
5. **commended** my friends for their behavior — **admonished**

Completing the Sentence

From the words in this unit, choose the one that best completes each of the following sentences. Write the word in the space provided.

1. The records of our club were in such a(n) **muddle** that we couldn't even determine which members had paid their dues.

2. The doctor became more and more fearful that her patient's weakened condition would **predispose** him to pneumonia.

3. The rug was rolled into such a(n) **cumbersome** bundle that it took four of us to carry it up the stairs.

4. He is so **opinionated** that he won't even consider the ideas or suggestions offered by other people.

5. The idea of a(n) **brigand** like Robin Hood who helps the poor appeals strongly to the popular imagination.

6. In order to capture the fleeing criminals, the police **commandeered** our car and raced after the vanishing truck.

7. The water pouring through the **breach(es)** in the dam threatened to flood the entire valley.

8. The nurse rushed into the hospital corridor to **admonish** the visitors who were creating a disturbance.

9. Though all modern scholars accept *Macbeth* as Shakespeare's work, there continue to be **spurious** allegations that other writers wrote the play.

10. Many a teenager's room is strewn with clothing, sports equipment, and all sorts of **debris**.

11. I added a few drops of food coloring to the liquid and watched as they slowly _____**diffused**_____ through it.

12. Before I make an investment, I study all aspects of the situation in a methodical and _____**circumspect**_____ manner.

13. Though his partner lost everything, he was able to _____**salvage**_____ a few dollars from the wreckage of the bankrupt business.

14. Once Great Britain had given up her vast overseas empire, she found that she had also _____**relinquished**_____ her position as a world power.

15. A man of towering pride and _____**unbridled**_____ ambition, he stopped at nothing to achieve his goals as quickly and directly as possible.

16. Since we do not want to replace the plants in our garden every year, we favor _____**perennials**_____ over annuals.

17. I have a(n) _____**dilemma**_____: If I don't get a job, I won't have the money to do what I want; and if I do get a job, I won't have the time.

18. Though my memory is getting dimmer and dimmer with the slow passage of time, I doubt that the exciting events of my childhood will ever be totally _____**effaced**_____ from my mind.

19. The two sides in the lawsuit reached a(n) _____**deadlock**_____ when neither was willing to meet the other partway.

20. Some people are subject to sudden seizures, during which their heads and legs may jerk about in a wild and _____**spasmodic**_____ manner.

Writing: Words in Action

Answers to both prompts will vary.

1. Look back at "I'll Wait for the Movie" (pages 12–13). How do the challenges of a filmmaker differ from those of an author? Write a short expository essay in which you explore how some of the major artistic decisions a filmmaker has to make differ from those a novelist has to make. Use at least two details from the passage and three unit words to support your understanding.

2. Do you prefer reading a book to seeing a movie, or do you think that movies tell a story in a more interesting way? In a brief essay, support your opinion with specific examples from your observations, studies, reading (refer to pages 12–13), or personal experience. Write at least three paragraphs, and use three or more words from this unit.

Writing prompt #2 is modeled on that of standardized tests.

C CCSS Vocabulary: 6; Writing: 1.c., 2.d. (See pp. T14–15.)

Vocabulary in Context: Informational Text for Unit 1 is available online at **vocabularyworkshop.com**.

1

Vocabulary in Context

Literary Text

The following excerpts are from Louisa May Alcott's novels Little Women *and* Little Men. *Some of the words you have studied in this unit appear in* **boldface** *type. Complete each statement below the excerpt by circling the letter of the correct answer.*

1. Laurie and his friends gallantly threw themselves into the **breach**, bought up the bouquets, encamped before the table, and made that corner the liveliest spot in the room. (*Little Women*)

A **breach** is a(n)

a. store   **c.** lake
b. opening   **d.** task

2. If Jo had not been otherwise engaged, Laurie's behavior would have amused her, for a faint twinge, not of jealousy, but something like suspicion, caused that gentleman to stand aloof at first, and observe the newcomer with brotherly **circumspection**. (*Little Women*)

Someone who observes with **circumspection** observes

a. eagerly   **c.** carefully
b. hatefully   **d.** uncomfortably

3. "I wouldn't leave a word out of it. You'll spoil it if you do, for the interest of the story is more in the minds than in the actions of the people, and it will be all a **muddle** if you don't explain as you go on," said Meg, who firmly believed that this book was the most remarkable novel ever written. (*Little Women*)

If something is in a **muddle** it is NOT

a. clear   **c.** useless
b. dirty   **d.** brilliant

A scene from the 1994 film version of *Little Women*, with Susan Sarandon as Mrs. March and Winona Ryder as Jo.

4. When little Vladimir finally **relinquished** her, with assurances that he was "desolated to leave so early," she was ready to rest, and see how her recreant knight had borne his punishment. (*Little Women*)

If someone is **relinquished** she is

a. let go   **c.** scolded
b. informed   **d.** conquered

5. "You must pay a pin apiece, or you can't see the show," said Stuffy, who stood by the wheelbarrow in which sat the band, consisting of a pocket-comb blown upon by Ned, and a toy drum beaten **spasmodically** by Rob. (*Little Men*)

Something that is beaten **spasmodically** is beaten

a. happily   **c.** skillfully
b. erratically   **d.** quietly

Snap the code, or go to **vocabularyworkshop.com**

Note that not all of the 20 unit words are used in this passage. *Feint*, *illegible*, *subjugate*, and *terse* are not included in the passage.

*Read the following selection, taking note of the **boldface** words and their contexts. These words are among those you will be studying in Unit 2. As you complete the exercises in this unit, it may help to refer to the way the words are used below.*

C CCSS Vocabulary: 4; Reading (Informational Text): 4, 6. (See pp. T14–15.)

Cowgirl Up!
<Historical Nonfiction>

People today may consider cowgirls to be folk heroines, but many of the women who helped open America's western cattle country would have **jeered** and laughed at the term. It had a hint of the **dissolute** until well into the 20ᵗʰ century. Cowgirls were associated with **comely** female sharpshooters, ropers, and trick riders of Wild West shows. At that time, working in entertainment meant **expulsion** from respectable society. But, it is said that you can't judge a horse by its color, and the West benefited from the work of all the women there.

Susan McSween

There was a precedent in the West for women ranchers in the areas governed by Spain from 1697 to 1848. Husbands and wives co-owned vast homesteads. Under Spanish law, wives could inherit property. Land ownership **fortified** the social status of women. Early generations of ranch women were **unflinching** and determined as they undertook all but the heaviest chores. They rode horses, herded cattle, and performed much of the work wealthy ranchers could **compensate** cowboys to do, and all the while, these women tended their homes and families. Their contributions helped turn struggling ranches into **lucrative** enterprises.

Some women of the old West are legends, while others have stories that have only been remembered by their families. Susan McSween lived in New Mexico at the time of Billy the Kid and the Lincoln County Wars. Rather than **adjourn** to a humdrum town life after her husband's murder in 1878, young Susan McSween purchased a ranch. Soon McSween, "The Cattle Queen of New Mexico," owned over 8,000 head of cattle. She lived much of her life running her ranch and selling real estate.

Lily Casey grew up in the early 1900s in a one-room house in West Texas, where, as a young child, she drove the family wagon to town to sell eggs. Her family bought a ranch in New Mexico when she was 11 years old. Casey's mother did not find

Calamity Jane

the **alien**, difficult ranch work **tantalizing**, so Casey began overseeing most of the ranch work when she was barely a teenager. Exhausted by running the ranch without support, Casey left home at age 15 to teach in a town 500 miles away. She rode a horse all the way and arrived at her new job, **sullied** and hungry, 28 days later. Casey taught for many years before returning to ranching during the 1930s.

Nobody would pin the label **mediocre** on the life of Martha Jane Canary. Born in 1852 in Missouri, she was separated from her family at an early age. To support herself, she worked **erratically** as a waitress, a nurse, a pony express rider, a mule- and ox-team driver, and a gold prospector. It was during her time as an army scout that she met Buffalo Bill and earned her famous nickname, "Calamity Jane." She traveled through much of the West, and stories of her adventures **proliferated**. She died in South Dakota in 1903. She is buried next to another western hero whose life is **fodder** for outrageous stories—Wild Bill Hickok.

While early ranch women were the first cowgirls, such women exist today. The National Cowgirl Hall of Fame in Texas first opened its doors in 1975 and has over 150 inductees. Among the cowgirls honored are a Pulitzer Prize winner, the first female chief of the Cherokee Nation, and a Supreme Court Justice.

Snap the code, or go to
vocabularyworkshop.com

Definitions

Note the spelling, pronunciation, part(s) of speech, and definition(s) of each of the following words. Then write the word in the blank spaces in the illustrative sentence(s) following. Finally, study the lists of synonyms and antonyms.

1. adjourn
(ə jərn')

(*v.*) to stop proceedings temporarily; move to another place

The judge _____**adjourned**_____ the hearing until ten o'clock the following morning.

SYNONYMS: postpone, discontinue
ANTONYMS: open, call to order

2. alien
(ā' lē ən)

(*n.*) a citizen of another country; (*adj.*) foreign, strange

Movies about _____**aliens**_____ from outer space have been extremely popular for decades.

An _____**alien**_____ species of plant or animal can upset the balance of an ecosystem.

SYNONYM: (*adj.*) exotic
ANTONYMS: (*adj.*) native, endemic

3. comely
(kəm' lē)

(*adj.*) having a pleasing appearance

The proud parents and their _____**comely**_____ children posed for a family portrait.

SYNONYMS: good-looking, attractive, bonny
ANTONYMS: plain, homely, ugly, repulsive

4. compensate
(käm' pən sāt)

(*v.*) to make up for; to repay for services

The manufacturer was ordered to _____**compensate**_____ customers injured by the defective product.

SYNONYMS: pay back, recompense
ANTONYMS: fail to reward, stiff

5. dissolute
(dis' ə lüt)

(*adj.*) loose in one's morals or behavior

The mad Roman emperor Caligula led an extravagant and _____**dissolute**_____ life.

SYNONYMS: dissipated, debauched, immoral, corrupt
ANTONYMS: chaste, moral, seemly, proper

6. erratic
(e rat' ik)

(*adj.*) not regular or consistent; different from what is ordinarily expected; undependable

Students who have an _____**erratic**_____ attendance record may find themselves disciplined by the principal.

SYNONYMS: irregular, inconsistent
ANTONYMS: steady, consistent, dependable

Ⓒ CCSS Vocabulary: 4.c., 4.d. (See pp. T14–15.)

7. expulsion
(ek spəl′ shən)

(*n.*) the process of driving or forcing out

The Biblical story of the _____ **expulsion** _____ of Adam and Eve from the Garden of Eden is told in Genesis.

SYNONYMS: ejection, removal, eviction
ANTONYMS: admittance, admission

8. feint
(fānt)

(*n.*) a deliberately deceptive movement; a pretense; (*v.*) to make a deceptive movement; to make a pretense of

The chess master's opening _____ **feint** _____ gave her an immediate advantage.

His uncanny ability to _____ **feint** _____ and counterpunch made the champ unbeatable.

SYNONYMS: (*n.*) trick, ruse, subterfuge, bluff

9. fodder
(fäd′ ər)

(*n.*) food for horses or cattle; raw material for a designated purpose

Every experience in life is _____ **fodder** _____ for a novelist's imagination.

SYNONYM: provender

10. fortify
(fôr′ tə fī)

(*v.*) to strengthen, build up

The soldiers _____ **fortified** _____ the garrison against the expected attack.

SYNONYMS: reinforce, shore up
ANTONYMS: weaken, undermine, sap, impair

11. illegible
(i lej′ ə bəl)

(*adj.*) difficult or impossible to read

The effects of air pollution have rendered the inscriptions on many old gravestones _____ **illegible** _____.

SYNONYMS: unreadable, scribbled
ANTONYMS: readable, distinct, clear

12. jeer
(jēr)

(*v.*) to make fun of rudely or unkindly; (*n.*) a rude remark of derision

To _____ **jeer** _____ at someone with a disability is absolutely inexcusable.

Umpires and other referees quickly become immune to the _____ **jeers** _____ of angry fans.

SYNONYMS: (*v.*) laugh at, mock, taunt (*n.*) gibe, insult
ANTONYMS: (*v.*) applaud, praise (*n.*) applause, plaudits

13. lucrative
(lü′ krə tiv)

(*adj.*) bringing in money; profitable

Many people find that they can turn a favorite hobby into a highly _____ **lucrative** _____ business.

SYNONYMS: gainful, moneymaking
ANTONYMS: unprofitable, losing, in the red

 CCSS Vocabulary: 4.c. (See pp. T14–15.)

14. mediocre
(mē dē ō′ kər)

(*adj.*) average, ordinary, undistinguished

The team's number-one draft pick turned out to be a rather _____**mediocre**_____ player, not a star who could lead them to the championship.

SYNONYM: run-of-the-mill
ANTONYMS: outstanding, distinguished

15. proliferate
(prō lif′ ə rāt)

(*v.*) to reproduce, increase, or spread rapidly

Because malignant cells _____**proliferate**_____, early detection of cancer is absolutely crucial to successful treatment.

SYNONYMS: multiply, mushroom, burgeon
ANTONYMS: decrease, diminish, dwindle, slack off

16. subjugate
(səb′ jü gāt)

(*v.*) to conquer by force, bring under complete control

"We must act quickly," the general said, "in order to _____**subjugate**_____ the rebel forces."

SYNONYMS: subdue, vanquish
ANTONYMS: be conquered, submit

17. sully
(səl′ ē)

(*v.*) to soil, stain, tarnish, defile, besmirch

The Nixon-era Watergate scandal _____**sullied**_____ the image of politicians in the minds of many voters.

SYNONYMS: pollute, taint, smear
ANTONYMS: cleanse, purify, decontaminate

18. tantalize
(tan′ tə līz)

(*v.*) to tease, torment by teasing

When I am on a diet, the treats in bakery windows seem to have been put there to _____**tantalize**_____ me.

SYNONYMS: tempt, lead on, make one's mouth water
ANTONYMS: satisfy, fulfill, gratify

19. terse
(tərs)

(*adj.*) brief and to the point

The manuscript for my short story was returned to me with a _____**terse**_____ letter of rejection.

SYNONYMS: succinct, crisp, short and sweet
ANTONYMS: wordy, diffuse, prolix

20. unflinching
(ən flin′ chiŋ)

(*adj.*) firm, showing no signs of fear, not drawing back

Everyone admires the _____**unflinching**_____ courage with which firefighters and other rescue workers carry out their dangerous jobs.

SYNONYMS: resolute, steadfast, unwavering
ANTONYMS: irresolute, wavering, vacillating

CCSS Vocabulary: 4.c. (See pp. T14–15.)

Choosing the Right Word

*Select the **boldface** word that better completes each sentence. You might refer to the selection on pages 22–23 to see how most of these words are used in context.*

1. We all experience fear and panic, but the leader of a great nation must be able to (**tantalize, subjugate**) such emotions.

2. Though a veteran soldier is often a well-tuned fighting machine, a raw recruit must be trained to avoid becoming cannon (**feint, fodder**).

3. His behavior is so (**erratic, terse**) that we never know what to expect from him.

4. When I first noticed how (**illegible, lucrative**) my roommate's handwriting was, I suggested that he sign up immediately for a course in penmanship.

Over 16 million men and women served in the United States armed forces during World War II.

5. I would be unwilling to vote for the (**expulsion, fodder**) of club members just because they are behind in their dues.

6. The desire to force everyone to accept the same set of ideas is completely (**illegible, alien**) to the spirit of democracy.

7. After the formal dinner was over, we (**adjourned, tantalized**) to the den in order to continue our conversation in a more relaxed atmosphere.

8. At one point in our fencing match, my opponent unexpectedly (**sullied, feinted**) to the left and threw me completely off guard.

9. *The Rake's Progress* paints a grim and uncompromising picture of some of the more (**dissolute, alien**) and degrading aspects of human behavior.

10. In my opinion, his writing is so bad that he will have to improve a great deal just to reach the level of (**mediocrity, compensation**).

11. To keep my self-respect, I must stand (**comely, unflinching**) before the authorities and tell them the truth as I see it.

12. For centuries people have turned to the support of their friends and family to (**fortify, proliferate**) themselves against the shocks of daily life.

13. "No," she said, "I won't (**sully, adjourn**) your ears by repeating those mean and nasty rumors."

14. All great athletes should know that the same fans who are cheering them today may be (**jeering, subjugating**) them tomorrow.

15. As soon as I entered that charming little cottage, I noticed that everything in it was neat and (**erratic, comely**).

16. Over the years I've noticed one thing about rumors: Where the facts are few, fictions (**proliferate, fortify**).

17. A best-selling book that is then made into a movie may be more (**dissolute, lucrative**) than the proverbial pot of gold at the end of the rainbow.

18. Even though I must work hard for a living, I feel that the company I'm with amply (**subjugates, compensates**) me for my time and effort.

19. Instead of all those long, flowery passages, why don't you try to write more in the (**mediocre, terse**) and direct style of a good newspaper reporter?

20. I can understand how ordinary people sometimes feel (**tantalized, jeered**) by the wealth and luxuries they see displayed on television programs.

21. When I asked my mother why she wouldn't let me borrow the car, she (**comely, tersely**) explained that she needed it for herself.

22. The (**feint, alien**), two-headed and covered with green scales, was grateful that the local people had welcomed him in spite of their misgivings.

23. The basketball team's uncharacteristic losing streak made the (**jeers, feints**) echoing throughout the arena sting even more.

24. The detective was frustrated by the (**illegibility, expulsion**) of the letter, which made it difficult to determine who had written it.

25. The little girl wanted to see her brother flinch, so she made a sudden (**sully, feint**).

Synonyms

*Choose the word from this unit that is the same or most nearly the same in meaning as the **boldface** word or expression in the phrase. Write that word on the line. Use a dictionary if necessary.*

1. found myself in **unfamiliar** territory — alien

2. ordered to **reimburse** the victims of the swindle — compensate

3. tried to **master** my hot temper — subjugate

4. a reputation for being **unpredictable** — erratic

5. ordered the **ouster** of seven career diplomats — expulsion

6. **dodged** to the left and ran for a touchdown — feinted

7. a supply of necessary **provisions** for our livestock — fodder

8. written in an **indecipherable** scrawl — illegible

9. **suspend** the discussion because of the late hour — adjourn

10. a **concise** answer — terse

C CCSS Vocabulary: 5. (See pp. T14–15.)

The synonyms and antonyms here do not appear on the Definitions page.

2

Antonyms

*Choose the word from this unit that is most nearly opposite in meaning to the **boldface** word or expression in the phrase. Write that word on the line. Use a dictionary if necessary.*

1. an **virtuous** lifestyle _____ dissolute

2. handwritten text that was **comprehensible** _____ illegible

3. delivered a **verbose** speech about the economy _____ terse

4. the villagers were forced to **yield** to the invaders _____ subjugate

5. judged the work to be **exceptional** _____ mediocre

Completing the Sentence

From the words in this unit, choose the one that best completes each of the following sentences. Write the word in the space provided.

1. Though he had a great sinker ball, he was so _____erratic_____ on the mound that fans started to call him "Wild Pitch Hickok."

2. When the national economy is expanding, new housing developments begin to _____proliferate_____; when times are lean, construction slacks off.

3. The fact that you say you are truly sorry does not _____compensate_____ for the pain I have suffered as a result of your cruelty.

4. Their so-called peace initiative proved to be nothing more than a clever _____feint_____ designed to lull the enemy into a false sense of security.

5. A telegram was usually as _____terse_____ as possible, since there was a charge for every word used in it.

6. A(n) _____mediocre_____ student is one who neither fails any subject nor receives any marks that are above average.

7. To enlarge the areas under their control, kings of old sent out their armies to _____subjugate_____ their neighbors.

8. The speaker advised us not to imitate the _____dissolute_____ kind of person who squanders time and money in the vain pursuit of pleasure.

9. In spite of all the adverse criticism her ideas have received, she remains _____unflinching_____ in her determination to improve our community.

10. Despite all my efforts to make this a(n) _____lucrative_____ enterprise, it continues to be a decidedly unprofitable organization.

CCSS Vocabulary: 4.a. (See pp. T14–15.)

Unit 2 ▪ *29*

11. When it is time to end one of our meetings, a member must make a motion to _____**adjourn**_____.

12. Their only response to my warnings was to _____**jeer**_____ at me scornfully and go ahead with their plans.

13. Our doctor's handwriting is so _____**illegible**_____ that my brother used one of his prescriptions as a teacher's pass.

14. Some people drink quantities of orange juice and swallow vitamin C tablets in a valiant attempt to _____**fortify**_____ themselves against winter colds.

15. Our laws protect not only citizens but also _____**aliens**_____ legally residing in this country.

16. The thoroughly disgraceful behavior of a few dissipated officers effectively _____**sullied**_____ the honor of the entire unit.

17. How can you be so cruel as to _____**tantalize**_____ those poor dogs by offering them tidbits that you will never let them have?

18. Though she is not a beautiful woman by conventional standards, she is certainly _____**comely**_____ and appealing.

19. The farmer must provide storage facilities for the _____**fodder**_____ he plans to set aside for his cattle during the long winter.

20. He was a changed young man after his _____**expulsion**_____ from West Point for "conduct unbecoming an officer and a gentleman."

Writing: Words in Action

Answers to both prompts will vary.

1. Look back at "Cowgirl Up!" (pages 22–23). The history of cowgirls is the history of individual women who embodied the independent spirit of the West. Which woman profiled seems like the most quintessential, or ideal, cowgirl? Write a short expository essay explaining your choice. Begin your essay with your own definition of what a cowgirl is and the traits she embodies, based on your reading of the passage. Use at least two details from the passage and three unit words to support your understanding.

2. Think of a job held by people today—men or women—that is often looked down upon by society or made to seem undesirable or unimportant. What judgments do people make about this job? Why is the job nevertheless important and necessary? Support your ideas with specific details from your own experience and observations, as well as information you have gained from your own reading or media viewing. Write at least three paragraphs explaining your viewpoint, and use three or more words from this unit.

Writing prompt #2 is modeled on that of standardized tests.

Vocabulary in Context: Informational Text for Unit 2 is available online at **vocabularyworkshop.com**.

2

Vocabulary in Context

Literary Text

The following excerpts are from Charlotte Brontë's novel Jane Eyre. *Some of the words you have studied in this unit appear in **boldface** type. Complete each statement below the excerpt by circling the letter of the correct answer.*

1. After dinner, we immediately **adjourned** to the schoolroom: lessons recommenced, and were continued till five o'clock.

   If you have **adjourned** you have
   a. turned your attention to
   (b.) moved to another place
   c. sent a message
   d. given up on

2. ""My dear children," pursued the black marble clergyman, with pathos, "this is a sad, a melancholy occasion; for it becomes my duty to warn you, that this girl, who might be one of God's own lambs, is a little castaway: not a member of the true flock, but evidently an interloper and an **alien**."

   Someone who is an **alien** is a(n)
   a. enemy
   b. orphan
   (c.) stranger
   d. spy

3. "I don't think she can ever have been pretty; but, for aught I know, she may possess originality and strength of character to **compensate** for the want of personal advantage."

   If you do NOT **compensate** for something, you
   a. fail to stay on schedule
   b. forget about it
   c. misplace it
   (d.) fail to make up for it

Joan Fontaine plays Jane Eyre and Orson Welles plays Mr. Rochester in the classic 1943 film *Jane Eyre*.

4. "I know how soon youth would fade and bloom perish, if, in the cup of bliss offered, but one dreg of shame, or one flavor of remorse were detected; and I do not want sacrifice, sorrow, **dissolution**—such is not my taste."

   A state of **dissolution** is characterized by
   (a.) corruption
   b. loneliness
   c. uncertainty
   d. madness

5. "You make me a liar by such language: you **sully** my honor."

   To **sully** is to
   a. ridicule
   b. praise
   (c.) tarnish
   d. proclaim

Interactive Quiz

Snap the code, or go to **vocabularyworkshop.com**

UNIT 3

Note that not all of the 20 unit words are used in this passage. *Cherubic*, *gluttony*, *pauper*, and *trite* are not included in the passage.

*Read the following selection, taking note of the **boldface** words and their contexts. These words are among those you will be studying in Unit 3. As you complete the exercises in this unit, it may help to refer to the way the words are used below.*

C CCSS Vocabulary: 4; Reading (Informational Text): 4, 6. (See pp. T14–15.)

A Polar Controversy
<Historical Nonfiction>

Today, traveling by air greatly **abridges** the time it once took to reach the North Pole. In the first decade of the 20th century, before airplanes, reaching that remote, frozen destination was no easy task. Those who attempted it had to **surmount** hazardous conditions, such as **rifts** in thick, drifting sea ice and bitter winds that made breathing painful. Nonetheless, reaching the Pole first was an elusive prize that adventurers ardently sought. Then toward the end of that decade, two **eminent** American explorers, Frederick Cook and Robert E. Peary, friends and cotravelers, each claimed to have done so. Which one actually hit the jackpot? After all, a "first" cannot be achieved twice!

The two men shared a passionate commitment to polar exploration, but diverged in their attitudes and methods. Cook took a keen interest in the indigenous hunters. He strove to learn their culture and language. In contrast, Peary, who had undertaken several Arctic journeys, treated the native peoples he encountered in a manner one would never **condone** today. He approached the Arctic dwellers as a **marauder** would, **pilfering** their grave sites and selling the remains.

Cook left his base camp in Annoatok, Greenland, in February of 1908, and he claimed later that he reached the Pole on April 21 after enduring two months of brutal conditions. Once he determined his location by sextant, he began his long trek back to Annoatok, arriving there a year later. In his exhuasted and emaciated state, he bore little **semblance** to a human being. Then, during his recovery, he learned that Peary had begun his own polar expedition eight months earlier, in August 1908. His strength restored, Cook journeyed overland by sled

Frederick Cook

to a Danish trading post that was 700 miles away, but he left behind most of his expedition records, intending to have them shipped later. In August 1909, several months after Cook's departure, Peary arrived at Annootok, convinced that he had been the first to reach the Pole on April 6, 1909. Hearing that Cook was claiming to have won the race the previous year made him **irate**. This news led him to try to discredit his fellow adventurer; he later accused Cook of **fabricating** accounts of such past achievements as his successful assault on the summit of Mount McKinley. Peary even refused to take Cook's expedition records with him aboard the ship that took him home, so they were lost forever.

Cook was heartsick that his former colleague would try to **usurp** his claim with these attacks. Their friendship was now **terminated**—and thus began a lifelong **altercation**. Once back in the United States, Peary and his associates kept busy casting doubts on Cook's reliability. Cook did not take these attacks lying down. He was in Europe, writing *My Attainment of the Pole* to make his case more forcefully.

Peary stayed on the offensive and soon gained public favor. A congressional committee investigated Peary's claims, and although it passed a bill honoring him, many **dissented**, remaining unconvinced

by his so-called proofs. The committee officially credited him—not with discovering the North Pole, but simply with Arctic exploration resulting in its discovery.

Both explorers claimed to have buried objects at the North Pole, but such evidence has never been found. Nor have Cook's records shown up. Both explorers have their **adherents**, and the question of who reached the Pole first remains unanswered, although Peary's name is the one that is most associated with the discovery. Peary's efforts notwithstanding, Cook's claim has proven hard to **exorcise**. One reason: More recent visitors to the polar region have confirmed as accurate his original vivid descriptions.

Snap the code, or go to
vocabularyworkshop.com

Robert E. Peary

Definitions

Note the spelling, pronunciation, part(s) of speech, and definition(s) of each of the following words. Then write the word in the blank spaces in the illustrative sentence(s) following. Finally, study the lists of synonyms and antonyms.

1. abridge
(ə brij')

(v.) to make shorter

Travel by air _____ **abridges** _____ the time needed to reach far-distant places.

SYNONYMS: shorten, condense, abbreviate
ANTONYMS: expand, enlarge, augment

2. adherent
(ad hēr' ənt)

(n.) a follower, supporter; (adj.) attached, sticking to

The senator's loyal _____ **adherent** _____ campaigned long and hard for her reelection.

Before we could repaint the walls of our living room, we had to remove an _____ **adherent** _____ layer of wallpaper.

SYNONYM: (n.) disciple
ANTONYMS: (n.) opponent, adversary, critic, detractor

3. altercation
(ôl tər kā' shən)

(n.) an angry argument

A noisy _____ **altercation** _____ in the next apartment kept me awake for hours

SYNONYMS: quarrel, dispute, squabble
ANTONYMS: agreement, accord

4. cherubic
(che rü' bik)

(adj.) resembling an angel portrayed as a little child with a beautiful, round, or chubby face; sweet and innocent

How well those photographs of the month-old twins capture the _____ **cherubic** _____ expressions on their faces!

SYNONYM: beatific
ANTONYMS: impish, devilish, diabolic, fiendish

5. condone
(kən dōn')

(v.) to pardon or overlook

Our parents have always made it crystal clear to us that they do not _____ **condone** _____ rude behavior.

SYNONYMS: ignore, wink at, look the other way
ANTONYMS: censure, condemn, disapprove, deprecate

6. dissent
(di sent')

(v.) to disagree; (n.) disagreement

Justices have an option to _____ **dissent** _____ from a ruling issued by a majority of the Supreme Court.

Some people give voice to their _____ **dissent** _____ on issues of public policy by writing letters to newspapers.

SYNONYMS: (v.) differ, dispute
ANTONYMS: (v.) agree, concur; (n.) unanimity

CCSS Vocabulary: 4.c., 4.d. (See pp. T14–15.)

7. eminent
(em′ ə nənt)

(*adj.*) famous, outstanding, distinguished; projecting

A group of _____ eminent _____ scientists met to discuss long-term changes in Earth's climate.

SYNONYMS: illustrious, renowned
ANTONYMS: nameless, unsung, lowly, humble

8. exorcise
(ek′ sôr sīz)

(*v.*) to drive out by magic; to dispose of something troublesome, menacing, or oppressive

We must do all we can to _____ exorcise _____ the evils of hatred and prejudice from our society.

SYNONYM: expel

9. fabricate
(fab′ rə kāt)

(*v.*) to make, manufacture; to make up, invent

Threads from the cocoons of caterpillars called silkworms are used to _____ fabricate _____ silk.

SYNONYMS: put together, devise, contrive, concoct
ANTONYMS: take apart, undo, destroy, demolish

10. gluttony
(glə′ tə nē)

(*n.*) engaging in extreme eating or drinking; greedy overindulgence

In the Middle Ages, _____ gluttony _____ was considered one of the Seven Deadly Sins.

SYNONYMS: overeating, ravenousness, rapaciousness
ANTONYM: abstemiousness

11. irate
(ī rāt′)

(*adj.*) angry

Long delays caused by bad weather are likely to make even the most unflappable traveler _____ irate _____.

SYNONYMS: incensed, infuriated, livid
ANTONYMS: calm, composed, cool, unruffled

12. marauder
(mə rôd′ ər)

(*n.*) a raider, plunderer

Edgar Allan Poe's story "The Gold Bug" concerns treasure buried by the _____ marauder _____ Captain Kidd.

SYNONYMS: looter, pirate

13. pauper
(pô′ pər)

(*n.*) an extremely poor person

During the Great Depression, many people were reduced to leading the desperate lives of _____ paupers _____.

SYNONYM: destitute person
ANTONYM: billionaire

CCSS Vocabulary: 4.c. (See pp. T14–15.)

14. pilfer
(pil' fər)

(v.) to steal in small quantities

An employee who _____pilfers_____ from the petty cash box will get caught sooner or later.

SYNONYMS: rob, swipe, purloin

---

15. rift
(rift)

(n.) a split, break, breach

Failure to repay a loan can be the cause of an angry _____rift_____ between longtime friends.

SYNONYMS: crack, fissure, gap, cleft
ANTONYM: reconciliation

---

16. semblance
(sem' bləns)

(n.) a likeness; an outward appearance; an apparition

Despite a bad case of stage fright, I tried to maintain a _____semblance_____ of calm as I sang my solo.

SYNONYMS: air, aura, facade
ANTONYMS: dissimilarity, contrast, total lack

---

17. surmount
(sər maúnt')

(v.) to overcome, rise above

Wilma Rudolph _____surmounted_____ childhood illness and physical disabilities to win three Olympic gold medals.

SYNONYMS: conquer, triumph over
ANTONYMS: be vanquished, be defeated, succumb to

---

18. terminate
(tər' mə nāt)

(v.) to bring to an end

If you fail to perform your job satisfactorily, your boss may _____terminate_____ your employment.

SYNONYMS: conclude, finish, discontinue
ANTONYMS: begin, commence

---

19. trite
(trīt)

(adj.) commonplace; overused, stale

When you write an essay or a story, be especially careful to avoid using _____trite_____ expressions.

SYNONYMS: banal, hackneyed, corny
ANTONYMS: original, innovative

---

20. usurp
(yü sərp')

(v.) to seize and hold a position by force or without right

The general who led the coup _____usurped_____ the office of the duly elected president.

SYNONYMS: seize illegally, supplant

C CCSS Vocabulary: 4.c. (See pp. T14–15.)

Choosing the Right Word

*Select the **boldface** word that better completes each sentence. You might refer to the essay on pages 32–33 to see how most of these words are used in context.*

1. The fact that Abraham Lincoln was able to (**surmount, terminate**) the handicap of a limited education does not mean that you should quit school.

2. It is the sacred duty of all Americans to oppose any attempt to (**abridge, condone**) or deny the rights guaranteed to us in the Constitution.

3. If you ever saw how vigorously my dog attacks his food, practically inhaling it, you would understand why I accuse him of (**gluttony, altercation**).

4. One can't become a good writer just by (**surmounting, adhering**) closely to rules laid down in standard grammar books.

President Lincoln before he delivered his Gettysburg Address

5. I do not entirely (**usurp, condone**) your misconduct, but I can understand, to a degree, why you behaved as you did.

6. The comforting presence of relatives did much to (**exorcise, pilfer**) the patient's feelings of alarm at the thought of undergoing major surgery.

7. Either party has the right to (**terminate, surmount**) the agreement that has been made whenever the partnership proves unprofitable.

8. His speech was so (**cherubic, trite**) that one could almost anticipate the phrases he would use next.

9. The robber barons of an earlier era often acted more like (**adherents, marauders**) than ethical businessmen in their dealings with the public.

10. Unless we repair the (**rifts, semblances**) in our party and present a united front, we will go down in crushing defeat in the upcoming election.

11. The few words that she grudgingly muttered were the only (**semblance, altercation**) of an apology that she offered for her rude behavior.

12. Like all literary sneak thieves, he has a truly nasty habit of (**pilfering, fabricating**) other people's ideas and then claiming them as his own.

13. I am very much flattered that you have referred to me as "an (**abridged, eminent**) educator," but I prefer to think of myself as just a good teacher.

14. I feel like a (**usurper, pauper**) now that my part-time job has come to an end and I no longer have any spending money.

15. In a dictatorship, people who (**abridge, dissent**) from the official party line usually wind up in prison—or worse.

C CCSS Vocabulary: 4.d. (See pp. T14–15.)

Unit 3 ■ 37

16. The fact that many citizens are (**trite, <u>irate</u>**) over the new taxes does not mean that these taxes are unjustifiable.

17. My cousin has so much imagination that he can (**dissent, <u>fabricate</u>**) an excuse that even an experienced principal would believe!

18. What began as a minor quarrel grew into a serious (**<u>altercation</u>, exorcism**) and then into an ugly brawl.

19. Their (**irate, <u>cherubic</u>**) faces and other-worldly voices almost made me believe that the music they were singing was coming from an ethereal place.

20. As a loyal (**<u>adherent</u>, pauper**), she was horrified by her political party's stance on the issue, feeling that it went against her principles.

21. In the new movie, the hero (**fabricates, <u>surmounts</u>**) the obstacles put in his path by his evil but clever brother, who has betrayed him.

22. There is nothing (**<u>trite</u>, irate**) about the saying "You can't go home again"; it is a wise expression that applies to many situations in life.

23. Apparently, our dog is a very successful (**<u>marauder</u>, adherent**) who finds toys and articles of clothing in neighbors' yards and brings them all home to us.

24. If you do not act quickly, they will (**pilfer, <u>terminate</u>**) the agreement, and you will have to start all over again with some other company.

25. You had no right to (**exorcise, <u>usurp</u>**) for yourself the role of gracious host at my party!

Synonyms

*Choose the word from this unit that is the same or most nearly the same in meaning as the **boldface** word or expression in the phrase. Write that word on the line. Use a dictionary if necessary.*

1. exhibited **voraciousness** at mealtime   gluttony

2. **timeworn** expression on a greeting card   trite

3. a **veneer** of friendliness   semblance

4. programs that aid **the needy**   paupers

5. **partisans** of the free market system   adherents

6. small change **filched** from the cash register   pilfered

7. **turned a blind eye to** corrupt practices   condoned

8. bravely faced the **enraged** crowd   irate

9. **commandeered** the reins of power   usurped

10. a positively **seraphic** appearance   cherubic

The synonyms and antonyms here do not appear on the Definitions page.

3

Antonyms

*Choose the word from this unit that is most nearly opposite in meaning to the **boldface** word or expression in the phrase. Write that word on the line. Use a dictionary if necessary.*

1. a **demonic** expression on the gargoyle's face _____cherubic_____

2. the social position of a **wealthy person** _____pauper_____

3. showed laudable **temperance** at the buffet table _____gluttony_____

4. **initiated** talks between the warring parties _____terminated_____

5. a **novel** approach to a familiar subject _____trite_____

Completing the Sentence

From the words in this unit, choose the one that best completes each of the following sentences. Write the word in the space provided.

1. Bands of _____marauders_____ broke through the frontier defenses of the province and began to plunder the rich farmlands of the interior.

2. "I am willing to wink at a harmless prank," the dean remarked, "but I will not _____condone_____ outright vandalism."

3. "It is a real tribute to the ingenuity of the human mind that for thousands of years people have been _____fabricating_____ new and interesting theories of the universe.

4. In this clever spoof of horror movies, the local witch doctor encounters hilarious difficulties when he tries to _____exorcise_____ a demon that has taken up residence in the heroine's body.

5. As the layer of clouds that hung over the city began to break up, the sun came pouring through the _____rift_____.

6. It is only through the exercise of their intelligence that people can begin to _____surmount_____ the difficulties they encounter in daily living.

7. A screenplay or television drama with the same old boy-meets-girl plot can certainly be criticized as _____trite_____.

8. After driving the lawful ruler out of the country for good, the villainous duke _____usurped_____ the throne and crowned himself king.

9. In movies, characters who engage in _____gluttony_____ are often used for comic relief, but in real-life extreme overeating is a serious problem.

10. In order to fit the newspaper article into the space available, the editor had to _____abridge_____ it by omitting secondary details.

11. The only way I could _____terminate_____ the argument peacefully was to walk away abruptly.

12. Although they have enough money to live on, the loss of most of their great wealth has left them feeling like _____paupers_____.

13. During a recent interdenominational service in our community center, the _____adherents_____ of various faiths met to worship as one.

14. Though I was hurt by the tactless comment, I tried to show pleasure in it by twisting my lips into a feeble _____semblance_____ of a smile.

15. "I think," said the salesclerk, "that the phrase 'hot under the collar' aptly describes the typical _____irate_____ customer we have to deal with."

16. A few of us who disagreed strongly with the committee's conclusions felt compelled to raise our voices in _____dissent_____.

17. No one but a heartless scoundrel would _____pilfer_____ nickels and dimes from a charity's collection fund.

18. Although I am not a particularly argumentative person, last week I found myself involved in a heated _____altercation_____ with a salesclerk.

19. "That child may have an angel's _____cherubic_____ features, but at heart he is a little demon," I exclaimed in disgust.

20. After so many years of distinguished service in the United States Senate, he can properly be called a(n) _____eminent_____ statesman.

Writing: Words in Action

Answers to both prompts will vary.

1. Look back at "A Polar Controversy" (pages 32–33). Suppose that you are one of the explorers. You want to persuade members of the National Explorers Club that you were the first to reach the North Pole. Write an argument using at least two details from the passage and three unit words to support your claim.

2. *"Twenty years from now you will be more disappointed by the things that you didn't do than by the ones you did do. So throw off the bowlines. Sail away from the safe harbor."*—Mark Twain

Do you agree with Twain's advice? In a brief essay, support your opinion with specific examples from your observations, studies, reading (refer to pages 32–33), or personal experience. Write at least three paragraphs, and use three or more words from this unit.

Writing prompt #2 is modeled on that of standardized tests.

C CCSS Vocabulary: 6; Writing: 1.c., 2.d. (See pp. T14–15.)

Vocabulary in Context: Informational Text for Unit 3 is available online at **vocabularyworkshop.com**.

3

Vocabulary in Context

Literary Text

The following excerpts are from Charles Dickens's novel Great Expectations. *Some of the words you have studied in this unit appear in* **boldface** *type. Complete each statement below the excerpt by circling the letter of the correct answer.*

1. As I was getting too big for Mr. Wopsle's great-aunt's room, my education under that preposterous female **terminated**.

   Whenever something is **terminated**, it

   a. begins
   b. ends
   c. pauses
   d. graduates

2. Besides, there had been no **altercation**; the assailant had come in so silently and suddenly, that she had been felled before she could look round.

   An **altercation** is a(n)

   a. sudden change
   b. loud noise
   c. angry argument
   d. warning signal

3. Mr. Jaggers suddenly became most **irate**. "Now, I warned you before," said he, throwing his forefinger at the terrified client, "that if you ever presumed to talk in that way here, I'd make an example of you. You infernal scoundrel, how dare you tell ME that?"

   Someone who is **irate** is definitely NOT

   a. calm
   b. upset
   c. irritated
   d. angry

A still from the 1934 English film adaptation of *Great Expectations*, with George Breakston as "Pip"

4. So, felons were not lodged and fed better than soldiers (to say nothing of **paupers**), and seldom set fire to their prisons with the excusable object of improving the flavor of their soup.

   Paupers are people who are extremely

   a. unlucky
   b. clever
   c. mischievous
   d. poor

5. My state of mind regarding the **pilfering** from which I had been so unexpectedly exonerated, did not impel me to frank disclosure; but I hope it had some dregs of good at the bottom of it.

   The act of **pilfering** involves

   a. beating
   b. stealing
   c. lying
   d. helping others

Interactive Quiz

Snap the code, or go to **vocabularyworkshop.com**

CCSS Vocabulary: 4.c.; Reading (Literature): 4. (See pp. T14–15.)

Unit 3 ■ **41**

Vocabulary for Comprehension

*Read the following selection in which some of the words you have studied in Units 1–3 appear in **boldface** type. Then answer the questions on page 43.*

This passage discusses the management of municipal common waste—in other words, trash disposal.

(Line)

In the early 1950s concern grew over the tons of trash produced in the United States and the limited amount of landfill space available
(5) for dumping. By the 1960s and 70s the public could no longer **condone** such enormous waste. Demands came from **eminent** scientists, politicians, and the general
(10) populace to address the problem by means *other* than landfill dumping. Many possible solutions emerged, including municipal solid waste incinerators (MSWIs).
(15) By burning trash in *very* hot incinerators and then harnessing the heat released to turn water into steam, MSWIs were predicted to reduce a city's trash volume by
(20) around 90% and produce 10% of their own electricity. But problems arose. The incinerators released carbon monoxide and other pollutants into the air, and the
(25) residue that remained contained toxic materials. Worse still, it was discovered that at extreme temperatures a family of toxic chemicals called *dioxins* might
(30) form. Airborne dioxins **diffuse** over local ecosystems and eventually

reach humans through the food chain. Cancer and other diseases have been linked to these dioxins.
(35) Requiring plants to clean up their harmful by-products is costly yet necessary for the public good. Does this dilemma spell the end for MSWIs? Answer: No. While fewer
(40) trash burners are in use than expected by the waste disposal industry, they may yet **proliferate**. In Europe and Japan efficient, super-clean incinerators are up and
(45) running. If our communities can pay for such plants, or if the cost of building and operating them comes down, our **perennial** effort to reduce trash will surely be **fortified**.
(50) But it is important to remember that all forms of waste management make a difference. Recycling plastic, glass, aluminum, and paper can make our resources last for
(55) years to come. Treating waste with biological and chemical agents often reduces its hazardous content. And most simply, using and consuming fewer products result in
(60) less waste.

C CCSS Vocabulary: 4.a.; Reading (Informational Text): 2, 4, 6. (See pp. T14–15.)

1. The primary purpose of the passage is to
   a. question the benefits of recycling
   b. discuss the benefits of combustion
   c. examine the use of waste incinerators
   d. provide data on waste generation
   e. promote landfill dumping

2. **Condone** (line 6) most nearly means
   a. support
   b. give
   c. conceal
   d. venerate
   e. overlook

3. **Eminent** (line 8) is best defined as
   a. qualified
   b. projecting
   c. dominant
   d. renowned
   e. irate

4. The meaning of **diffuse** (line 30) is
   a. dispense
   b. disperse
   c. rambling
   d. concentrate
   e. fall

5. In the third paragraph (lines 35–49), the author suggests that safe MSWIs are
   a. expensive
   b. common
   c. unnecessary
   d. imported
   e. unavailable

6. **Proliferate** (line 42) is best defined as
   a. explode
   b. operate
   c. lessen
   d. disappear
   e. increase

7. In lines 43–45, the author cites the incinerators in Europe and Japan as examples of
   a. an alternate form of waste management
   b. waste source reduction efforts
   c. MSWIs that are environmentally sound
   d. international cooperation
   e. MSWIs that need to be regulated

8. **Perennial** (line 48) most nearly means
   a. plant
   b. devoted
   c. resistant
   d. persistent
   e. intermittent

9. The meaning of **fortified** (line 49) is
   a. strengthened
   b. multiplied
   c. enriched
   d. nullified
   e. defended

10. The focus of the last paragraph (lines 50–60) is on
    a. federal regulations for protecting the environment
    b. other solutions for the trash problem
    c. questionable waste management practices
    d. burning municipal solid wastes
    e. identifying the best waste disposal method

11. Evidently the author believes that
    a. we have adequately addressed the problem of waste disposal
    b. MSWIs can be the most effective means of waste disposal
    c. the waste disposal problem requires more than one solution
    d. the scientists and politicians of the 1960s and 70s were alarmists
    e. MSWIs are not a good alternative to landfills

12. All of the following statements about MSWIs are true EXCEPT
    a. MSWIs burn 90% of the waste produced in most cities.
    b. Some day MSWIs may fulfill their promise.
    c. MSWIs reduce the amount of landfill space needed.
    d. Not only do MSWIs reduce waste, but they also produce electricity.
    e. MSWIs emit toxic materials that pollute the environment.

C CCSS Vocabulary: 4.a.; Reading (Informational Text): 2, 4, 6. (See pp. T14–15.)

Review Units 1–3 ■ **43**

Two-Word Completions

Select the pair of words that best complete the meaning of each of the following passages.

1. The earthquake had more or less reduced our house to a pile of worthless rubble. Nevertheless, we picked carefully through the _____, trying to _____ items of value. Unfortunately, very little could be saved.
   a. deadlock . . . relinquish
   b. muddle . . . efface
   c. debris . . . salvage
   d. dilemma . . . condone

2. Minor squabbles may cause temporary _____ in our friendship, but such _____, however heated and noisy, have never resulted in a permanent breach.
   a. feints . . . dilemmas
   b. rifts . . . altercations
   c. deadlocks . . . abridgments
   d. dissents . . . semblances

3. "If you always act cautiously, you should be able to _____ many of life's obstacles," Dad told me. "Still, some difficulties cannot be overcome, even by the most _____ behavior.
   a. surmount . . . circumspect
   b. abridge . . . alien
   c. commandeer . . . erratic
   d. relinquish . . . mediocre

4. Though I am prepared to wink at an occasional petty offense against my moral code, I absolutely refuse to _____ behavior that is consistently wicked or _____.
   a. condone . . . dissolute
   b. efface . . . erratic
   c. abridge . . . unbridled
   d. exorcise . . . circumspect

5. Although the auditorium was packed with the candidate's supporters, who greeted his remarks with thunderous cheers and applause, there were a few _____ in the crowd who seemed inclined only to boo and _____.
   a. brigands . . . feint
   b. dissenters . . . jeer
   c. paupers . . . condone
   d. adherents . . . admonish

6. Though he began life little better than a(n) _____, with only his hands in his pockets, his highly _____ business deals turned him into a multimillionaire before the age of forty.
   a. adherent . . . cumbersome
   b. usurper . . . spurious
   c. brigand . . . mediocre
   d. pauper . . . lucrative

7. He was thrown out of the club for constantly _____ small items from the supply room. According to club rules, that type of petty theft constitutes valid grounds for _____.
   a. tantalizing . . . termination
   b. sullying . . . subjugation
   c. fabricating . . . admonishment
   d. pilfering . . . expulsion

Idioms

In the essay about the controversy over whether Robert Peary or Frederick Cook was first to reach the North Pole (see pages 32–33), the author asks the question, "Which one actually hit the jackpot?"

"Hit the jackpot" is an idiom that means "succeed" or "win the prize." An **idiom** is an informal expression or figure of speech that means something different from the literal meaning of the words that form it. Because the meanings of idioms are not obvious or self-explanatory, they must be learned, just like new or unfamiliar words.

Choosing the Right Idiom

Read each sentence. Use context clues to figure out the meaning of each idiom in **boldface** *print. Then write the letter of the definition for the idiom in the sentence.*

1. **To make ends meet**, Lefty Smalls lets a neighbor graze her sheep on his land. _____c_____

2. The value of good herding dogs to a shepherd is **as plain as the nose on your face**. _____f_____

3. After a long day directing sheep, my collie just wanted to get back home and **hit the hay**. _____g_____

4. I buy herding dogs from a trainer who **drives a hard bargain**. _____h_____

5. Ranchers who do not use guardian dogs for their herds are **skating on thin ice**. _____d_____

6. The awkward new ranch hand **is all thumbs**. _____a_____

7. After much training, the dog finally **got the hang of it**. _____e_____

8. When her dog did not win first prize, the young girl was **down in the dumps**. _____b_____

9. After losing sheep, it **dawned on** the farmer that she needed more dogs to protect the flock. _____j_____

10. One judge at the dog show was very skinny. He must **eat like a bird**. _____i_____

a. very clumsy

b. discouraged

c. earn enough to pay one's bills

d. taking a dangerous chance

e. learned how to do something

f. something that is obvious

g. go to bed

h. makes a deal to one's advantage

i. consume very little food

j. began to grow plain

Writing with Idioms

Find the meaning of each idiom. (Use an online or print dictionary if necessary.) Then write a sentence for each idiom. **Answers will vary.**

1. get the ball rolling
   Sample response: If no one else will get the ball rolling, I will start the meeting.

2. get up on the wrong side of the bed

3. a green thumb

4. a half-baked idea

5. catch a cold

6. on the house

7. go fly a kite

8. out of the woods

9. hold a candle to

10. call it a day

11. it's about time

12. get in touch

Denotation and Connotation

The literal meaning of a word is its **denotation**. It is the formal meaning of the word found in a dictionary. A word's denotation conveys a *neutral* tone.

Conversely, a word's **connotation** is the informal, implied meaning a reader or listener associates with it. That connotation can be either *positive* or *negative*.

Consider these synonyms for the neutral word *smell*:

fragrance   aroma   odor   stench

Fragrance and *aroma* have positive connotations, while *odor* and *stench* have negative connotations.

> **Think:** Perfume has a fragrance or an aroma, but garbage has an odor or a stench.

Look at these examples of words that are similar in denotation but have different connotations.

NEUTRAL	POSITIVE	NEGATIVE
show	display	flaunt
work	profession	drudgery
interested	inquisitive	nosy

Understanding connotation is important for readers and writers alike. Readers who understand the connotation of a word can better grasp the author's intended meaning. Writers can make their work richer and more expressive by choosing words with just the right connotation. But connotations can be subjective. Good writers keep in mind how a word's connotation may affect their audience.

Shades of Meaning

Write a plus sign (+) in the box if the word has a positive connotation. Write a minus sign (–) if the word has a negative connotation. Put a zero (0) if the word is neutral.

1. altercation [–]

2. breach [–]

3. relinquish [–]

4. jeer [–]

5. cherubic [+]

6. cumbersome [–]

7. feint [–]

8. fortify [+]

9. spurious [–]

10. abridge [0]

11. comely [+]

12. sully [–]

13. lucrative [+]

14. circumspect [+]

15. surmount [+]

16. efface [–]

Expressing the Connotation

Read each sentence. Select the word in parentheses that expresses the connotation (positive, negative, or neutral) given at the beginning of the sentence.

negative **1.** The secret agent's (**dilemma, situation**) was that his disguise was weak.

positive **2.** The woman's (**comely, gorgeous**) appearance made for a good stage presence.

positive **3.** The winning debater's closing argument was an example of (**eminent, satisfactory**) speech making

neutral **4.** The police showed restraint when they refused to (**admonish, jeer**) the unreliable suspect.

negative **5.** The heavy bag felt (**full, cumbersome**) after I had lugged it around for a few hours.

negative **6.** The tour group's (**predictable, perennial**) favorite was a visit to Yellowstone Park.

neutral **7.** The girl was such a snob that she refused to (**risk, sully**) her reputation as a diva by applauding the regional theatre group.

positive **8.** The student's scheme to make a few bucks over the summer turned out to be a (**gainful, lucrative**) idea that brought in considerable profits.

Challenge: Using Connotation

Choose vocabulary words from Units 1–3 to replace the highlighted words in the sentences below. Then explain how the connotation of the replacement word changes the tone of the sentence. **Answers will vary.**

tersely	**irate**	**admonished**
dissolute	**mediocre**	**lucrative**

1. Eva's mother **told** _____admonished_____ her to work harder in math, or Eva would not be able to go on the field trip.
Sample response: *Admonished* makes the tone of the sentence more negative, suggesting that the mother is warning Eva in a strict way.

2. The **corrupt** _____dissolute_____ mayor turned out to be even less honorable than we had expected.
Sample response: *Dissolute* adds a more formal tone and may seem less harsh than *corrupt*, even though the meanings of the words are similar.

3. Mrs. Li was so **angry** _____irate_____ with her neighbor that they ended up in a big feud and never spoke again.
Sample response: *Irate* adds a more negative tone, suggesting a greater degree of hostility and lasting animosity than *angry* implies.

Classical Roots

pos, pon—to put, place

The root *pos* appears in **predispose** (page 16). The literal meaning is "to put away before," but the word has come to mean "to incline" or "to make susceptible." Some other words based on the same root are listed below.

component	impose	composite	juxtapose
depose	repository	disposition	transpose

From the list of words above, choose the one that corresponds to each of the brief definitions below. Write the word in the blank space in the illustrative sentence below the definition. Use an online or print dictionary if necessary.

1. to put or place upon or over something else

Digital software allows creative photographers to _____**impose**_____ a second image over the first to create an original picture.

2. to put out of office; to declare under oath (*"to put down"*)

She was shocked to learn of a secret plot to _____**depose**_____ the king.

3. to interchange positions; to shift

Jeff will _____**transpose**_____ the harmony into a different key that better suits the singer's voice.

4. a part, element

At the last minute we replaced a central _____**component**_____ of our presentation.

5. a place where things are stored or kept

They rented an off-site warehouse as a _____**repository**_____ for company records.

6. to place side by side or close together (*"to place next to"*)

They will _____**juxtapose**_____ incongruous celebrity photos in order to make a lampoon.

7. one's temperament; a tendency, inclination; a settlement, arrangement

That pony's pleasing _____**disposition**_____ makes it a perfect choice for children.

8. made up of distinct parts; combining elements or characteristics; such a combination (*"put together"*)

The forensic artist made a _____**composite**_____ drawing of the primary suspect.

UNIT 4

Note that not all of the 20 unit words are used in this passage.
Hoodwink, *inanimate*, and *pompous* are not included in the passage.

*Read the following selection, taking note of the **boldface** words and their contexts. These words are among those you will be studying in Unit 4. As you complete the exercises in this unit, it may help to refer to the way the words are used below.*

C CCSS Vocabulary: 4; Reading (Informational Text): 4, 6. (See pp. T14–T15.)

Elephant Culture and Conservation
<Expository Writing>

Throughout history, humans have admired elephants for their strength, their intelligence, and their courageous, **intrepid** behavior. The largest land mammal, elephants are divided into two species, named for the continents on which each is found. The African elephant (*Loxodonta africana*) stands twelve feet high and weighs up to eight tons. The Asian elephant (*Elephas maximus*) is slightly less massive. For centuries, Asian elephants have been carefully trained to perform the most **arduous** of tasks, such as carrying heavy loads and patrolling protected forests over rough terrain. Asian elephants have proved more **pliant** than

Asian elephants are strong work animals that can be trained to carry heavy loads.

the African species. They can respond to more than thirty vocal commands from their handlers, called *mahawats* in India.

Elephants are highly social creatures, living in herds under the leadership of a matriarch. Without the coordination this senior female provides, **anarchy** might prevail in the herd. The animals show affection by wrapping their trunks around one another, and they are especially attentive to the young calves. Elephants sleep little because they are always on the move in search of far-flung sources of food and water. In Africa, drought is a herd's biggest threat. Recently, elephants have been shown to communicate using infrasound—deep rumbles inaudible to the human ear—to ensure **access** to water and to keep the herd together. Elephants are peaceful animals, with no natural predators except humans. An elephant's trunk is a remarkable limb that could serve as an ancient **prototype** for a modern precision tool. Two fingers at the end of the trunk are so delicate that an elephant can hold an egg without breaking it.

There is one appendage, however, that critically endangers elephants: their ivory tusks. The tusks have made elephants vulnerable to poaching in both Africa and Asia. Poachers employ a variety of brutal methods to kill a wild elephant. They then slash off the animals' tusks for the illegal ivory trade and **abscond** with their loot, a clear-cut case of **larceny**.

It has proved especially difficult to **disentangle** the complex issues surrounding poaching and the ivory trade, a practice that puts all elephants at risk. The threat to elephants is serious enough to have made them one of the

To discourage poaching and the illegal trade in ivory, Kenyan authorities destroyed $3 million worth of elephant tusks.

chief concerns of wildlife conservationists, especially in Asia. Advocates of tough antipoaching laws argue that only severe penalties will **rectify** the situation and ease the threat to Asian elephants, now numbering only 30,000 to 50,000 spread over thirteen countries. India has the largest population by far. Fortunately, elephants have an **auspicious** reputation in India, and in 1992, it established Project Elephant as a national agency to protect *Elephas maximus*. In Africa, certain countries assert that they have too many elephants. These countries have,

therefore, devised culling campaigns to reduce the herds. Such programs are **reviled** as cruel by many conservationists, who warn that elephants are teetering on a **precipice** that could lead to extinction. So though it is said that an elephant never forgets, it appears that people might forget the elephant. The many challenges posed by conservation efforts are **daunting**. Are these majestic animals **fated** to suffer extinction? Or can well-designed conservation programs afford them a **reprieve** from such a bleak future? In 1989, conservationist Richard Leakey convinced Kenya's president to kick off a vigorous antipoaching campaign by publicly **incinerating** a 12-ton pile of elephant tusks. The pile was 20 feet high and worth $3 million. This celebrated bonfire drew worldwide attention.

iWords

Snap the code, or go to **vocabularyworkshop.com**

Definitions

Note the spelling, pronunciation, part(s) of speech, and definition(s) of each of the following words. Then write the word in the blank spaces in the illustrative sentence(s) following. Finally, study the lists of synonyms and antonyms.

1. abscond
(ab skänd′)

(*v.*) to run off and hide

The thieves who _____**absconded**_____ with several of the museum's most valuable paintings have never been found.

SYNONYMS: bolt, make off, skip town

2. access
(ak′ ses)

(*n.*) approach or admittance to places, persons, things; an increase; (*v.*) to get at, obtain

_____**Access**_____ to information on a seemingly unlimited number of topics is available over the Internet.

You need a password in order to _____**access**_____ your e-mail accounts.

SYNONYMS: (*n.*) entry, ingress
ANTONYM: (*n.*) total exclusion

3. anarchy
(an′ ər kē)

(*n.*) a lack of government and law; confusion

In the final days of a war, civilians may find themselves living in _____**anarchy**_____.

SYNONYMS: chaos, disorder, turmoil, pandemonium
ANTONYMS: law and order, peace and quiet

4. arduous
(är′ jü əs)

(*adj.*) hard to do, requiring much effort

No matter how carefully you plan for it, moving to a new home is an _____**arduous**_____ chore.

SYNONYMS: hard, difficult, laborious, fatiguing
ANTONYMS: easy, simple, effortless

5. auspicious
(ô spish′ əs)

(*adj.*) favorable; fortunate

My parents describe the day that they first met as a most _____**auspicious**_____ occasion.

SYNONYMS: promising, encouraging, propitious
ANTONYMS: ill-omened, sinister

6. daunt
(dônt)

(*v.*) to overcome with fear, intimidate; to dishearten, discourage

Despite all its inherent dangers, space flight did not _____**daunt**_____ the Mercury program astronauts.

SYNONYMS: dismay, cow
ANTONYMS: encourage, embolden, reassure

7. **disentangle**
(dis en taŋ' gəl)

(*v.*) to free from tangles or complications

Rescuers worked for hours to _____ **disentangle** _____ a whale from the fishing net wrapped around its jaws.

SYNONYMS: unravel, unwind, unscramble, unsnarl
ANTONYMS: tangle up, ensnarl, snag

8. **fated**
(fā' tid)

(*adj.*) determined in advance by destiny or fortune

The tragic outcome of Shakespeare's *Romeo and Juliet* is _____ **fated** _____ from the play's very first scene.

SYNONYMS: destined, preordained, doomed
ANTONYMS: fortuitous, chance, random

9. **hoodwink**
(hùd' wiŋk)

(*v.*) to mislead by a trick, swindle

Many sweepstakes offers _____ **hoodwink** _____ people into thinking they have already won big prizes.

SYNONYMS: put one over on, fool
ANTONYMS: disabuse

10. **inanimate**
(in an' ə mit)

(*adj.*) not having life; without energy or spirit

Although fossils are _____ **inanimate** _____, they hold many clues to life on Earth millions of years ago.

SYNONYMS: dead, spiritless
ANTONYMS: living, alive, energetic, sprightly

11. **incinerate**
(in sin' ər āt)

(*v.*) to burn to ashes

Because of environmental concerns, many cities and towns no longer _____ **incinerate** _____ their garbage.

SYNONYMS: burn up, cremate, reduce to ashes

12. **intrepid**
(in trep' id)

(*adj.*) very brave, fearless, unshakable

_____ **Intrepid** _____ Polynesian sailors in outrigger canoes were the first humans to reach the Hawaiian Islands.

SYNONYMS: valiant, audacious, daring
ANTONYMS: timid, cowardly, craven, pusillanimous

13. **larceny**
(lär' sə nē)

(*n.*) theft

Someone who steals property that is worth thousands of dollars commits grand _____ **larceny** _____.

SYNONYMS: stealing, robbery

14. **pliant**
(plī' ənt)

(*adj.*) bending readily; easily influenced

The _____ **pliant** _____ branches of the sapling sagged but did not break under the weight of the heavy snow.

SYNONYMS: supple, flexible, elastic, plastic
ANTONYMS: rigid, stiff, inflexible, set in stone

15. pompous
(päm′ pəs)

(*adj.*) overly self-important in speech and manner; excessively stately or ceremonious

Political cartoonists like nothing better than to mock _____**pompous**_____ public officials.

SYNONYMS: highfalutin, bombastic
ANTONYMS: unpretentious, plain

16. precipice
(pres′ ə pis)

(*n.*) a very steep cliff; the brink or edge of disaster

During the Cuban Missile Crisis, the world hovered on the _____**precipice**_____ of nuclear war.

SYNONYMS: crag, bluff, ledge
ANTONYMS: abyss, chasm, gorge

17. prototype
(prō′ tə tīp)

(*n.*) an original model on which later versions are patterned

The assembly line managers studied the _____**prototype**_____ of the new car for weeks before production began.

SYNONYMS: example, sample
ANTONYM: copy

18. rectify
(rek′ tə fī)

(*v.*) to make right, correct

The senators debated a series of measures designed to _____**rectify**_____ the nation's trade imbalance.

SYNONYM: set right
ANTONYMS: mess up, botch, bungle

19. reprieve
(ri prēv′)

(*n.*) a temporary relief or delay; (*v.*) to grant a postponement

A vacation is a kind of _____**reprieve**_____ from the cares and responsibilities of everyday life.

A judge may _____**reprieve**_____ a first-time offender from jail time until sentencing.

SYNONYMS: (*n.*) stay, respite; (*v.*) delay
ANTONYM: (*v.*) proceed

20. revile
(ri vīl′)

(*v.*) to attack with words, call bad names

The enraged King Lear _____**reviles**_____ the daughters who have cast him out into a fierce storm.

SYNONYMS: inveigh against, malign, vilify
ANTONYMS: praise, acclaim, revere, idolize

C CCSS Vocabulary: 4.c. (See pp. T14–15.)

Choosing the Right Word

*Select the **boldface** word that better completes each sentence. You might refer to the selection on pages 50–51 to see how most of these words are used in context.*

1. The voters may seem unaware of the underlying issues, but in the long run they cannot be (**disentangled, hoodwinked**) by self-serving politicians.

2. The general feared that the latest attacks on the city would push the situation over the (**precipice, access**), leading directly to a full-blown war.

3. Despite the threats made against his life, the (**arduous, intrepid**) district attorney was able to obtain a conviction of the corrupt official.

4. His broad education gave him a(n) (**auspicious, fated**) view of cultures different from his own.

5. When her eyes suddenly blazed with such fury, I felt that the heat of her glance would all but (**disentangle, incinerate**) me.

Frequent elections allow voters to change their leaders.

6. A great playwright's characters always seem to come alive; those of a third-rate hack stubbornly remain (**pliant, inanimate**).

7. His speech and manners were so (**auspicious, pompous**) and stiff that he cut a somewhat ridiculous figure at our informal little get-together.

8. How can you accuse me of (**absconding, reviling**) with all your brilliant ideas when you have never had an original thought in your life?

9. Though the dangers and uncertainties of a westward passage to the Orient cowed many a brave sailor, they did not (**rectify, daunt**) Columbus.

10. Only by admitting your fault and trying to make up for it can you obtain a(n) (**reprieve, access**) from the pangs of conscience.

11. We should begin studying foreign languages at an early age because it is during those years that our minds are most (**pompous, pliant**) and receptive.

12. The team of accountants spent hours trying to locate and then to (**rectify, prototype**) the error I had so carelessly made.

13. Spring, with its ever-renewing promise of life, is for me the most (**arduous, auspicious**) of seasons.

14. For most retired athletes, the comeback trail is an (**arduous, inanimate**) one, and few ever get to the end of it.

15. Anyone who takes the writings of other people and presents them as his or her own is guilty of literary (**larceny, anarchy**).

16. Although the hero and the heroine were parted by circumstance, I knew that they were (**intrepid, fated**) to meet again before the last commercial.

17. There is a vast difference between democracy, under which everyone has duties and privileges, and (**larceny, anarchy**), under which no one has.

18. Like farmers separating the wheat from the chaff, the members of a jury must (**disentangle, daunt**) the truth from the evidence presented to them.

19. Far from being useless, mathematics will give you (**reprieve, access**) to many fields of scientific study.

20. Instead of recognizing that he caused his own troubles, he continues to (**revile, hoodwink**) all the people who were "unfair" to him.

21. Although she looks young and inexperienced, it is not easy to (**hoodwink, rectify**) her, since she is a private detective by profession.

22. At the design firm, the most well-received (**reprieves, prototypes**) for the new line of evening gowns were the ones made from a new silk blend.

23. To (**access, disentangle**) the large safe we will need the five-digit combination to the lock.

24. I was not completely surprised when my aunt decided to (**daunt, reprieve**) her decision to let me borrow her car next weekend.

25. My uncle can be so (**pompous, intrepid**) when he lectures me about politics.

Synonyms

*Choose the word from this unit that is the same or most nearly the same in meaning as the **boldface** word or expression in the phrase. Write that word on the line. Use a dictionary if necessary.*

1. an **inert** stone   *inanimate*

2. ostentatious style of dress   *pompous*

3. editorials that **denounced** the mayor's actions   *reviled*

4. gained **entrée** to an exclusive club   *access*

5. scheduled to stand trial for **burglary**   *larceny*

6. courageous in the face of danger   *intrepid*

7. duped into buying a flawed diamond   *hoodwinked*

8. granted a thirty-day **deferral**   *reprieve*

9. tried to **remedy** their mistaken impression of me   *rectify*

10. a house built on a **promontory**   *precipice*

   ⓒ CCSS Vocabulary: 5. (See pp. T14–15.)

The synonyms and antonyms here do not appear on the Definitions page.

4

Antonyms

*Choose the word from this unit that is most nearly opposite in meaning to the **boldface** word or expression in the phrase. Write that word on the line. Use a dictionary if necessary.*

1. their **unaffected** way of expressing themselves _____ pompous _____

2. **undeceived** by the joke _____ hoodwinked _____

3. the author's surprisingly **vigorous** prose _____ inanimate _____

4. an **accidental** meeting _____ fated _____

5. a series of **ominous** events _____ auspicious _____

Completing the Sentence

From the words in this unit, choose the one that best completes each of the following sentences. Write the word in the space provided.

1. This master key will give you _____ access _____ to any of the rooms in the building.

2. No matter how much protective legislation we pass, there will probably always be gullible consumers for swindlers to _____ hoodwink _____.

3. One of the most controversial figures of his time, the former president was revered by some and _____ reviled _____ by others.

4. This handmade chair is a(n) _____ prototype _____ for the machine-built ones we will produce by the thousands.

5. With no government around to restore order, the small country remained in a state of _____ anarchy _____ for weeks after the revolution.

6. Since everything had gone so smoothly, we felt that the campaign to elect Ellen captain was off to a(n) _____ auspicious _____ beginning.

7. Though somewhat massively built, the gymnast's body was as supple and _____ pliant _____ as a ballet dancer's.

8. The treasurer who had _____ absconded _____ with the company's funds was quickly captured by alert federal agents.

9. The film had gotten so badly entwined in the malfunctioning old movie projector that I had a hard time _____ disentangling _____ it.

10. As soon as I discovered that the project was being mismanaged, I tried my best to _____ rectify _____ the situation.

CCSS Vocabulary: 4.a. (See pp. T14–15.)

Unit 4 ■ *57*

11. Though many people firmly believe that life-forms exist somewhere in outer space, everything that our astronauts have so far encountered has been decidedly _____ **inanimate** _____.

12. The youths who had "borrowed" the car for joyriding were caught by the police and charged with _____ **larceny** _____.

13. Since I'm only an average linguist, mastering the irregular verbs in French was one of the most _____ **arduous** _____ tasks I have ever undertaken.

14. Without the slightest hesitation, _____ **intrepid** _____ firefighters will enter a blazing building to rescue anyone who may be trapped.

15. The guardrail was reinforced to prevent cars from skidding over the edge of the _____ **precipice** _____ and falling into the abyss below.

16. Her extraordinary faith in her own abilities enabled her to overcome many obstacles that would have _____ **daunted** _____ someone less confident.

17. Since I did not feel well prepared, the three-day postponement of final exams was a most welcome _____ **reprieve** _____.

18. The steak I'd accidentally left in the broiler too long wasn't just overdone; it was positively _____ **incinerated** _____.

19. The overly ornate style of many eighteenth-century writers seems rather forced and _____ **pompous** _____ to us today.

20. Ancient astrologers developed the idea that what is _____ **fated** _____ to happen to a person is determined by the stars.

Writing: Words in Action

Answers to both prompts will vary.

1. Look back at "Elephant Culture and Conservation" (pages 50–51). Which kind of elephant seems more likely to survive in today's world—the Asian or the African elephant? Write a short expository essay in which you compare and contrast the two species in order to arrive at a conclusion about their possible futures. Use at least two details from the passage and three unit words to support your conclusions.

2. Protecting endangered species can be a difficult undertaking. In a brief essay, explain some of the challenges people and organizations face in their efforts to save endangered animals. Support your views with specific examples from your observations, studies, reading (refer to pages 50–51), or your own experience. Write at least three paragraphs, and use three or more words from this unit.

Writing prompt #2 is modeled on that of standardized tests.

CCSS Vocabulary: 6; Writing: 1.c., 2.d. (See pp. T14–15.)

Vocabulary in Context: Informational Text for Unit 4 is
available online at **vocabularyworkshop.com**.

4

Vocabulary in Context

Literary Text

The following excerpts are from Daniel Defoe's novels The Life and Adventures of Robinson Crusoe *and* A Journal of the Plague Year. *Some of the words you have studied in this unit appear in* **boldface** *type. Complete each statement below the excerpt by circling the letter of the correct answer.*

1. … and then I entered into a long discourse with him about the devil…and the many stratagems he made use of to delude mankind to their ruin; how he had a secret **access** to our passions and to our affections…so as to cause us even to be our own tempters, and run upon our destruction by our own choice. (*Robinson Crusoe*)

If you have **access** you have

a. envy of
b. love for
c. hatred of
d. admittance to *(circled)*

2. … [H]e approached the mountains another way; and though it is true the hills and **precipices** looked dreadful…we insensibly passed the height of the mountains without being much encumbered with the snow…. (*Robinson Crusoe*)

A **precipice** is a

a. very steep cliff *(circled)*
b. pile of rocks
c. large canopy
d. group of trees

3. They who know what it is to have a **reprieve** brought to them upon the ladder, or to be rescued from thieves just going to murder them, or who have been in such extremities, may guess what my present surprise of joy was…. (*Robinson Crusoe*)

If you have a **reprieve**, you have been given

a. a meal
b. relief *(circled)*
c. praise
d. a reward

Robinson Crusoe sitting with his dog, from an old book illustration.

4. … [T]he corpse was always left till the officers had notice to come and take them away, or till night, when the bearers attending the dead-cart would take them up and carry them away. Nor did those **undaunted** creatures…fail to search their pockets, and sometimes strip off their clothes if they were well dressed, as sometimes they were, and carry off what they could get. (*A Journal of the Plague Year*)

If you are **undaunted** you are NOT

a. eager
b. courageous
c. frightened *(circled)*
d. bold

5. … [S]ome that stayed [were] not only boasting too much of themselves, but **reviling** those that fled, branding them with cowardice, deserting their flocks, and acting the part of the hireling, and the like. (*A Journal of the Plague Year*)

To **revile** is to

a. attack with words *(circled)*
b. beat with sticks
c. admire greatly
d. take pleasure in

Interactive Quiz

Snap the code, or go to
vocabularyworkshop.com

CCSS Vocabulary: 4.c.; Reading (Literature): 4. (See pp. T14–15.)

Unit 4 ▪ 59

UNIT 5

Note that not all of the 20 unit words are used in this passage. *Morose*, *prattle*, *reprimand*, *servitude*, and *slapdash* are not included in the passage.

*Read the following selection, taking note of the **boldface** words and their contexts. These words are among those you will be studying in Unit 5. As you complete the exercises in this unit, it may help to refer to the way the words are used below.*

C CCSS Vocabulary: 4; Reading (Informational Text): 4, 6. (See pp. T14–15.)

The Leopard: Unlikely Survivor

<Expository Essay>

"**A** leopard cannot change its spots." So runs a well-known proverb. But this statement is easily **rebutted**. It turns out that leopards are remarkably adaptable animals whose **latent** ability to adapt to new situations has made them one of the few big cats not facing extinction in the wild. Africa, the Middle East, Asia, and Russia all have leopard populations. Half a million leopards roam in areas as different as the plains of South Africa to the snows of the Russian Far East. That's as many leopards as there are cheetahs, lions, and tigers combined. The leopard ranks first among cats in its ability to survive.

An **paramount** factor in the leopard's success is its diet—this cat is a generalist. The leopard does not discriminate when it comes to food and the list of its many prey seems almost **arbitrary**: Baboons, lizards, insects, and antelope are all possible meals. Cats whose diets are limited to a few species are in danger when populations of their favored prey dwindle.

Their wide-ranging diet also means that leopards can live in different types of ecosystems. Species that can only survive in a specific landscape have one of two choices when their habitats shrink or become overpopulated: **exodus** or death. Polar bears, for example, can only exist in very cold climates, and they are in danger of loosing that habitat. However, leopards can live in jungles, where they eat monkeys; islands, where they eat fish; and mountains, where they eat rodents. This wide-ranging habitat ensures that while one population may be struggling, another is surviving.

Black panther, a melanistic form of leopard

Leopards are excellent hunters. When hunting, leopards seldom rely on an **accomplice** from their own species to bring down their prey, since the animal is an **incorrigible** hermit that prefers a solitary existence. The leopard's jaw muscles are so powerful that it can catch and kill animals larger than itself. After a stealthy stalk, a leopard will charge at speeds of up to 35 miles per hour to catch its prey. Its remarkable strength **facilitates** its ability to carry quarry three times its size into trees. This practice protects the food from scavengers. Leopards prefer to stalk their prey when the **opaque** shadows of the night allow them to remain hidden hunters, but the animals also **brazenly** hunt during the day. This flexibility allows for a wider-ranging diet and increased hunting opportunities—another example of the species' unique ability to survive.

Humans also have had a hand in the rise and fall of leopard populations though. Leopards faced a serious threat from the fashion industry in the mid-20th century. Jacqueline Kennedy's appearance in a leopard-skin coat in 1964 served as a **catalyst**, leading to the rising popularity of the fur. Demand for leopard skins almost **annihilated** wild populations. A **militant** and ultimately successful campaign in the 1960s and 1970s opposing the use of leopard skins as fashion items is another reason that this animal's populations are now thriving.

While some subspecies of leopards have **stagnant** population growth or are even close to extinction, such as the Amur Leopard of Russia, the species population worldwide is impressive. According to current estimates by international conservation groups, it is highly unlikely that wild leopards will **succumb** to extinction any time soon.

Snap the code, or go to **vocabularyworkshop.com**

Left: African leopard;
Above: Indian snow leopard

Definitions

Note the spelling, pronunciation, part(s) of speech, and definition(s) of each of the following words. Then write the word in the blank spaces in the illustrative sentence(s) following. Finally, study the lists of synonyms and antonyms.

1. accomplice
(ə käm′ plis)

(*n.*) a person who takes part in a crime

The driver of the getaway car was arrested and tried as an _____**accomplice**_____ in the daring bank robbery.

SYNONYM: partner in crime

2. annihilate
(ə nī′ ə lāt)

(*v.*) to destroy completely

Throughout history, nations that are bitter enemies have sought to _____**annihilate**_____ each other.

SYNONYMS: obliterate, decimate
ANTONYMS: foster, promote, encourage, nurture

3. arbitrary
(är′ bə trer ē)

(*adj.*) unreasonable; based on one's wishes or whims without regard for reason or fairness

A judge may be criticized for rulings that appear to be _____**arbitrary**_____ and without legal precedent.

SYNONYMS: capricious, high-handed, autocratic
ANTONYMS: reasoned, rational, objective, equitable

4. brazen
(brā′ zən)

(*adj.*) shameless, impudent; made of brass

Behavior considered _____**brazen**_____ in one era may be deemed perfectly acceptable in another.

SYNONYMS: saucy, bold
ANTONYMS: deferential, respectful, self-effacing

5. catalyst
(kat′ əl ist)

(*n.*) a substance that causes or hastens a chemical reaction; any agent that causes change

Enzymes are _____**catalysts**_____ that aid in the digestion of food.

SYNONYMS: stimulus, spur, instigator

6. exodus
(ek′ sə dəs)

(*n.*) a large-scale departure or flight

The _____**exodus**_____ of African Americans to the industrialized northern states is known as the Great Migration.

SYNONYMS: escape, hegira
ANTONYMS: immigration, influx, arrival, entrance

Ⓒ CCSS Vocabulary: 4.c., 4.d. (See pp. T14–15.)

7. facilitate
(fə sil′ ə tāt)

(*v.*) to make easier; to assist

The Federal Reserve Board may lower interest rates in order to _____ **facilitate** _____ economic growth.

SYNONYMS: ease, smooth the way, simplify
ANTONYMS: hamper, hinder, obstruct, impede

8. incorrigible
(in kä′ rə jə bəl)

(*adj.*) not able to be corrected; beyond control

Criminals deemed _____ **incorrigible** _____ can expect to receive maximum sentences for their offenses against society.

SYNONYMS: unruly, intractable, incurable, inveterate
ANTONYMS: tractable, docile, curable, reparable

9. latent
(lāt′ ənt)

(*adj.*) hidden, present but not realized

Don't you think it's sad that many people use only a small fraction of their _____ **latent** _____ abilities?

SYNONYMS: dormant, inactive, undeveloped
ANTONYMS: exposed, manifest, evident

10. militant
(mil′ ə tənt)

(*adj.*) given to fighting; active and aggressive in support of a cause; (*n.*) an activist

In the struggle for civil rights, Martin Luther King, Jr., advocated peaceful rather than _____ **militant** _____ protest.

Elizabeth Cady Stanton was a _____ **militant** _____ in the fight for woman suffrage.

SYNONYM: (*adj.*) truculent
ANTONYMS: (*adj.*) unassertive, peaceable, passive

11. morose
(mə rōs′)

(*adj.*) having a gloomy or sullen manner; not friendly or sociable

Heathcliff is the _____ **morose** _____ and vengeful protagonist in Emily Brontë's novel *Wuthering Heights*.

SYNONYM: morbid
ANTONYMS: blithe, jaunty, buoyant

12. opaque
(ō pāk′)

(*adj.*) not letting light through; not clear or lucid; dense, stupid

I have read that book twice, but I still find the author's meaning completely _____ **opaque** _____ .

SYNONYMS: hazy, cloudy, foggy, murky, dull, obtuse
ANTONYMS: transparent, clear, bright, perceptive

13. paramount
(par′ ə maủnt)

(*adj.*) chief in importance, above all others

Voters should insist that candidates for high office address the _____ **paramount** _____ issues facing our society.

SYNONYMS: supreme, primary, dominant
ANTONYMS: secondary, subordinate, ancillary

14. prattle
(prat′ əl)

(v.) to talk in an aimless, foolish, or simple way; to babble; (n.) baby talk; babble

Some people can _____prattle_____ away on the phone for hours on end.

Over time, recognizable words become part of a toddler's cheerful _____prattle_____ .

SYNONYMS: (n.) twaddle, gibberish, piffle

---

15. rebut
(ri bət′)

(v.) to offer arguments or evidence that contradict an assertion; to refute

It is a defense lawyer's job to _____rebut_____ the charges made by the prosecutor.

SYNONYMS: disprove, confute, shoot holes in
ANTONYMS: confirm, corroborate, substantiate

---

16. reprimand
(rep′ rə mand)

(v.) to scold; find fault with; (n.) a rebuke

A judge may need to _____reprimand_____ a lawyer for repeatedly harassing a witness.

An employee who frequently violates a company's rules may receive a written _____reprimand_____ .

SYNONYMS: (v.) reproach; (n.) reproof
ANTONYM: (v.) pat on the back

---

17. servitude
(sər′ və tüd)

(n.) slavery, forced labor

In *Les Misérables*, Jean Valjean is sentenced to many years of _____servitude_____ for stealing a loaf of bread.

SYNONYMS: bondage, thralldom; ANTONYM: liberty

---

18. slapdash
(slap′ dash)

(adj.) careless and hasty

Landlords who routinely make _____slapdash_____ repairs should be considered negligent.

SYNONYMS: cursory, perfunctory, slipshod
ANTONYMS: painstaking, thorough, in-depth

---

19. stagnant
(stag′ nənt)

(adj.) not running or flowing; foul from standing still; inactive

It is dangerous for hikers to drink water from any source that appears to be _____stagnant_____ .

SYNONYMS: still, motionless, inert, sluggish, dull
ANTONYMS: flowing, running, fresh, sweet

---

20. succumb
(sə kəm′)

(v.) to give way to superior force, yield

Most dieters occasionally _____succumb_____ to the lure of a high-calorie dessert.

SYNONYMS: submit, die, expire
ANTONYMS: overcome, master, conquer

CCSS Vocabulary: 4.c. (See pp. T14–15.)

Choosing the Right Word

*Select the **boldface** word that better completes each sentence. You might refer to the selection on pages 60–61 to see how most of these words are used in context.*

1. Most historians agree that military disasters during World War I were the (**exodus, catalyst**) that sparked the Russian Revolution of 1917.

2. During the summer, urban "sun worshippers" begin their weekly (**exodus, servitude**) from the city at around 3:00 P.M. on Friday.

3. Since they are firmly based on the logic of a sentence, the rules of punctuation should not be considered purely (**arbitrary, slapdash**).

4. (**Accomplices, Militants**), disgusted with the government's policies, took to the streets to register a vote of no confidence.

The Bolsheviks, a party of workers led by Vladimir Lenin, seized power during the Russian Revolution of 1917 and formed the Soviet Union.

5. It is up to us to get rid of any (**latent, arbitrary**) prejudices that we may still unwittingly hold against members of other races and nationalities.

6. He has deceived me so many times that I am forced to conclude that he is simply a(n) (**incorrigible, morose**) liar.

7. The brook (**prattling, annihilating**) along its rocky course seemed to be conversing wordlessly with the wind murmuring in the trees.

8. For the world's starving millions, finding enough food to keep body and soul together has become the (**paramount, latent**) concern in life.

9. With their bigger, faster, more experienced players, South High simply (**succumbed, annihilated**) our team, 56 to 7.

10. The best way to (**facilitate, rebut**) the contention that something is not possible to do is to go out and do it.

11. I refuse to believe that our society will (**reprimand, succumb**) to the weaknesses which have destroyed other nations.

12. While his (**accomplices, militants**) acted as decoys, one of the youngsters attempted to filch a couple of apples from the unguarded bin.

13. Her excellent command of both French and Spanish should (**rebut, facilitate**) her efforts to get a position in the foreign service.

14. Even people who appear to be free may be in (**catalyst, servitude**) to their own passions and prejudices.

15. The leaden silence of the afternoon was shattered by the (**opaque, brazen**) voices of trumpets braying fanfares for the returning hero.

16. People who never give any assignment more than a "lick and a promise" may be said to belong to the (**stagnant, slapdash**) school of working.

17. On rare occasions, the U.S. Senate will (**reprimand, prattle**) one of its members who has violated the rules.

18. Unemployment will stay at a high level so long as a nation's economy remains (**stagnant, paramount**).

19. I don't think it is fair to call him a(n) (**incorrigible, morose**) person just because he was in a dejected mood when you met him.

20. You may think that his explanation is perfectly clear, but I find it confused and (**brazen, opaque**).

21. The boss's (**servitude, reprimand**) stung his employee especially hard, as it was delivered in front of the entire staff.

22. His (**stagnant, brazen**) demeanor might help him to be a successful salesperson, but it could also alienate potential customers.

23. The family's (**servitude, catalyst**) to the local lords had begun generations earlier, when an ancestor's misfortunes had resulted in a loss of wealth and status.

24. After the police secured the evidence, it became (**paramount, arbitrary**) to track down the witnesses before they left the scene.

25. I worried that the toddler's (**reprimand, prattle**) would continue throughout the film.

Synonyms

*Choose the word from this unit that is the same or most nearly the same in meaning as the **boldface** word or expression in the phrase. Write that word on the line. Use a dictionary if necessary.*

1. a **doleful** stare — morose

2. **demolished** our rivals in the playoffs — annihilated

3. the **emigration** of refugees from the war zone — exodus

4. **chastised** them for their discourteous behavior — reprimanded

5. a **fetid** pond clogged with debris — stagnant

6. a moving account of life in **captivity** — servitude

7. refused to accept such **sloppy** work — slapdash

8. searched for the forger's **confederates** — accomplices

9. **chattered** about nothing in particular — prattled

10. the **foremost** authority on the subject — paramount

C CCSS Vocabulary: 5. (See pp. T14–15.)

The synonyms and antonyms here do not appear on the Definitions page.

5

Antonyms

*Choose the word from this unit that is most nearly opposite in meaning to the **boldface** word or expression in the phrase. Write that word on the line. Use a dictionary if necessary.*

1. a consistently **cheerful** personality .... morose

2. will **speak concisely** for a few minutes .... prattle

3. the native people's **freedom** .... servitude

4. **meticulous** cleaning .... slapdash

5. **praise** the students for their work .... reprimand

Completing the Sentence

From the words in this unit, choose the one that best completes each of the following sentences. Write the word in the space provided.

1. Mom and Dad said nothing when I failed the examination, but the disappointed looks on their faces hurt more than the most severe _____ reprimand _____.

2. Though she had always loved art, Grandma Moses did not discover her own _____ latent _____ artistic talents until well into her seventies.

3. The helpful librarian did much to _____ facilitate _____ the research for my term paper.

4. In large areas of the huge swamp, there were _____ stagnant _____ pools of water covered with unmoving masses of green slime.

5. When he was suddenly deprived of everything he valued in life, the poor man became extremely gloomy and _____ morose _____.

6. After both of the opposing speakers had presented their cases, they were allowed time to _____ rebut _____ each other's arguments.

7. The fact that you cannot control those small children does not mean that they are _____ incorrigible _____.

8. The doctor warned relatives that if the patient's condition deteriorated any further, he would _____ succumb _____ to pneumonia.

9. It is an unfortunate fact that the _____ militant _____ attitudes of Germany's kaiser and his saber-rattling cronies helped make World War I inevitable.

10. If we are going to use this space as a darkroom for photography, we must have a completely _____ opaque _____ covering over the window.

C CCSS Vocabulary: 4.a. (See pp. T14–15.)

Unit 5 ■ *67*

11. In certain industrial processes, _____**catalysts**_____ speed up the desired reaction by lessening the amount of energy needed to produce it.

12. It is a frightening fact of modern life that we now possess the weaponry to _____**annihilate**_____ not only our enemies but all humankind.

13. No matter what make of automobile you have, it is of _____**paramount**_____ importance that you learn to drive safely before you use it.

14. The second book of the Old Testament is named for the story it recounts of the _____**exodus**_____ of the Israelites from the land of Egypt.

15. The youth did not actually steal the car, but he was an _____**accomplice**_____.

16. Many people came to the Americas after they had been sentenced to terms of penal _____**servitude**_____ for crimes they had committed.

17. In guaranteeing the right to "due process of law," the Constitution protects Americans against _____**arbitrary**_____ arrest and imprisonment.

18. "If you spent more time and effort on your essays, they would cease to be such _____**slapdash**_____ affairs," my older sister priggishly observed.

19. Fighting is considered such a(n) _____**brazen**_____ violation of the rules of a game that the offending players are usually severely penalized.

20. His friends call him "Motormouth" because he has a remarkable capacity to _____**prattle**_____ endlessly about the most trivial matters.

Writing: Words in Action

Answers to both prompts will vary.

1. Look back at "The Leopard: Unlikely Survivor" (pages 60–61). Which of the leopard's traits make it best suited to survival in today's world? Write a short persuasive essay in which you try to convince an audience that one of the leopard's survival techniques most accounts for the animal's continued survival in the 21st century. Use at least two details from the passage and three unit words to support your argument.

2. "The leopard cannot change its spots" is a common proverb that means people cannot change their essential natures. Do you agree with the idea behind the proverb? Is it true that people cannot really change who they are? In a brief essay, present your opinion about the truth of this proverb. Support your opinion with specific examples from your observations, studies, or your own experience. Write at least three paragraphs, and use three or more words from this unit.

Writing prompt #2 is modeled on that of standardized tests.

Vocabulary in Context: Informational Text for Unit 5 is available online at **vocabularyworkshop.com**.

5

Vocabulary in Context

Literary Text

The following excerpts are from Henry James's novels Washington Square *and* The Portrait of a Lady. *Some of the words you have studied in this unit appear in **boldface** type. Complete each statement below the excerpt by circling the letter of the correct answer.*

1. ... she averted herself rigidly from the idea of marrying other people. Her opportunities for doing so were not numerous, but they occurred often enough to test her disposition. ...Mr. Macalister, the widower, had desired to make a marriage of reason, and had chosen Catherine for what he supposed to be her **latent** matronly qualities.... (*Washington Square*)

Latent qualities are
a. hidden   c. visible
b. excellent   d. developed

2. "If you **succumb** to the dread of your father's wrath," she said, "I don't know what will become of us." (*Washington Square*)

If you **succumb** to something, you
a. fight it   c. yield to it
b. call attention to it   d. anticipate it

3. They came back into the first of the rooms... but as the two other ladies were still on the terrace, and as Isabel had not yet been made acquainted with the view, the **paramount** distinction of the place, Mr. Osmond directed her steps into the garden without more delay. (*The Portrait of a Lady*)

Jennifer Jason Leigh plays Catherine Sloper in the 1997 film *Washington Square*.

If something is **paramount,** it is NOT
a. noticeable   c. insignificant
b. central   d. predominant

4. "Well, I don't know that it's right to make everything so easy for a person."

"It surely depends upon the person. When the person's good, your making things easy is all to the credit of virtue. To **facilitate** the execution of good impulses, what can be a nobler act?" (*The Portrait of a Lady*)

If you can **facilitate** something, you can
a. report on it   c. force it
b. relate to it   d. make it easier

5. "Oh dear, no," said Lord Warburton **brazenly**; "our talk had no such solemn character as that." (*The Portrait of a Lady*)

Someone who talks **brazenly** is speaking
a. shyly   c. beautifully
b. boldly   d. falsely

Interactive Quiz

Snap the code, or go to **vocabularyworkshop.com**

UNIT 6

Note that not all of the 20 unit words are used in this passage. *Doleful*, *ghastly*, *prim*, *sardonic*, and *taunt* are not included in the passage.

*Read the following selection, taking note of the **boldface** words and their contexts. These words are among those you will be studying in Unit 6. As you complete the exercises in this unit, it may help to refer to the way the words are used below.*

C CCSS Vocabulary: 4; Reading (Informational Text): 4, 6. (See pp. T14–15.)

Modernize the School Calendar

<Persuasive Essay>

"Should the school day be longer?" "Should administrators lengthen the school year?" Some people would answer both questions with "No." Insisting that students already work **incessantly** during the day, they argue that students need those after-school hours and summer days to earn money, help at home, or pursue key interests. Supporters of the current school year argue that keeping schools open later and longer will cost too much. Such advocates **hew** to the argument that school time need not be longer, just better spent. Those contentions are **lucid** and **credible**—anyone can see that. But for the sake of the students' futures, the answer to both questions must be "Yes."

The current school year in the United States is a product of 19th-century thinking. School schedules were shaped by the harsh demands of city life or were in **bondage** to the unyielding hold of farm life. In rural areas, children had to be available for spring planting and fall harvesting. Thus, they customarily were in school only from December to March and from mid-May through August. But as the population of the urban United States ballooned, the educational experts of the day shifted their attention to city schools. Prominent educators, Horace Mann among them, believed that students needed a long break to avoid over-stimulation. Physicians worried that students would suffer nervous disorders from work pressures. Doctors predicted

One-room schoolhouses were abundant in the 20th century.

A typical urban class in 1914 did not meet during the heat of the summer.

Students in South Korea meet 220 days a year.

illnesses caused by the heat of the classrooms in summer. These concerns resulted in the two-month summer holiday, and even though there is nothing permanent about such a long break, belief in adherence to the 180-day school year retains its **tenacious** hold on the thinking of many educators. These apprehensions are **superfluous** today.

How can the United States stay competitive in the global economy when so many of its students' international peers are in classrooms for more days and longer days? In fact, Japanese students have a 243-day school year, and South Korean students are in school for 220 days a year. Despite the **diligence** of our hardworking teachers and the high quality of our educational institutions, our students are struggling to keep pace, **hampered** by a 20th-century school schedule that holds back the 21st-century student. The argument that the expense of keeping schools open longer would **impoverish** school districts is easily refuted. First of all, buildings kept open later can serve other vital community needs and be rented to civic groups. Secondly, the costs would be **defrayed** by the improved skills students would bring to medicine, science, and business. Horace Mann might **posthumously** agree that modern conveniences make schools comfortable year round.

Many today see the writing on the wall. They understand that having hardworking and caring educators as well as fresh, thoughtful curricula are not enough to **atone** for the short school year. In March 2009, President Obama spoke of the **intricacies** of the issue. He stated that in order to compete favorably with their international peers, students in the U.S. need to spend more time in school. To guarantee a brighter future for the country it is necessary to **supplant** the current school schedule with a modern one.

Snap the code, or go to **vocabularyworkshop.com**

Definitions

Note the spelling, pronunciation, part(s) of speech, and definition(s) of each of the following words. Then write the word in the blank spaces in the illustrative sentence(s) following. Finally, study the lists of synonyms and antonyms.

1. atone
(ə tōn')

(*v.*) to make up for

At one time or another, everyone has done something for which he or she needs to _____ atone _____.

SYNONYM: expiate

2. bondage
(bän' dij)

(*n.*) slavery; any state of being bound or held down

Many people escaped the cruel _____ bondage _____ of slavery with the help of the Underground Railroad.

SYNONYMS: servitude, subjection, dependence
ANTONYMS: freedom, liberty, independence

3. credible
(kred' ə bəl)

(*adj.*) believable

Do you have a _____ credible _____ explanation for not completing your assignment on time?

SYNONYMS: plausible, acceptable, likely
ANTONYMS: unbelievable, implausible, improbable

4. defray
(dē frā')

(*v.*) to pay for

Corporate sponsors helped to _____ defray _____ the cost of the charity's annual telethon.

SYNONYMS: bear the cost, foot the bill

5. diligent
(dil' ə jənt)

(*adj.*) hardworking, industrious, not lazy

_____ Diligent _____ employees are likely to be well rewarded for their dedication and hard work.

SYNONYMS: assiduous, sedulous
ANTONYMS: lazy, indolent, cursory, perfunctory

6. doleful
(dōl' fəl)

(*adj.*) sad; dreary

One look at the players' _____ doleful _____ faces told me that the team had lost the championship game.

SYNONYMS: sorrowful, mournful, dolorous
ANTONYMS: blithe, jaunty, buoyant

7. ghastly
(gast' lē)

(*adj.*) frightful, horrible; deathly pale

Some people are almost afraid to go to sleep because they suffer from _____ ghastly _____ recurring nightmares.

SYNONYMS: dreadful, appalling, grisly
ANTONYMS: pleasant, agreeable, attractive

CCSS Vocabulary: 4.c., 4.d. (See pp. T14–15.)

8. hamper
(ham' pər)

(*v.*) to hold back

Poor grades will _____**hamper**_____ you in your effort to get a college education.

SYNONYMS: hinder, obstruct, impede, inhibit
ANTONYMS: facilitate, ease, smooth the way

9. hew
(hyü)

(*v.*) to shape or cut down with an ax; to hold to

Even in a crisis, we must _____**hew**_____ to this nation's principles of liberty, equality, and justice.

SYNONYMS: chop, hack, fell, adhere, conform

10. impoverished
(im päv' risht)

(*adj.*) poor, in a state of poverty; depleted

After World War II, _____**impoverished**_____ European countries received U.S. aid under the Marshall Plan.

SYNONYMS: poverty-stricken, destitute, indigent
ANTONYMS: rich, wealthy, affluent, prosperous

11. incessant
(in ses' ənt)

(*adj.*) never stopping, going on all the time

The loud and _____**incessant**_____ chatter of the people at the next table made it hard for us to hear each other.

SYNONYMS: ceaseless, constant, uninterrupted
ANTONYMS: occasional, sporadic, intermittent

12. intricate
(in' trə kət)

(*adj.*) complicated; difficult to understand

Our teacher took us through the _____**intricate**_____ solution to the equation step by step.

SYNONYM: convoluted
ANTONYMS: simple, uninvolved, uncomplicated

13. lucid
(lü' sid)

(*adj.*) easy to understand, clear; rational, sane

The ability to speak in a _____**lucid**_____ and persuasive fashion is a great asset to a politician.

SYNONYMS: limpid, intelligible
ANTONYMS: murky, muddy, obscure, unintelligible

14. posthumous
(päs' chə məs)

(*adj.*) occurring or published after death

Many artists and writers have been ignored during their lifetimes only to achieve _____**posthumous**_____ fame.

ANTONYM: prenatal

15. prim
(prim)

(*adj.*) overly neat, proper, or formal; prudish

How is it that such a _____ **prim** _____ and tidy person and such a messy one can be such good friends?

SYNONYMS: fussy, fastidious, squeamish
ANTONYMS: dowdy, frumpy, sloppy, untidy, loose

16. sardonic
(sär dän′ ik)

(*adj.*) grimly or scornfully mocking, bitterly sarcastic

Great satirists save their most _____ **sardonic** _____ wit for the greedy, the corrupt, and the hypocritical.

SYNONYMS: mordant, acerbic, wry
ANTONYMS: bland, saccharine, good-natured

17. superfluous
(sü pər′ flü wəs)

(*adj.*) exceeding what is sufficient or required, excess

Neat and well-organized people know how to eliminate all _____ **superfluous** _____ clutter.

SYNONYMS: surplus, supererogatory
ANTONYMS: necessary, essential, vital, indispensable

18. supplant
(sə plant′)

(*v.*) to take the place of, supersede

Computers rapidly _____ **supplanted** _____ typewriters in the workplace, just as photocopiers replaced carbon paper.

SYNONYMS: replace, displace, oust

19. taunt
(tônt)

(*v.*) to jeer at, mock; (*n.*) an insulting or mocking remark

It is not at all unusual for brothers and sisters to tease and _____ **taunt** _____ one another good-naturedly.

For umpires and referees, the _____ **taunts** _____ of angry fans are just part of the job.

SYNONYMS: (*v.*) ridicule (*n.*) insult
ANTONYMS: (*v.*) cheer, acclaim (*n.*) praise

20. tenacious
(tə nā′ shəs)

(*adj.*) holding fast; holding together firmly; persistent

Athletes must be _____ **tenacious** _____ in the pursuit of excellence if they hope to become Olympic champions.

SYNONYMS: obstinate, stubborn, dogged
ANTONYMS: yielding, weak, gentle, slack

⊂ CCSS Vocabulary: 4.c. (See pp. T14–15.)

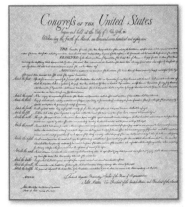

Choosing the Right Word

*Select the **boldface** word that better completes each sentence. You might refer to the essay on pages 70–71 to see how most of these words are used in context.*

1. If we were to lose the basic freedoms guaranteed by the Bill of Rights, we would be truly (**taunted, impoverished**).

2. When I looked through the microscope, I observed the (**incessant, intricate**) pattern of blood vessels in the specimen's body.

3. The penniless adventurer is a character so familiar to fiction readers that further description of the type is (**sardonic, superfluous**).

4. Loss of blood very quickly turned the victim's normally rosy face a (**prim, ghastly**) hue of white.

5. In a totalitarian state, people who do not (**hew, supplant**) firmly to the party line are likely to find themselves in hot water with the authorities.

The first 10 amendments to the U.S. Constitution are known as the Bill of Rights.

6. That village is famous all over the world for its demure cottages, well-manicured lawns, and (**prim, diligent**) gardens.

7. "The witness has changed his story so often that no jury on earth is likely to find his testimony (**lucid, credible**)," the district attorney observed.

8. (**Hampered, Impoverished**) by the weight of my backpack, it took me longer than usual to reach the bus stop.

9. Frankly, I am tired of your endless (**credible, doleful**) complaints about all the people who have been unfair to you.

10. If we want government to provide services, we must pay taxes to (**defray, hamper**) the costs.

11. "Sticks and stones may break my bones, but names will never hurt me" is an old saying I try to keep in mind whenever someone (**hews, taunts**) me.

12. The author's writing style is as (**lucid, intricate**) as the sparkling waters of a mountain lake on a spring morning.

13. In some early societies, people who had committed certain crimes could (**atone, defray**) for them by paying sums of money to their victims.

14. The novel's grim humor and (**posthumous, sardonic**) portrayal of the futility of all human endeavor make it an intensely disturbing book.

15. What real use is financial independence if a person remains forever in (**bondage, tenacity**) to foolish fears and superstitions?

16. Royalties from a novel that is published (**superfluously, <u>posthumously</u>**) normally go to the author's estate.

17. She is very slow to form opinions; but once she does, she holds on to them (**<u>tenaciously</u>, dolefully**).

18. Even after the most systematic and (**ghastly, <u>diligent</u>**) search, we could not find the missing documents.

19. His feverish and (**lucid, <u>incessant</u>**) activity cannot hide the fact that he doesn't know what he's doing.

20. I know that love is fickle, but I never expected to be (**atoned, <u>supplanted</u>**) in her affections by a man like that.

21. The details of the peace accord among the four nations, worked out by a host of foreign affairs officials over a period of months, were (**tenacious, <u>intricate</u>**).

22. I refuse to (**taunt, <u>atone</u>**) for something that I still believe was the right thing to do, even if no one else agrees with me.

23. The gold medal was completely (**incessant, <u>superfluous</u>**), as the pleasure of winning was all that mattered to her.

24. Once he adopted the puppy, his enjoyment of the new pet began to (**<u>supplant</u>, defray**) the sadness he felt over the death of the dog he'd had since childhood.

25. She could never quite forget her sister's hurtful childhood (**bondage, <u>taunts</u>**).

Synonyms

*Choose the word from this unit that is the same or most nearly the same in meaning as the **boldface** word or expression in the phrase. Write that word on the line. Use a dictionary if necessary.*

1. a **prudish** way of dress .... prim

2. averted my eyes from the **gruesome** scene .... ghastly

3. a fund to **settle** the cost of room and board .... defray

4. freed the hostages from **captivity** .... bondage

5. **complex** and beautiful designs .... intricate

6. a **postmortem** analysis of the patient's condition .... posthumous

7. a target of the writer's **caustic** criticism .... sardonic

8. writes **melancholy** songs about lost love .... doleful

9. **made amends** for their misdeeds .... atoned

10. refuses to respond to **derision** .... taunts

C CCSS Vocabulary: 5. (See pp. T14–15.)

The synonyms and antonyms here do not appear on the Definitions page.

6

Antonyms

*Choose the word from this unit that is most nearly opposite in meaning to the **boldface** word or expression in the phrase. Write that word on the line. Use a dictionary if necessary.*

1. a **cheerful** individual _____doleful_____

2. a **delightful** sight _____ghastly_____

3. a rather **lax** attitude toward the rules _____prim_____

4. a **mild** response _____sardonic_____

5. **applaud** the competitor _____taunt_____

Completing the Sentence

From the words in this unit, choose the one that best completes each of the following sentences. Write the word in the space provided.

1. For thousands of years Native Americans used stone implements to _____hew_____ canoes out of logs and tree trunks.

2. I shall never forget the _____ghastly_____ sight that greeted us when we arrived at the scene of the incident.

3. Although the survivors were still in a state of shock, some of them were _____lucid_____ enough to answer the questions posed by the police.

4. When the stock market collapsed in 1929, many wealthy speculators found themselves as _____impoverished_____ as proverbial church mice.

5. The wily old senator derived a certain amount of _____sardonic_____ amusement from watching his enemies turn on and destroy one another.

6. A student who is _____diligent_____ and systematic in study habits will often do better than one who is brilliant but lazy.

7. Because my home is located at a busy intersection, I have been forced to accustom myself to the _____incessant_____ hum of traffic outside.

8. I suppose bloodhounds may be as happy as other dogs, but they have the _____doleful_____ look of creatures who have lost their last friend.

9. He is a rather _____prim_____ sort of man who is easily shocked by other people's less exacting standards of conduct.

10. Saying "I'm sorry" is a good way to begin to _____atone_____ for the suffering or harm that you have done to another person.

11. To help _____ **defray** _____ the expenses that I would incur on the senior class trip to Washington, I worked as a babysitter.

12. Our football team would do a great deal better if we mastered a few simple plays, instead of trying to use all those _____ **intricate** _____ formations.

13. A woman of strong character and noble bearing, she endured the jibes and _____ **taunts** _____ of her adversaries with great patience and fortitude.

14. The huge piles of snow that cover the roads will greatly _____ **hamper** _____ the efforts of the rescue team to reach the stranded skiers.

15. On the steps of the Capitol, the president awarded _____ **posthumous** _____ Medals of Honor to soldiers who had recently fallen in defense of the country.

16. "Since their heroic deeds clearly speak for themselves," the president remarked, "further comment on my part would be _____ **superfluous** _____."

17. I know that he will say anything to save his own skin, but I feel that in this case his account of the incident is _____ **credible** _____ and should be accepted.

18. Lincoln said: "Familiarize yourself with the chains of _____ **bondage** _____ and you prepare your own limbs to wear them."

19. "Someone with such a(n) _____ **tenacious** _____ grip on life doesn't give up the ghost easily," I thought as I watched the old man celebrate another birthday.

20. During World War II, artificial rubber began to _____ **supplant** _____ natural rubber in American automobile tires.

Writing: Words in Action

Answers to both prompts will vary.

1. Look back at "Modernize the School Calendar" (pages 70–71). Which of the author's arguments in favor of a year-round school calendar do you believe is the strongest? Write a persuasive essay explaining the single best reason for extending students' time in school. Use at least two details from the passage and three unit words to support your argument.

2. *"To find out what one is fitted to do and to secure an opportunity to do it is the key to happiness."— John Dewey*

Do you agree that happiness comes from discovering one's talents and finding work that utilizes them? Does Dewey's idea refer only to finding the right occupation, or is his idea broader than that? How can schooling help with this quest for "the right work"? In a brief essay, support your opinion with examples from your studies, readings, or your own experiences. Write at least three paragraphs, and use three or more words from this unit.

Writing prompt #2 is modeled on that of standardized tests.

C CCSS Vocabulary: 6; Writing: 1.c., 2.d. (See pp. T14–15.)

Vocabulary in Context: Informational Text for Unit 6 is available online at **vocabularyworkshop.com**.

6

Vocabulary in Context

Literary Text

The following excerpts are from Sir Arthur Conan Doyle's novel The Hound of the Baskervilles, *featuring the famous detective Sherlock Holmes. Some of the words you have studied in this unit appear in **boldface** type. Complete each statement below the excerpt by circling the letter of the correct answer.*

1. All day today the rain poured down, rustling on the ivy and dripping from the eaves. I thought of the convict out upon the bleak, cold, shelterless moor. Poor devil! Whatever his crimes, he has suffered something to **atone** for them.

To **atone** for something means to

a. make up for it   c. repeat it
b. be punished for it   d. be very hurt by it

2. Our conversation was **hampered** by the presence of the driver of the hired wagonette, so that we were forced to talk of trivial matters when our nerves were tense with emotion and anticipation. It was a relief to me, after that unnatural restraint, when we at last passed Frankland's house and knew that we were drawing near to the Hall and to the scene of action.

Something that is **hampered** is

a. overheard   c. enjoyed
b. enhanced   d. hindered

3. He spoke unconcernedly, but his small light eyes glanced **incessantly** from the girl to me.

If someone's eyes move **incessantly,** they are moving

a. fiercely   c. questioningly
b. continually   d. sleepily

Poster for the 1939 film
The Hound of the Baskervilles,
starring Basil Rathbone as
Sherlock Holmes.

4. "...[S]everal people had seen a creature upon the moor which corresponds with this Baskerville demon, and which could not possibly be any animal known to science. They all agreed that it was a huge creature, luminous, **ghastly**, and spectral.... [A]ll tell the same story of this dreadful apparition...."

Something that is **ghastly** is

a. smelly   c. frightful
b. wet   d. colorful

5. It was not a brutal countenance, but it was **prim**, hard, and stern, with a firm-set, thin-lipped mouth, and a coldly intolerant eye.

Something that is **prim** is NOT

a. proper   c. neat
b. formal   d. relaxed

Snap the code, or go to
vocabularyworkshop.com

Vocabulary for Comprehension

*Read the following passage, in which some of the words you have studied in Units 4–6 appear in **boldface** type. Then answer the questions on page 81.*

Marjory Stoneman Douglas, an environmentalist known as the "Grandmother of the Glades," is the subject of the following passage.

(Line)

Most people in the early years of the twentieth century thought that the Everglades in South Florida was little more than **stagnant** swampland

(5) that had no evident or **latent** value. Had it not been for the zealous industry of one woman to save that unappreciated land, the Everglades might have been **fated** for

(10) destruction and would now be nothing more than a memory.

Born in Minnesota in 1890, Marjory Stoneman Douglas became a feminist, journalist, author,

(15) playwright, and all-around environmental advocate. She moved to Florida in 1915 to work for her father's fledgling newspaper (later to become the *Miami Herald*). She

(20) became smitten with South Florida's blindingly clear light and regarded the Everglades as a unique and inspiring region that had to be saved at all costs. When President Truman

(25) declared it a national park in 1947, Douglas happily attended the dedication ceremony.

Marjory Stoneman Douglas could not be **hampered** by adversity. She

(30) was the first Florida woman to serve in the U.S. Naval Reserve, and she began social action programs to help the needy. She simply would

not be **daunted** by challenges or by

(35) people who disagreed with her deeply held ideals. In 1947 she wrote *The Everglades: River of Grass*. She spent five long years researching her subject, and in the

(40) end she helped people understand that the Everglades provide clean water for Florida and that the ecosystem is far more than "an alligator alley." The passions that the

(45) work instilled in her would guide her throughout her life.

When she was in her late seventies, she founded Friends of the Everglades to continue her

(50) important work. Douglas lived to be 108 years old and was in fairly good health until her death. As her last request, her ashes were spread over her beloved Everglades.

(55) Her **posthumous** induction into the National Women's Hall of Fame in 2000 ensures that future generations will know of Marjory Stoneman Douglas and of her

(60) dedication to the Everglades she so deeply cherished. Thanks to her, the Everglades ecosystem will thrive for years to come.

CCSS Vocabulary: 4.a.; Reading (Informational Text): 2, 4, 6. (See pp. T14–15.)

1. The passage is best described as
   a. a psychological portrait
   b. an environmental study
   c. an autobiographical sketch
   d. a biographical sketch
   e. a sociological study

2. The meaning of **stagnant** (line 4) is
   a. motionless
   b. sweet
   c. dynamic
   d. flowing
   e. careless

3. **Latent** (line 5) most nearly means
   a. lasting
   b. hidden
   c. commercial
   d. sentimental
   e. monetary

4. **Fated** (line 9) is best defined as
   a. adapted
   b. considered
   c. examined
   d. destined
   e. scheduled

5. The meaning of **hampered** (line 29) is
   a. expected
   b. exceeded
   c. aided
   d. persuaded
   e. impeded

6. **Daunted** (line 34) most nearly means
   a. destined
   b. entangled
   c. depressed
   d. intimidated
   e. encouraged

7. According to the passage, Douglas's book on the Everglades led her to
   a. found the National Women's Hall of Fame
   b. become an advocate for the protection of alligators
   c. leave Minnesota for Miami
   d. work for the preservation of the region
   e. join the fight against the over-development of the Everglades

8. Douglas recognized that the Everglades are needed to
   a. supply fresh water for the region
   b. ensure commercial development
   c. facilitate the agricultural use of the land
   d. draw visitors to Florida
   e. provide a breeding ground for mosquitoes

9. **Posthumous** (line 55) is best defined as
   a. good-natured
   b. speedy
   c. after death
   d. believable
   e. poverty-stricken

10. According to the passage, Douglas is largely responsible for the
    a. current perception of the Everglades
    b. interest of women in ecology
    c. recruitment of women in the navy
    d. economic development of Florida
    e. destruction of the wetlands

11. Based on the passage, Douglas can be described as all of the following EXCEPT
    a. forward-thinking
    b. civic-minded
    c. highly principled
    d. persistent
    e. easily daunted

12. The author's attitude toward Douglas is best described as
    a. scornful
    b. indifferent
    c. ambivalent
    d. respectful
    e. astonished

C CCSS Vocabulary: 4.a.; Reading (Informational Text): 2, 4, 6. (See pp. T14–15.)

Two-Word Completions

Select the pair of words that best complete the meaning of each of the following passages.

1. "A(n) _____ is supposed to _____ the commission of a crime," the burglar growled at his sidekick. (The latter had just set off the alarm system to the bank the pair were robbing.) "But all *you* can seem to do," the burglar continued, "is make this job more difficult!"
   a. catalyst . . . revile
   b. accomplice . . . facilitate
   c. rebuttal . . . incinerate
   d. precipice . . . reprimand

2. They could no longer sit idly by while a gross injustice went uncorrected. For that reason, they joined a group of _____ reformers actively trying to get the government to _____ the situation.
   a. militant . . . rectify
   b. incorrigible . . . disentangle
   c. arbitrary . . . taunt
   d. morose . . . defray

3. Though learning a foreign language never comes easily for me, I've found that I can _____ the process if I imitate the ant in the old fable and apply myself to the task as _____ as possible.
   a. defray . . . credibly
   b. rectify . . . brazenly
   c. hamper . . . tenaciously
   d. facilitate . . . diligently

4. His lies sounded so much like the truth that I was completely taken in by them. If they hadn't seemed so _____, I don't think I would have been _____ quite so easily.
   a. intrepid . . . impoverished
   b. intricate . . . disentangled
   c. credible . . . hoodwinked
   d. ghastly . . . annihilated

5. Shakespeare's Timon of Athens is a bitter misanthrope who spends much of his time on stage _____ the world and those in it with _____ taunts and caustic jests.
   a. reviling . . . sardonic
   b. reprimanding . . . posthumous
   c. rebutting . . . prim
   d. daunting . . . lucid

6. Tourists always gasp in amazement when _____ Mexican daredevils climb to the top of a lofty _____ in Acapulco and dive fearlessly into the sea hundreds of feet below.
   a. brazen . . . access
   b. intrepid . . . precipice
   c. prim . . . catalyst
   d. pliant . . . exodus

7. "I'm trying to help you, not _____ you," I said. "I want to make your task easier, not more _____."
   a. reprieve . . . slapdash
   b. hamper . . . arduous
   c. revile . . . pliant
   d. supplant . . . latent

Proverbs

In the essay about the survival advantages of the leopard (see pages 60–61), the author mentions the proverb, "A leopard cannot change its spots."

"A leopard cannot change its spots" is a proverb that means a person or thing cannot change its essential nature. A **proverb** is a condensed but memorable saying that makes an observation about an important aspect of life; the insight the proverb provides is accepted as true by many people. Because the meanings of proverbs are not always obvious or self-explanatory, they must be learned, just like new or unfamiliar words.

Choosing the Right Proverb

*Read each sentence. Use context clues to figure out the meaning of each proverb in **boldface** print. Then write the letter of the definition for the proverb in the sentence.*

1. **Curiosity killed the cat** when I broke an expensive antique while exploring a friend's house. _____h_____

2. Whoever said "**A wise man never knows all, only fools know everything**" must have been talking about my know-it-all friend Tim. _____g_____

3. **No one can paddle two canoes at the same time**, so what makes you think that you can do your homework while watching television? _____f_____

4. Keeping my new smartphone in my locker is probably a good idea, since it's better to **lock a door than accuse your neighbor.** _____i_____

5. He asked what Sue and I had been fighting about, but I told him to **let sleeping dogs lie**. _____j_____

6. Even though they say that a **brave man dies but once, a coward many times,** I couldn't work up the nerve to dive into the deep swimming hole. _____e_____

7. When it's pouring rain outside, **any port in a storm will do**, even if it means being stranded under an umbrella with my obnoxious sister. _____c_____

8. **Familiarity breeds contempt**, which may be why I am often antagonistic to my roommate. _____a_____

9. **A friend in need is a friend indeed,** especially when that friend is someone like Lily, who came to visit me every day in the hospital. _____b_____

10. I knew **many hands make light work** when two of us raked the yard in half the time it takes just me. _____d_____

a. The better you know somebody, the more you find fault with that person.

b. Someone who helps you in a time of difficulty is a true friend.

c. In a tough situation, any safe place is better than none.

d. The more people who pitch in, the faster the work gets done.

e. It's better to face your fears than hesitate to take action.

f. You can only do one thing at a time well.

g. People who think they know everything are probably not that smart.

h. Nosiness and prying can lead to trouble.

i. Don't make it easy for someone to steal from you.

j. Don't bring up old business that might reopen a touchy issue.

CCSS Vocabulary: 5.a. (See pp. T14–15.)

Word Study ■ 83

WORD STUDY

Writing with Proverbs

Find the meaning of each proverb. (Use an online or print dictionary if necessary.) Then write a sentence for each proverb. **Answers will vary.**

1. A bird in the hand is worth two in the bush. **Sample response:**
   I tried to reach the picnic table to snatch another hamburger, but when I saw
   people glaring at me I decided that a bird in the hand is worth two in the bush.

2. A closed mouth catches no flies.
   _____

3. Every cloud has a silver lining.
   _____
   _____

4. Don't look a gift horse in the mouth.
   _____
   _____

5. Appearances can be deceptive.
   _____
   _____

6. The only way to have a friend is to be one.
   _____

7. You can't have your cake and eat it too.
   _____

8. The bee has a sting, but honey too.
   _____

9. Don't put all your eggs in one basket.
   _____

10. Two wrongs don't make a right.
    _____

11. The more you get, the more you want.
    _____

12. The early bird catches the worm.
    _____

Denotation and Connotation

A word's **denotation** is its literal meaning—the formal meaning of the word provided by a dictionary. A word's denotation conveys a *neutral* tone.

Words also have informal, implied meanings, or **connotations**—associations that readers or listeners make to the word. Connotations can be either *positive* or *negative*.

Consider these synonyms for the neutral word *bold*:

> *intrepid*   *fearless*   *brazen*   *impudent*

Intrepid and *fearless* have positive connotations, while *brazen* and *impudent* have negative connotations.

> **Think:** An explorer can be intrepid or fearless, but a friend with an overbearing manner can be brazen or impudent.

Look at these examples of words that are similar in denotation but have different connotations.

NEUTRAL	POSITIVE	NEGATIVE
extra	abundant	superfluous
talk	elucidate	prattle
associate	partner	accomplice

Keep in the mind the importance of the various shades of meaning of the words you use in speech or writing. Speakers and writers who use a word with a negative connotation in a situation that calls for a positive or at least neutral term can be unintentionally insulting. Although connotations may be subjective, it pays to take seriously the difference between the right word and the "not quite right" word.

Shades of Meaning

Write a plus sign (+) in the box if the word has a positive connotation.
Write a minus sign (–) if the word has a negative connotation. Put a zero (0)
if the word is neutral.

1. reprieve +   **2.** diligence +   **3.** credible +   **4.** ghastly –

5. tenacious +   **6.** hoodwink –   **7.** morose –   **8.** access 0

9. pompous –   **10.** slapdash –   **11.** rectify +   **12.** larceny –

13. latent 0   **14.** lucid +   **15.** facilitate +   **16.** arduous –

Expressing the Connotation

Read each sentence. Select the word in parentheses that expresses the connotation (positive, negative, or neutral) given at the beginning of the sentence.

neutral
1. My sister (**absconded with, acquired**) our mother's jewels after the funeral.

negative
2. He discovered many (**undeveloped, latent**) qualities in himself during his time in the Peace Corps.

positive
3. The rising applause was a(n) (**superfluous, auspicious**) sign of the quality of our performance.

negative
4. Despite its interesting subject matter, the painting seemed (**fated, destined**) to not attract anyone's attention.

positive
5. The mountain climber was (**daunted, emboldened**) by the fog and snow up ahead.

neutral
6. The (**lifeless, inanimate**) carousel provided a contrast to the group of horses and riders parading beside it.

positive
7. The tennis player's (**intrepid, brazen**) dive for the ball secured her the winning point.

neutral
8. My cousin has a(n) (**confirmed, incorrigible**) habit of taking my phone without asking.

Challenge: Using Connotation

Choose vocabulary words from Units 4–6 to replace the highlighted words in the sentences below. Then explain how the connotation of the replacement word changes the tone of the sentence. **Answers will vary.**

reprimand	**succumb**	**tenacious**
ghastly	**slapdash**	**pliant**

1. I did not receive a good grade on the assignment; my teacher said it was **quick** ____slapdash____ work. **Sample response:**
   The negative connotation of *slapdash* makes it clear that the
   teacher thinks the student was sloppy and careless, not just hasty.

2. The head chef would **correct** ____reprimand____ me whenever I put too much pepper in the soup. **Sample response:**
   The negative connotation of *reprimand* gives a more disapproving
   tone, suggesting that the head chef was angry and not just critical.

3. To make it to the next level of the video game, I had to be very **persistent** ____tenacious____. **Sample response:**
   The positive connotation of *tenacious* suggests that the effort took more than
   mere persistence; it took strong dedication and energy.

Classical Roots

ten, tain, tin—to hold, keep

This root appears in **tenacious** (page 74), which means, literally, "full of holding power." Some other words based on the same root are listed below.

abstention	detention	retinue	tenor
detain	pertain	sustenance	tenure

From the list of words above, choose the one that corresponds to each of the brief definitions below. Write the word in the blank space in the illustrative sentence below the definition. Use an online or print dictionary if necessary.

1. confinement; holding in custody

The temporary holding cells in that impoverished country were dank and filthy places of _____**detention**_____ .

2. the flow of meaning through something written or spoken, drift; the highest adult male voice

He auditioned for the lead _____**tenor**_____ role in the opera *Tosca*.

3. to have reference to; to be suitable; to belong, as an attribute or accessory

An attorney can only introduce evidence that directly _____**pertains**_____ to the case.

4. the means of support or subsistence; nourishment

During her ordeal, she drew _____**sustenance**_____ from her supportive family.

5. to prevent from going on, delay, hold back; hold as a prisoner

"This traffic jam may _____**detain**_____ us for so long that we miss our flight," he complained.

6. the act of doing without; refraining

The doctor advised the patient to observe total _____**abstention**_____ from fatty foods to prevent another heart attack.

7. the time during which something is held; a permanent right to an office or position after a trial period

The Constitution limits a president's _____**tenure**_____ to two consecutive 4-year terms of office.

8. a body of followers, group of attendants

The delegation consisted of the king and his loyal _____**retinue**_____ of advisors and protectors.

UNIT 7

Note that not all of the 20 unit words are used in this passage. *Apex*, *assimilate*, *pensive*, and *tirade* are not included in the passage.

*Read the following selection, taking note of the **boldface** words and their contexts. These words are among those you will be studying in Unit 7. As you complete the exercises in this unit, it may help to refer to the way the words are used below.*

C CCSS Vocabulary: 4; Reading (Informational Text): 4, 6. (See pp. T14–15.)

City Critters

<Humorous Essay>

The **metropolis** is full of life. Millions of people live together in the city, coming and going, day and night. They stream from their homes each morning, off to work and school. The city's an exciting place, full of things to discover: restaurants and shops, playgrounds and parks, theaters and concert halls. But it's a crowded place, and if there's anything millions of people are good at doing when they get together, it's creating **exorbitant** amounts of trash. The trash bags pile up higher each day, while careless citizens litter in the streets, and all this mess attracts unwelcome guests.

Beneath the **obstreperous** traffic of the streets, rats scavenge for food among the waste we leave behind. The **vagrant** rats that wander through our cities can grow to be ten inches long and two pounds in weight. Some urban rats live underground, **meandering** through the sewers and subways, while others nest in alleyways and in proximity to parks or garbage cans. A few creep into our homes through water pipes and holes in walls. Do you think you might like to see a two-pound rat staring at you from the kitchen sink? Think again: A meeting with a **surly** rat can be a **perilous** situation.

Less nasty than the rat is the mighty cockroach. The largest roach you'll find in most American cities is only two inches long. But if you've ever seen one speeding across the floor, or seen a countertop **inundated** with **sprightly** roaches scrambling for cover, you won't forget the sight. No wonder the cockroach is so often **maligned**! Roaches sneak into homes, like rats, through cracks and pipes or through tiny spaces left by **shoddy** repairs. What do you suppose these creepy insects are doing in human dwellings? They're looking for food, just like rats.

The bedbug is even smaller than the cockroach—only ¼-inch in length and difficult to spot. Bedbugs hide in mattresses, in carpeting and furniture, and in cracks and crevices in walls. They creep out while you're asleep, attracted by your body heat and breath. These little critters aren't looking for the food you've dropped; they aim to feed on you! In the **interim** between the time you go to bed and wake up in the moring, a bedbug will crawl onto your body and feed on your blood, like a mosquito does, for up to five minutes. The next day, you'll find a small, red, irritating bump, the telltale sign of the bedbug bite. Once bedbugs have infested your home, they're difficult to get rid of without the assistance of an exterminator. The best way to prevent infestation is to frequently vacuum dusty areas in your home, including mattresses.

The **advent** of pesticides has limited the spread of vermin, but with so many pests to keep at bay, keeping our homes and cities clean remains a **momentous** task. Don't make **bogus** excuses: Keep kitchens and bathrooms clean and dry, and put food away when you're finished eating. Don't let much time pass between housecleaning days, and refrain from littering in streets and public spaces. We may not ever say **adieu** to all the pests that dwell among us. But we can each do something to keep the places where we live clean and free of pests that thrive in the mess that humans leave behind.

Definitions

Note the spelling, pronunciation, part(s) of speech, and definition(s) of each of the following words. Then write the word in the blank spaces in the illustrative sentence(s) following. Finally, study the lists of synonyms and antonyms.

1. adieu
(ə dü′; ə dyü′)

(*int.*) "Farewell!"; (*n.*) a farewell

As my friends boarded the airplane, I waved to them and shouted, "_____**Adieu**_____! Have a safe trip."

I made my _____**adieus**_____ to the hosts and left.

SYNONYMS: (*int.*) "So long"; (*n.*) good-bye
ANTONYMS: (*int.*) "Hello"; (*n.*) greeting

2. advent
(ad′ vent)

(*n.*) an arrival; a coming into place or view

The _____**advent**_____ of spring is particularly welcome after a long, harsh winter.

SYNONYM: approach; ANTONYMS: departure, going away, exodus

3. apex
(ā′ peks)

(*n.*) the highest point, tip

If you want to reach the _____**apex**_____ of the Washington Monument, take the stairs or an elevator.

SYNONYMS: peak, summit, acme; ANTONYMS: nadir, lowest point

4. assimilate
(ə sim′ ə lāt)

(*v.*) to absorb fully; to adopt as one's own; to adapt fully

A well-read person _____**assimilates**_____ knowledge of a wide range of subjects.

SYNONYMS: digest, blend in

5. bogus
(bō′ gəs)

(*adj.*) false, counterfeit

Cashiers receive special training so that they will be able to identify _____**bogus**_____ currency.

SYNONYMS: phony, fake, spurious; ANTONYMS: genuine, authentic

6. exorbitant
(eg zôr′ bə tənt)

(*adj.*) unreasonably high; excessive

Management rejected the union's demands for higher wages and better benefits as _____**exorbitant**_____.

SYNONYMS: extreme, inordinate, overpriced
ANTONYMS: inexpensive, affordable, reasonable

7. interim
(in′ tər əm)

(*n.*) the time between; (*adj.*) temporary, coming between two points in time

In the _____**interim**_____ between landing and takeoff, the ground crew cleaned and refueled the plane.

The team played well under an _____**interim**_____ coach for the final three months of the season.

SYNONYMS: (*n.*) interval, interlude; (*adj.*) provisional, stopgap

8. inundate
(in′ ən dāt)

(*v.*) to flood, overflow; to overwhelm by numbers or size
Torrential rains and high tides _____**inundated**_____ the streets of the picturesque seaside community.

SYNONYMS: submerge, deluge, swamp

9. malign
(mə līn′)

(*v.*) to speak evil of, slander; (*adj.*) evil
In every office, there are gossips who are only too willing to _____**malign**_____ their coworkers.

Iago reveals his _____**malign**_____ motives to the audience in a series of soliloquies.

SYNONYMS: (*v.*) defame, vilify, badmouth; (*adj.*) wicked
ANTONYMS: (*v.*) praise, commend; (*adj.*) kind, benevolent

10. meander
(mē an′ dər)

(*v.*) to wander about, wind about; (*n.*) a sharp turn or twist
When I travel, I like to _____**meander**_____ through unfamiliar towns and cities.

Lombard Street in San Francisco is famous for its many _____**meanders**_____.

SYNONYMS: (*v.*) ramble, zigzag, twist

11. metropolis
(mə träp′ ə ləs)

(*n.*) a large city; the chief city of an area
Archaeologists have learned much about the Mayans from the ruins of the _____**metropolis**_____ Palenque.

SYNONYM: large urban center
ANTONYMS: hamlet, village

12. momentous
(mō men′ təs)

(*adj.*) very important
A _____**momentous**_____ decision by the Supreme Court in 1954 declared public school segregation unconstitutional.

SYNONYMS: consequential, weighty
ANTONYMS: inconsequential, trivial, slight, unimportant

13. obstreperous
(əb strep′ ər əs)

(*adj.*) noisy; unruly, disorderly
Our teacher will not tolerate _____**obstreperous**_____ behavior in the classroom.

SYNONYMS: wild, uncontrolled, riotous
ANTONYMS: quiet, well-behaved, docile

14. pensive
(pen′ siv)

(*adj.*) thoughtful; melancholy

We admired the skill with which the artist captured the child's ____**pensive**____ expression.

SYNONYMS: dreamy, contemplative

15. perilous
(per′ ə ləs)

(*adj.*) dangerous

Episodes of old-time movie serials usually ended with the hero or heroine in ____**perilous**____ circumstances.

SYNONYMS: risky, chancy, hazardous, unsafe
ANTONYMS: safe, secure, harmless

16. shoddy
(shäd′ ē)

(*adj.*) of poor quality; characterized by inferior workmanship

That designer watch I bought from a street vendor turned out to be a ____**shoddy**____ knockoff.

SYNONYMS: cheap, tacky, imitative
ANTONYMS: well-made, solid, durable, superior

17. sprightly
(sprīt′ lē)

(*adj.*) lively, full of life; spicy, flavorful

Though Grandmother is well into her eighties, she is still as ____**sprightly**____ as a teenager.

SYNONYMS: frisky, peppy, spirited, buoyant
ANTONYMS: sullen, spiritless, dull, morose, sluggish

18. surly
(sər′ lē)

(*adj.*) angry and bad-tempered; rude

Passengers stranded in an airport because their flight is canceled may become quite ____**surly**____.

SYNONYMS: gruff, sullen, cranky, grouchy, hostile
ANTONYMS: polite, gracious, civil, friendly, genial

19. tirade
(tī′ rād)

(*n.*) a long, angry speech, usually very critical

The dictator's televised ____**tirade**____ against his opponents lasted for four hours.

SYNONYMS: diatribe, tongue-lashing

20. vagrant
(vā′ grənt)

(*n.*) an idle wanderer, tramp; (*adj.*) wandering aimlessly

During the Great Depression, many people lost everything and were forced to live as ____**vagrants**____.

Advertisers continually vie with one another to capture the ____**vagrant**____ attention of fickle consumers.

SYNONYMS: (*n.*) vagabond, hobo, nomad
ANTONYMS: (*n.*) stay-at-home, resident

ⓒ CCSS Vocabulary: 4.c. (See pp. T14–15.)

Choosing the Right Word

*Select the **boldface** word that better completes each sentence. You might refer to the essay on pages 88–89 to see how most of these words are used in context.*

1. I feel that a symphony orchestra is just as important to a (**vagrant, <u>metropolis</u>**) as a big department store or a major-league sports team.

2. The (**tirade, <u>advent</u>**) of texting has revolutionized the way in which people communicate with one another.

3. His talk (**maligned, <u>meandered</u>**) aimlessly through memories of his youth, descriptions of his children, and criticisms of the administration.

4. I have no respect for people who are unfailingly courteous to their superiors but (**sprightly, <u>surly</u>**) to the employees under them.

5. I don't know which is worse—your failure to keep your promise to me or your (**<u>shoddy</u>, momentous**) excuse for lying about it.

Many major cities in the U.S. have a symphony orchestra.

6. The bylaws state that any member who speaks in a(n) (**<u>obstreperous</u>, perilous**) manner is to be quieted by the sergeant at arms.

7. I lay there quietly, looking at the clouds and allowing (**<u>vagrant</u>, surly**) thoughts to pass through my mind.

8. When we asked for suggestions on how to improve our school's athletic program, we were (**assimilated, <u>inundated</u>**) by "bright ideas" from all sides.

9. The governor appointed a member of the state assembly to serve as a(n) (**bogus, <u>interim</u>**) senator until a new election can be held.

10. Only after Lincoln's death did most people appreciate the great qualities of the man who had been so (**<u>maligned</u>, inundated**) in his own lifetime.

11. Churchill once said that if a nation tries to avoid everything that is hard and (**shoddy, <u>perilous</u>**), it will weaken its own security.

12. I suffered a substantial financial loss and an even greater loss of faith in human nature when I tried to cash his (**obstreperous, <u>bogus</u>**) check.

13. Most people agree that Elizabethan drama reached its (**<u>apex</u>, metropolis**) in the matchless plays of Shakespeare.

14. One of the glories of America has been its ability to (**<u>assimilate</u>, inundate**) immigrants from every part of the globe.

15. You have reached the stage of life where you must expect to say (**interim, <u>adieu</u>**) to childhood and take on the responsibilities of a young adult.

16. My mother's recipe for lemon meringue pie is a (**pensive, sprightly**) blend of tartness and sweetness.

17. Was any event in American history more (**momentous, exorbitant**) than the decision of the Continental Congress in 1776 to break away from Great Britain?

18. I know that you're eager to have that pretty dress for the junior prom, but don't you think the price is a little (**perilous, exorbitant**)?

19. When the new recruits refused to budge from their foxholes, the enraged sergeant let loose with a(n) (**apex, tirade**) of insults and abuse.

20. It was amazing to see how that quiet, (**pensive, exorbitant**) teenager changed into a tough, hard-driving leader.

21. The trail that winds through the park (**inundates, meanders**) through a variety of settings: the Japanese garden, the koi pond, the rose garden, and the pavilion area.

22. If we have to wait for her to arrive before starting the show, it would be a good idea for us to practice our act in the (**interim, advent**).

23. She admired her supervisor and could not believe that any of her coworkers could possibly have made a (**malign, shoddy**) comment against him.

24. My uncle, an accomplished musician who can play several instruments, is always (**assimilated, inundated**) with requests to play at weddings and parties.

25. "(**Adieu, Tirade**)," she said softly as the train pulled out of the station.

Synonyms

*Choose the word from this unit that is the same or most nearly the same in meaning as the **boldface** word or expression in the phrase. Write that word on the line. Use a dictionary if necessary.*

1. a group of **rowdy** fans — obstreperous

2. made of **flimsy** material — shoddy

3. music that suits my **wistful** state of mind — pensive

4. refused to respond to my opponent's **harangue** — tirade

5. enjoyed the **animated** conversation — sprightly

6. the **crowning point** of a brilliant career — apex

7. **roamed** through the beautiful gardens — meandered

8. a **portentous** meeting of world leaders — momentous

9. foreign words **incorporated** into English — assimilated

10. provides **drifters** with hot meals and shelter — vagrants

The synonyms and antonyms here do not appear on the Definitions page.

7

Antonyms

*Choose the word from this unit that is most nearly opposite in meaning to the **boldface** word or expression in the phrase. Write that word on the line. Use a dictionary if necessary.*

1. an **unreflective** mood _____ pensive _____

2. a **brief friendly chat** _____ tirade _____

3. to **reject** new ideas _____ assimilate _____

4. the **bottom** of the mountain _____ apex _____

5. a confirmed **homebody** _____ vagrant _____

Completing the Sentence

From the words in this unit, choose the one that best completes each of the following sentences. Write the word in the space provided.

1. The senator departed from his prepared remarks to deliver an intemperate _____ tirade _____ attacking the administration's foreign policy.

2. It takes many long hours of study to _____ assimilate _____ all the technical information you need to know if you wish to become a computer programmer.

3. It is sad to have to bid _____ adieu _____ to friends we have known for many years.

4. When the head of your golf club has reached the _____ apex _____ of the swing, pause for a second before you begin the downward motion.

5. Shakespeare's wicked characters often assume the guise of kindness to cloak their _____ malign _____ natures.

6. "This great _____ metropolis _____ has many problems," the mayor said, "but it also has much to offer both residents and visitors."

7. Is there anything more unpleasant than to go to a store and find yourself in the hands of a(n) _____ surly _____ salesperson?

8. Many students take jobs during the _____ interim _____ between the end of one school year and the beginning of the next.

9. When vacant apartments are in short supply, landlords can often get away with charging _____ exorbitant _____ rents.

10. In the streets of all our great cities, you will find _____ vagrants _____ who wander about without homes, jobs, or friends.

11. The people living in the valley will have to leave their homes because the area will be _____ **inundated** _____ when a new dam is constructed across the river.

12. My friend interrupted my _____ **pensive** _____ mood with the quip "A penny for your thoughts."

13. The food processor certainly looked impressive, but its construction was so _____ **shoddy** _____ that within a few months it began to fall apart.

14. When the band struck up a(n) _____ **sprightly** _____ tune, even the most reserved party guests began to laugh, dance, and have fun.

15. King's Highway, an old American Indian trail, _____ **meanders** _____ through Brooklyn, crossing many streets and almost retracing its path at some points.

16. The notorious jewel thief evaded capture for years by adopting numerous clever disguises and _____ **bogus** _____ identities.

17. How can you criticize me for the way I behaved during the emergency when you have never been in such a _____ **perilous** _____ position yourself?

18. The difficult choice between going to college and getting a job is indeed a(n) _____ **momentous** _____ one for a young person.

19. With the _____ **advent** _____ of fast-food restaurants, the appearance of many a main street was forever transformed.

20. Babysitters often find that children described by their parents as well behaved become _____ **obstreperous** _____ brats as soon as those parents leave the house.

Writing: Words in Action

Answers to both prompts will vary.

1. Look back at "City Critters" (pages 88–89). If you had to choose from bedbugs, roaches, and rats, which pest would you *least* want in your home, based on the dangers each poses? Use at least two details from the passage and three unit words to support your observations.

2. The humorous essay "City Critters" makes it clear that humans, with their creation of vast amounts of waste, have a great deal of responsibility for the "pest problem" in cities. In a brief problem-and-solution essay, describe at least one way in which humans can be "pests" themselves in causing harm to the environment, and suggest one way in which this problem can be improved or even solved. Support your views with specific examples from your observations, studies, reading (refer to pages 88–89), or your own experience. Write at least three paragraphs, and use three or more words from this unit.

Writing prompt #2 is modeled on that of standardized tests.

Vocabulary in Context: Informational Text for Unit 7 is available online at **vocabularyworkshop.com**.

7

Vocabulary in Context

Literary Text

The following excerpts are from Jules Verne's novel Around the World in Eighty Days. *Some of the words you have studied in this unit appear in* **boldface** *type. Complete each statement below the excerpt by circling the letter of the correct answer.*

1. He bade **adieu** to Phileas Fogg, wishing him all success, and expressing the hope that he would come that way again in a less original but more profitable fashion.

   If you have bid **adieu,** you have said
   a. "Good night!"   c. "Hello!"
   b. "Good luck!"   **d.** "Good-bye!"

2. This voyage of eight hundred miles was a **perilous** venture on a craft of twenty tons, and at that season of the year. The Chinese seas are usually boisterous, subject to terrible gales of wind, and especially during the equinoxes; and it was now early November.

   Something that is **perilous** is NOT
   a. safe   c. difficult
   b. hazardous   d. lengthy

3. John Bunsby, himself, a man of forty-five or thereabouts, vigorous, sunburnt, with a **sprightly** expression of the eye, and energetic and self-reliant countenance, would have inspired confidence in the most timid.

   The character Phileas Fogg and his valet Passepartout in the great hot-air balloon from the classic 1956 film *Around the World in 80 Days*.

   Someone described as **sprightly** is
   a. weathered   c. bright
   b. spirited   d. undependable

4. Everybody knows that the great reversed triangle of land, with its base in the north and its **apex** in the south, which is called India, embraces fourteen hundred thousand square miles, upon which is spread unequally a population of one hundred and eighty millions of souls.

   An **apex** is a
   a. slope   **c.** peak
   b. capital   d. direction

5. Then they came upon vast tracts extending to the horizon, with jungles inhabited by snakes and tigers, which fled at the noise of the train; succeeded by forests penetrated by the railway, and still haunted by elephants which, with **pensive** eyes, gazed at the train as it passed.

Snap the code, or go to **vocabularyworkshop.com**

   A **pensive** expression is
   a. thoughtful   c. squinting
   b. uncaring   d. hostile

UNIT 8

Note that not all of the 20 unit words are used in this passage. *Asylum*, *dilate*, *immunity*, and *rabid* are not included in the passage.

*Read the following selection, taking note of the **boldface** words and their contexts. These words are among those you will be studying in Unit 8. As you complete the exercises in this unit, it may help to refer to the way the words are used below.*

C CCSS Vocabulary: 4; Reading (Informational Text): 4, 6. (See pp. T14–15.)

A History of Sound Recording

<Encyclopedia Entry>

Sound recording is the mechanical or electrical re-creation of sound waves, such as the spoken voice, singing, or instrumental music. Musical clocks and music boxes, some dating to the 1600s, were the first devices to re-create sound. Able to delight a family or **console** a child, these devices had obvious limitations. Most played only one melody, and they could not record a live performance. They also had to be cranked by hand, and the music quickly faded away as the spring mechanism wound down.

Early Sound Recording

Thomas Edison invented the first "talking machine" in 1877. This device recorded sounds on tinfoil wrapped around a cylinder. With every **assurance** of success, the inventor **instituted** the Edison Record Company. Flat disks, invented by Emil Berliner in 1887, improved the quality of the sound, and by 1900, the production of records was an international industry.

Early sound recordings relied on acoustical means to amplify the sound. Huge, **preposterous**-looking horns on early record players were needed to magnify the sound. The invention of vacuum tubes in the early 1920s eliminated this **liability**. Microphones replaced acoustic horns, and the modern electric phonograph was born. The 78 rpm record, made of shellac and later plastic, became the standard.

Sound Recording and Popular Culture

In the **realm** of popular culture, recorded sound had a major impact. In the home, piano-playing and other live music became less common as people listened to records instead. The number of jobs for bands **dwindled**, and many musicians lost their jobs. On the other hand, sound recording **remunerated** popular singers well, and

Early phonographs had huge horns to amplify the sound.

Record players were a popular way to listen to music at home for much of the 20th century.

Long playing record (above)
and tape cassettes (below)

Reel-to-reel tape deck

Digital recording has many
modern applications.

many became rich. When movie makers
began recording sound on film in the late
1920s, movies became even more popular.

Later Developments

As new inventions **rejuvenated** the
industry, the **dross** of old equipment was
replaced by new technology. In 1948, long-
playing records (LPs) appeared, allowing
30 minutes of playing time per side. Ten
years later, stereophonic recordings made
their debut. With two channels of sound in
each groove of the record, stereo produced
sound of **sterling** quality.

Recording tape, a thin film coated with
magnetic material, had been used to
record sound in radio stations since the
1950s. By the mid-1960s, portable tape
recorders were available for consumers.
Unlike records, tapes did not scratch or
warp, and people liked the convenience of
small tape cassettes, which could be used
in cars and portable players. As a result,
tape cassettes wound up shouldering out
traditional LPs, and the next two decades
saw an increasingly **sparse** demand for
records.

Digital Recording

Unlike earlier types of sound recording,
digital recording converts sound into
binary (base-2) numbers. These numbers
are then recorded on tape as a series
of pulses. Digital compact discs (CDs),
read by a laser, came on the market in the
early 1980s. Within a decade, CDs were
by far the most common way to listen
to music, although some music lovers
pugnaciously defended the sound quality
of vinyl records. The rise of the Internet in
the 1990s led to a new **venture** in sound
recording. Digital downloads of music
to personal listening devices became
popular, cutting into CD sales.

While it is often **flippant** to predict the
future, the rapid pace of change in sound
recording is likely to continue. New ways
to listen to music are sure to come.

Related Articles

Acoustics
Digital Technology
Edison, Thomas
Microphone
Phonograph

Snap the code, or go to
vocabularyworkshop.com

Definitions

Note the spelling, pronunciation, part(s) of speech, and definition(s) of each of the following words. Then write the word in the blank spaces in the illustrative sentence(s) following. Finally, study the lists of synonyms and antonyms.

1. assurance
(ə shŭr′ əns)

(*n.*) a pledge; freedom from doubt, self-confidence

The airport was built with the _____ **assurance** _____ that all the people displaced by its construction would be fairly compensated.

SYNONYMS: promise, sureness, poise, self-possession
ANTONYMS: uncertainty, doubt, insecurity

2. asylum
(ə sī′ ləm)

(*n.*) an institution for the care of children, elderly people, etc.; a place of safety

Some refugees are political fugitives who have fled their homeland to seek _____ **asylum** _____ in another country.

SYNONYMS: sanatorium, sanctuary

3. console
(*v.,* kən sōl′; *n.,* kän′ sōl)

(*v.*) to comfort; (*n.*) the keyboard of an organ; a control panel for an electrical or mechanical device

A neighbor tried to _____ **console** _____ the sobbing child whose cat had wandered away.

The _____ **console** _____ of the large church organ had an assortment of keys, knobs, and pedals.

SYNONYMS: (*v.*) solace, alleviate
ANTONYMS: (*v.*) distress, aggravate, bother, vex, torment

4. dilate
(dī′ lāt)

(*v.*) to make or become larger or wider; to expand upon

The ophthalmologist said she would _____ **dilate** _____ the pupil before examining the injured eye.

SYNONYMS: enlarge, expand, prolong
ANTONYMS: compress, constrict

5. dross
(drôs)

(*n.*) refuse, waste products

The _____ **dross** _____ from the manufacturing process turned out to be highly toxic.

SYNONYMS: trash, detritus, dregs, scum

6. dwindle
(dwin′ dəl)

(*v.*) to lessen, diminish

During the coldest weeks of winter, the pile of firewood slowly _____ **dwindled** _____ until there were no logs left.

SYNONYMS: decrease, shrink, fade, peter out
ANTONYMS: increase, enlarge, swell, proliferate

Ⓒ CCSS Vocabulary: 4.c., 4.d. (See pp. T14–15.)

7. flippant
(flip′ ənt)

(*adj.*) lacking in seriousness; disrespectful, saucy

Parents and other adults are often upset by a teenager's _____**flippant**_____ responses.

SYNONYMS: frivolous, impudent, impertinent, insolent
ANTONYMS: serious, respectful, deferential, obsequious

8. immunity
(i myü′ nə tē)

(*n.*) resistance to disease; freedom from some charge or obligation

Most babies are vaccinated so that they develop an _____**immunity**_____ to measles.

SYNONYM: exemption; ANTONYMS: vulnerability, exposure

9. institute
(in′ stə tüt)

(*v.*) to establish, set up; (*n.*) organization that promotes learning

Congress has been reluctant to _____**institute**_____ new guidelines for campaign spending.

After graduating from high school, I plan to attend an accredited _____**institute**_____ of technology.

SYNONYMS: (*v.*) found, bring about; (*n.*) academy
ANTONYMS: (*v.*) terminate, discontinue, demolish, raze

10. liability
(lī ə bil′ ə tē)

(*n.*) a debt; something disadvantageous

A limited attention span is his biggest _____**liability**_____ as a student.

SYNONYMS: difficulty, impediment; ANTONYMS: advantage, asset

11. preposterous
(prē päs′ tər əs)

(*adj.*) ridiculous, senseless

The theory that Stonehenge was constructed by alien life-forms is utterly _____**preposterous**_____.

SYNONYMS: nonsensical, absurd, incredible
ANTONYMS: sensible, reasonable, realistic, plausible

12. pugnacious
(pəg nā′ shəs)

(*adj.*) quarrelsome, fond of fighting

The fox terrier is a particularly _____**pugnacious**_____ breed of dog known for its aggressive behavior.

SYNONYMS: combative, belligerent
ANTONYMS: peace-loving, friendly, amicable, congenial

13. rabid
(rab′ id)

(*adj.*) furious, violently intense, unreasonably extreme; mad; infected with rabies

Police arrived in force to quell the riot set off by _____**rabid**_____ soccer fans.

SYNONYMS: zealous, raving, infuriated, berserk
ANTONYMS: moderate, blasé, indifferent

14. realm
(relm)

(n.) a kingdom; a region or field of study

While astronomy falls within the _____ **realm** _____ of science, astrology does not.

SYNONYMS: domain, duchy, bailiwick, jurisdiction

15. rejuvenate
(ri jü' və nāt)

(v.) to make young again; to make like new

A few minutes of conversation with my best friend helped to _____ **rejuvenate** _____ my flagging spirits.

SYNONYM: renew
ANTONYMS: wear out, exhaust, enervate, debilitate

16. remunerate
(ri myü' nə rāt)

(v.) to reward, pay, reimburse

The couple promised to _____ **remunerate** _____ the artist handsomely for a portrait of their child.

SYNONYMS: satisfy, profit, benefit

17. sparse
(spärs)

(adj.) meager, scant; scattered

Unlike its neighboring metropolis, the area has quite a _____ **sparse** _____ population.

SYNONYMS: thin, scanty, few and far between
ANTONYMS: plentiful, abundant, profuse, teeming

18. sterling
(stər' liŋ)

(adj.) genuine, excellent; made of silver of standard fineness

The reviewer noted the young actor's _____ **sterling** _____ performance in *A Midsummer Night's Dream*.

SYNONYMS: first-rate, outstanding, worthy, pure
ANTONYMS: shoddy, second-rate, sham

19. venture
(ven' chər)

(n.) a risky or daring undertaking; (v.) to expose to danger; to dare

An overseas voyage was a daunting and dangerous _____ **venture** _____ during the Age of Exploration.

It takes courage to _____ **venture** _____ out into unknown territory.

SYNONYMS: (n.) gamble; (v.) try, chance, undertake
ANTONYMS: (v.) withdraw, retire, shrink from, shy away

20. warp
(wôrp)

(v.) to twist out of shape; (n.) an abnormality

The carpenter explained that humidity caused the kitchen door to _____ **warp** _____.

Criminal behavior often shows a striking lack of judgment or a _____ **warp** _____ in thinking.

SYNONYMS: (v.) bend, distort, misshape; (n.) irregularity
ANTONYMS: (v.) straighten, unbend, rectify

CCSS Vocabulary: 4.c. (See pp. T14–15.)

Choosing the Right Word

*Select the **boldface** word that better completes each sentence. You might refer to the selection on pages 98–99 to see how most of these words are used in context.*

1. When you write so imaginatively about "life on other planets," you are entering the (**realm, dross**) of science fiction.

2. Generally, (**pugnacious, sterling**) behavior on the football field is more effective in drawing penalties than in gaining ground.

3. Clear away the (**immunity, dross**) of false ideas from your mind and take a long, hard look at reality.

4. The college swim team went on an overseas (**asylum, venture**) to compete with teams from all parts of Southeast Asia.

5. Do you expect me to be (**instituted, consoled**) by the fact that I was not the only one to fail the exam?

In 2007, the Pulitzer Prize Board awarded science fiction writer Ray Bradbury a Special Citation for his contributions to American literature.

6. A sound understanding of the principles of freedom and self-government is the best way to gain (**immunity, liability**) from totalitarian propaganda.

7. Many Americans think that the United States should continue to provide (**assurance, asylum**) to people fleeing from tyranny in other lands.

8. The hired man agreed to testify against his boss in exchange for (**immunity, assurance**) against charges related to the crime.

9. Patriotism is a fine quality, but not when it is (**dwindled, warped**) into a hatred of other nations.

10. The outworn ideas of the past cannot be (**rejuvenated, dilated**) simply by expressing them in snappy, modern slang.

11. I agree with some of the speaker's ideas, but I find his (**rabid, sparse**) enthusiasm for crackpot causes hard to take.

12. An unwillingness to listen to suggestions from others is a grave (**liability, realm**) in a leader.

13. I support the team captain because of the (**sterling, preposterous**) leadership she has given us during the long, hard season.

14. In order to meet stricter industry standards, manufacturers will have to (**institute, remunerate**) new systems of quality control.

15. How quickly interest in the program (**dwindles, rejuvenates**) when students realize that it calls for so much work, with little chance for glory!

16. I would not agree to run for public office before receiving (**assurance, asylum**) of support from important groups in the community.

17. I like humor as well as anyone, but I don't believe in being (**flippant, rabid**) on so solemn an occasion.

18. No doubt the instructor knows a great deal about ecology, but is there any need for her to (**venture, dilate**) on threats to the environment at such great length?

19. Today scientists smile wryly at the (**preposterous, pugnacious**) notion that the earth is flat, but in earlier times it was an accepted fact.

20. When the thief stepped up to the computer (**realm, console**), I knew at once that he had the secret passwords.

21. I know better than to (**warp, venture**) into a canoe that a novice will paddle upstream against a crosswind.

22. The (**institute, console**) had a strict policy that new members could not be admitted without a thorough review and background check.

23. My dog's behavior in obedience class is usually (**pugnacious, sterling**), but yesterday he was more interested in playing with the other dogs than in paying attention to commands.

24. In spite of all his talk about his great wealth, I noticed that the penny-pincher did not offer to (**console, remunerate**) us for expenses.

25. As usual, there are plenty of *talkers,* but the supply of *doers* is (**flippant, sparse**).

 **Synonyms**

*Choose the word from this unit that is the same or most nearly the same in meaning as the **boldface** word or expression in the phrase. Write that word on the line. Use a dictionary if necessary.*

1. a potion to **revitalize** and energize _____ rejuvenate

2. seek **refuge** from incessant strife _____ asylum

3. without any **drawback** _____ liability

4. the **rubbish** from the metal plant _____ dross

5. with **impunity** from prosecution _____ immunity

6. an **argumentative** person ready to take offense _____ pugnacious

7. **soothe** the family in their sorrow _____ console

8. **compensate** the baby sitter for his time _____ remunerate

9. cause blood vessels to **swell** _____ dilate

10. the **fanatical** ravings of a rabble-rouser _____ rabid

CCSS Vocabulary: 5. (See pp. T14–15.)

The synonyms and antonyms here do not appear on the Definitions page.

8

Antonyms

*Choose the word from this unit that is most nearly opposite in meaning to the **boldface** word or expression in the phrase. Write that word on the line. Use a dictionary if necessary.*

1. a policy calling for the **expulsion** of immigrants _____asylum_____

2. a medication that causes blood vessels to **contract** _____dilate_____

3. **susceptibility** to colds and flu _____immunity_____

4. the fans' **restrained** response to the celebrity's appearance _____rabid_____

5. a person of **mediocre** reputation _____sterling_____

Completing the Sentence

From the words in this unit, choose the one that best completes each of the following sentences. Write the word in the space provided.

1. The philanthropist devoted his time, energy, and funds to establishing a(n) _____institute_____ for promoting world peace.

2. Despite intense heat, meager rainfall, and _____sparse_____ vegetation, many animals have adapted to life in the desert.

3. Although I cannot support her in the election, I fully appreciate her many _____sterling_____ qualities.

4. You will need experience, ability, financing, and good luck to have any chance of succeeding in so risky a business _____venture_____.

5. As the snake came into view and slithered across her path, the archaeologist's eyes _____dilated_____ with fear.

6. The wooden staircase we had worked so hard to build was now irregularly curved because the boards had _____warped_____.

7. The main point of my father's speech was that all the riches of the world are so much worthless _____dross_____ without the support of one's friends.

8. The idea that an incoming president can miraculously solve all of the nation's problems is simply _____preposterous_____.

9. Weary from months of hard work, she was hopeful that a week at a spa would _____rejuvenate_____ her.

10. Calling upon his many years of experience, the retired warden discussed with great _____assurance_____ the topic of the evening: "Can Criminals Be Rehabilitated?"

11. I consider myself a very peaceful person, but if anyone approaches me in a(n) _____**pugnacious**_____ manner, I am prepared to defend myself.

12. Can any amount of money _____**remunerate**_____ someone for years sacrificed to a hopeless cause?

13. As days passed without a phone call, a letter, or an e-mail, his hopes for even a small role in the production _____**dwindled**_____.

14. When my pet hamster died suddenly, even my closest friends were unable to _____**console**_____ me during my hours of grief.

15. Because his army was stronger than his rival's, the pretender to the throne was able to seize power throughout the entire _____**realm**_____.

16. Did you know that the English word *bedlam* was taken from the name of an infamous _____**asylum**_____ for the insane in medieval London?

17. He is such a(n) _____**rabid**_____ sports enthusiast that he spends almost all of his spare time either playing ball or watching ball games on TV.

18. When we are discussing serious social issues, I feel that _____**flippant**_____ remarks are in bad taste.

19. Doctors hope to lessen the number, length, and severity of common colds, even if they cannot provide complete _____**immunity**_____ from them.

20. She is an excellent ball handler and a very good shot; her only serious _____**liability**_____ as a basketball player is lack of speed.

Writing: Words in Action

Answers to both prompts will vary.

1. Look back at "A History of Sound Recording" (pages 98–99). Write a brief cause-and-effect essay in which you explore the effects of one specific technological advancement in sound recording from the era of your choice. Identify at least one positive (or intended) and one negative (or unintended) effect of the advancement. Use at least two details from the passage and three unit words to support your choice.

2. Technological advances often have a significant impact on popular culture. Think of a technological advancement in your lifetime that has affected some aspect of popular entertainment that you enjoy, such as movies, sports, music, books, or gaming. In a brief essay, describe this advancement and its effects on your chosen form of entertainment, using specific examples from your observations, studies, reading (refer to pages 98–99), or your own experience. Write at least three paragraphs, and use three or more words from this unit.

Writing prompt #2 is modeled on that of standardized tests.

Vocabulary in Context: Informational Text for Unit 8 is available online at **vocabularyworkshop.com**.

8

Vocabulary in Context

The following excerpts are from H. G. Wells's novels The Time Machine *and* The War of the Worlds. *Some of the words you have studied in this unit appear in* **boldface** *type. Complete each statement below the excerpt by circling the letter of the correct answer.*

1. All the time, with the certainty that sometimes comes with excessive dread, I knew that such **assurance** was folly, knew instinctively that the machine was removed out of my reach. (*The Time Machine*)

   If you have **assurance**, you have
   a. arrogance
   b. apprehension
   c. ignorance
   (d.) confidence

2. I might have **consoled** myself by imagining the little people had put the mechanism in some shelter for me, had I not felt assured of their physical and intellectual inadequacy. (*The Time Machine*)

   To **console** is to
   (a.) comfort
   b. agitate
   c. fantasize
   d. reflect on

The Martians in their frightening tripods try to destroy Earth in the 2005 film *War of the Worlds,* directed by Steven Spielberg.

3. ...[T]he balanced civilization that was at last attained must have long since passed its zenith, and was now far gone in decay. The too-perfect security of the Upper-worlders had led them to a slow movement of degeneration, to a general **dwindling** in size, strength, and intelligence. (*The Time Machine*)

   Something that is **dwindling** is
   a. enlarging
   (b.) diminishing
   c. evolving
   d. accelerating

4. But the Martians now understood our command of artillery and the danger of human proximity, and not a man **ventured** within a mile of either cylinder, save at the price of his life. (*The War of the Worlds*)

   If a man has NOT **ventured** within a mile he has
   a. come closer
   b. gone out
   (c.) stayed away
   d. explored

5. Here, moved by curiosity, I turned aside to find, among a tangle of red fronds, the **warped** and broken dog cart with the whitened bones of the horse scattered and gnawed. (*The War of the Worlds*)

   Something that is **warped** is
   (a.) twisted
   b. discolored
   c. forgotten
   d. shabby

Interactive Quiz

Snap the code, or go to **vocabularyworkshop.com**

UNIT 9

Note that not all of the 20 unit words are used in this passage.
Cubicle, envoy, incredulous, monologue, and *rasping* are not
included in the passage.

*Read the following selection, taking note of the **boldface** words and their contexts.
These words are among those you will be studying in Unit 9. As you complete the
exercises in this unit, it may help to refer to the way the words are used below.*

C CCSS Vocabulary: 4; Reading (Informational Text): 4, 6. (See pp. T14–15.)

Ringl and Pit: Witnesses to the Weimar

<Profile>

There is an old adage that says, "Success is not measured by what you accomplish but by the opposition you have encountered." Two women who knew the meaning of that type of success generations ago were the pioneering photographers Ellen Rosenberg Auerbach and Grete Stern, better known as Ringl + Pit.

Auerbach and Stern were born in Germany in the early 1900s to middle-class Jewish families. They met in Berlin at the studio of a photography professor at the Bauhaus, the world-famous art and design school, and became fast friends. These creative women discovered that they had a **flair** for photography. They were also ambitious: As so-called new women, they refused to settle for **auxiliary** roles in the workplace. They had no intention of **feigning** interest in the more traditional careers open to women at the time. They wanted the same freedom and choices their male colleagues took for granted. So when their friend from the Bauhaus decided to close his private studio, the young women took over the premises and renamed the business Foto Ringl + Pit. (*Ringl* and *Pit* were the childhood nicknames, respectively, of Stern and Auerbach.)

It was a great time to set up shop because the advertising industry was booming, despite the fragile economic and political state of the Weimar Republic (the period of German history from 1919 to 1933, between the two world wars). Their career move proved to be **expedient**, and Foto Ringl + Pit was a commercial and artistic success. The women discovered they could earn a living using their artistic talents in advertising, publicity, and fashion

Ellen Rosenberg Auerbach and Grete Stern, shown here in 1995, named their groundbreaking photography business after their childhood nicknames, Ringl and Pit.

photography. Their striking photographs were praised for their unique, playful style. While some of their shots were **candid**, most were staged and posed. They also turned their cameras on many celebrated writers, artists, and performers of the day.

But the **prognosis** for peace and longed-for prosperity in Germany was not promising. The country's Jews were already experiencing **grievous** hardships. The **repugnant** beliefs of Hitler and the Nazis soon replaced the tolerant views of the Weimar era. **Hordes** of Jews and other "undesirables" were rounded up and taken to concentration camps; most didn't survive the **drudgery**, illness, starvation, or gas chambers there.

Anti-Semitism **escalated** once Hitler came to power, forcing Ringl and Pit to **scuttle** their plans and working partnership. They were

"Elegant Lady", advertisement

impelled to leave Germany. As Ellen Auerbach said years later in a documentary about Ringl + Pit, "In a country with concentration camps, you cannot live." The women eventually settled in Buenos Aires and in New York, places with more open, **heterogeneous** populations than Germany. They continued to work in photography and had impressive solo careers.

Ellen Rosenberg Auerbach and Grete Stern both lived long, extraordinary lives. Although the talented duo of Ringl + Pit never worked together again after the mid-1930s, they stayed lifelong friends. These days, you can see their groundbreaking photographs on display in galleries and museums around the world, and their original prints are highly sought-after (a photo **inscribed** with "Ringl + Pit" can be worth thousands).

Snap the code, or go to **vocabularyworkshop.com**

Hat and Gloves, 1932

Pit with Veil, 1930

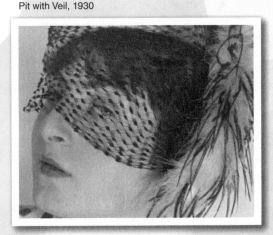

Definitions

Note the spelling, pronunciation, part(s) of speech, and definition(s) of each of the following words. Then write the word in the blank spaces in the illustrative sentence(s) following. Finally, study the lists of synonyms and antonyms.

1. auxiliary
(ôg zil′ yə rē)

(*adj.*) giving assistance or support; (*n.*) a helper, aid

If the main motor fails, the instructions say to turn on the _____**auxiliary**_____ motor.

Someone second in command is an _____**auxiliary**_____ to the person in charge.

SYNONYMS: (*adj.*) additional; (*n.*) reserve, accessory
ANTONYMS: (*adj.*) main, primary, principal

2. candid
(kan′ did)

(*adj.*) frank, sincere; impartial; unposed

It is safe to be _____**candid**_____ about our faults with friends and loved ones.

SYNONYMS: forthright, plainspoken, unbiased
ANTONYMS: insincere, evasive, misleading, artful

3. cubicle
(kyü′ bə kəl)

(*n.*) a small room or compartment

The tiniest _____**cubicle**_____ is usually assigned to the newest employee.

SYNONYM: hole-in-the-wall
ANTONYMS: vast hall, auditorium

4. drudgery
(drəj′ ə rē)

(*n.*) work that is hard and tiresome

Trade unions lobby to relieve the endless _____**drudgery**_____ of factory workers.

SYNONYMS: toil, labor, grind
ANTONYMS: play, frolic, amusement, recreation, fun

5. envoy
(en′ voi; än′ voi)

(*n.*) a representative or messenger (as of a government)

On more than one occasion, a former President has been asked to act as a special _____**envoy**_____ to the United Nations.

SYNONYMS: ambassador, emissary, minister

6. escalate
(es′ kə lāt)

(*v.*) to elevate; to increase in intensity

A small dispute can _____**escalate**_____ into a major conflict unless the opposing parties sit down and talk.

SYNONYMS: raise, ascend, mount
ANTONYMS: decrease, lessen, descend, defuse

Ⓒ CCSS Vocabulary: 4.c., 4.d. (See pp. T14–15.)

7. expedient
(ek spē′ dē ənt)

(*n.*) a means to an end; (*adj.*) advantageous, useful

As an _____**expedient**_____, we chose to use a rock as a makeshift hammer.

An opportunist is someone who is always ready to do whatever is most _____**expedient**_____.

SYNONYMS: (*n.*) contrivance, device; (*adj.*) serviceable
ANTONYMS: (*adj.*) inconvenient, untimely, disadvantageous

8. feign
(fān)

(*v.*) to pretend

Children sometimes _____**feign**_____ illness to avoid going to school.

SYNONYMS: fake, sham, affect, simulate

9. flair
(flâr)

(*n.*) a natural quality, talent, or skill; a distinctive style

An opera singer needs a _____**flair**_____ for the dramatic as well as a good voice.

SYNONYMS: bent, knack, gift, style, panache
ANTONYMS: inability, incapacity

10. grievous
(grē′ vəs)

(*adj.*) causing sorrow or pain; serious

Reporters should take careful notes when interviewing to avoid making _____**grievous**_____ errors in print.

SYNONYMS: painful, heartrending, onerous, flagrant
ANTONYMS: joyful, uplifting, cheery, upbeat, comforting

11. heterogeneous
(het ə rə jē′ nē əs)

(*adj.*) composed of different kinds, diverse

Most college admissions officers actively seek a student body that is both talented and _____**heterogeneous**_____.

SYNONYMS: miscellaneous, mixed, variegated
ANTONYMS: uniform, homogeneous, of a piece

12. horde
(hôrd)

(*n.*) a vast number (as of people); a throng

When the doors opened, a _____**horde**_____ of shoppers headed toward the sales racks.

SYNONYMS: crowd, mass, multitude, host, swarm
ANTONYMS: few, handful

13. impel
(im pel′)

(*v.*) to force, drive forward

Hunger often _____**impels**_____ people to leave their homes in search of food.

SYNONYMS: urge, push, spur, propel, incite
ANTONYMS: discourage, check, restrain, curb

14. incredulous
(in krej′ ə ləs)

(*adj.*) disbelieving, skeptical

When the testimony of a witness contradicts the evidence, you can expect _____incredulous_____ stares from the jury.

SYNONYMS: mistrustful, doubting; ANTONYMS: believing, trustful

15. inscribe
(in skrīb′)

(*v.*) to write or engrave; to enter a name on a list

The young man asked the jeweler to _____inscribe_____ the locket with his fiancée's name.

SYNONYMS: enroll, enlist
ANTONYMS: erase, rub out, delete, efface, obliterate

16. monologue
(män′ ə läg)

(*n.*) a speech by one actor; a long talk by one person

By means of a _____monologue_____, a playwright shares a character's private thoughts with the audience.

SYNONYM: soliloquy; ANTONYMS: conversation, colloquy

17. prognosis
(präg nō′ səs)

(*n.*) a forecast of the probable course and outcome of a disease or situation

Doctors are particularly happy to deliver a _____prognosis_____ of a speedy recovery.

SYNONYM: projection

18. rasping
(ras′ piŋ)

(*adj.*) with a harsh, grating sound; (*n.*) a harsh sound

Chronic bronchitis can lead to a _____rasping_____ cough that is difficult to cure.

The _____rasping_____ of metal scraping against metal sets my teeth on edge.

SYNONYMS: (*adj.*) scraping, abrasive, gravelly
ANTONYMS: (*adj.*) smooth, satiny, silky

19. repugnant
(rē pəg′ nənt)

(*adj.*) offensive, disagreeable, distasteful

Despite their _____repugnant_____ lack of cleanliness, pigs are endearing to many people.

SYNONYMS: hateful, odious, revolting, repulsive
ANTONYMS: pleasing, attractive, tempting, wholesome

20. scuttle
(skət′ əl)

(*v.*) to sink a ship by cutting holes in it; to get rid of something in a decisive way; to run hastily, scurry; (*n.*) a pail

Pirates would not wish to _____scuttle_____ a captured galleon before looting its cargo.

Years ago, it was possible to buy a _____scuttle_____ of coal at the corner grocery store.

SYNONYMS: (*v.*) abandon, discard, scrap, ditch, dump
ANTONYMS: (*v.*) keep afloat, salvage, rescue, preserve

ⓒ CCSS Vocabulary: 4.c. (See pp. T14–15.)

Choosing the Right Word

*Select the **boldface** word that better completes each sentence. You might refer to the selection on pages 108–109 to see how most of these words are used in context.*

1. Despite the doctor's gloomy (**prognosis, flair**) when I entered the hospital, I was up and about in a matter of days.

2. I must admit now that I was hurt when the coach took me out in the last minutes of the game, but I tried to (**scuttle, feign**) indifference.

3. How can you say that the TV interview was spontaneous and (**heterogeneous, candid**) when it was all carefully rehearsed?

4. I don't consider it (**drudgery, rasping**) to prepare meals every day because I love good food and good cooking.

5. The building is equipped with a(n) (**repugnant, auxiliary**) generator, ready to go into service whenever the main power source is cut off.

6. "The noble Brutus has told you Caesar was ambitious; if it were so, it was a (**grievous, candid**) fault."

7. I work in an office compartment, travel in a midget car, and sleep in a tiny bedroom. My life seems to take place in a series of (**envoys, cubicles**)!

8. Instead of sending your little sister as a(n) (**envoy, horde**) to explain what went wrong, why don't you stand up and speak for yourself?

9. The poet Browning tells us that if we were to open his heart, we would find the word "Italy" (**inscribed, impelled**) inside it.

10. After examining the price tag, I gingerly replaced the coat on the rack, (**incredulous, grievous**) at the preposterous sum the store was asking for it.

11. People who boast of their high moral principles are often the ones who will (**scuttle, escalate**) them most quickly to serve their own interests.

12. The expression of satisfaction that comes over her face when she talks of the failures of other people is highly (**expedient, repugnant**) to me.

13. An army without strong leadership and firm discipline is no more than an armed (**horde, drudgery**).

14. I searched in vain through the (**auxiliary, heterogeneous**) pile of odds and ends for the spare part I had inadvertently thrown away.

15. It's one thing to be interested in writing; it's quite another to have a (**flair, monologue**) for it.

16. Political analysts, students of statecraft, and historians tried to determine what caused a minor border incident to (**escalate, feign**) into a full-scale war.

17. As soon as I heard (**incredulous, rasping**) noises coming from the workshop, I knew that someone was using a saw or a file.

18. Was it patriotism, a desire to show off, or just self-interest that (**inscribed, impelled**) the foreign minister to take those terrible risks?

19. Since the person I was trying to interview wouldn't let me get a word in edgewise, our conversation quickly turned into a (**prognosis, monologue**).

20. Cut off from all supplies, the soldiers had to use various (**expedients, cubicles**) to keep their equipment in working order.

21. It was wrong of me to be so curt with her, but it was the (**expedient, incredulous**) thing to do, since I was already running late to my appointment.

22. I practiced my theatrical (**feign, monologue**) for weeks, hoping that a flawless performance would land me the part I wanted.

23. When I jolted awake last night to the sound of a desperate (**prognosis, rasping**), I was cold with fear until I realized that it was my old dog, who sometimes has breathing problems.

24. He handed me a (**scuttle, cubicle**) of slop for the pigs, and suddenly I was glad that this was a job I did not have to do very often.

25. If I'm not available, ask my (**cubicle, auxiliary**) to sign the papers.

Synonyms

*Choose the word from this unit that is the same or most nearly the same in meaning as the **boldface** word or expression in the phrase. Write that word on the line. Use a dictionary if necessary.*

1. the small, dark **enclosure** _____cubicle_____

2. an **agent** of a foreign government _____envoy_____

3. the **scratchy** tone of an old vinyl record _____rasping_____

4. rely on the **back-up** speakers _____auxiliary_____

5. an extraordinary **aptitude** for numbers _____flair_____

6. continue to **climb** rapidly _____escalate_____

7. remained **dubious** of stories about aliens _____incredulous_____

8. an endless **recitation** of petty complaints _____monologue_____

9. an optimistic **prediction** for economic recovery _____prognosis_____

10. the names **imprinted** on a monument _____inscribed_____

C CCSS Vocabulary: 5. (See pp. T14–15.)

The synonyms and antonyms here do not appear on the Definitions page.

9

Antonyms

*Choose the word from this unit that is most nearly opposite in meaning to the **boldface** word or expression in the phrase. Write that word on the line. Use a dictionary if necessary.*

1. an **enemy** who has infiltrated a foreign nation _____ envoy

2. directed to a **capacious office** _____ cubicle

3. a **gullible** child _____ incredulous

4. create a lively **dialogue** _____ monologue

5. a **sonorous** sound _____ rasping

Completing the Sentence

From the words in this unit, choose the one that best completes each of the following sentences. Write the word in the space provided.

1. It is a(n) ___heterogeneous___ population that accounts for the wide variety of cultures found in some neighborhoods.

2. In times of rapid inflation, prices of goods ___escalate___ at a dizzying rate.

3. The New York City Marathon begins with a(n) ___horde___ of runners swarming across the Verrazano-Narrows Bridge.

4. A(n) ___flair___ for color and texture is an indispensable asset to an aspiring dress designer.

5. While some people relish Limburger cheese, others find its strong odor truly ___repugnant___.

6. It is all very well to be ___candid___, but there are times when you should keep certain thoughts and opinions to yourself.

7. We must have the courage and the clear-sightedness to realize that what is ___expedient___ is not always right.

8. The names of all four members of the record-breaking relay team are ___inscribed___ on the trophy awarded to our school.

9. A strong sense of fair play should ___impel___ you to admit your mistake.

10. In many cities, groups of private citizens have volunteered to serve as ___auxiliary___ police to help combat crime.

CCSS Vocabulary: 4.a. (See pp. T14–15.)

Unit 9 ∎ 115

11. I maintain that my _____ cubicle _____ in the dormitory is so small that I have to walk into the hallway to change my mind or stretch my imagination.

12. My rather lame excuse for failing to complete my homework was greeted with a(n) _____ incredulous _____ snort by the teacher.

13. I can't help but admire your ability to _____ feign _____ interest when someone prattles on endlessly about nothing.

14. An unwilling pupil is apt to look upon hours of practice at the piano as so much boredom and _____ drudgery _____.

15. Hopelessly cut off from the main fleet, the captain of the vessel decided to _____ scuttle _____ his ship rather than allow it to fall into enemy hands.

16. Her voice is so _____ rasping _____ that I find it painful to listen to her speak.

17. In his opening _____ monologue _____, the talk-show host often pokes fun at political candidates and elected officials.

18. I hope you will listen attentively to your parents' dire _____ prognosis _____ of the probable effect that a third bowl of chili will have on your digestion.

19. When Lincoln had been in the White House for about a year, he suffered a(n) _____ grievous _____ loss in the death of his son Willie.

20. A special _____ envoy _____ was named by the President to negotiate a settlement in the war-torn region.

Writing: Words in Action

Answers to both prompts will vary.

1. Look back at "Ringl and Pit: Witnesses to the Weimar" (pages 108–109). Imagine that you are a career counselor about to speak to a group of recent graduates in order to give them confidence and courage in planning the next phase of their lives. Write a brief speech in which you summarize the story of Ringl and Pit, using it as an inspiring anecdote to show your audience that they too can overcome difficult circumstances. Use at least two details from the passage and three unit words to support your points.

2. Ellen Rosenberg Auerbach and Grete Stern carved a unique path for themselves in spite of—or perhaps because of—the persecution of the Nazi regime, which thwarted their careers in Germany. In a brief essay, write about how difficulties can impel people to take creative risks and build successful lives in spite of challenging and even dangerous circumstances. Support your points with specific examples from your observations, studies, reading (refer to pages 108–109), or your own experiences. Write at least three paragraphs, and use three or more words from this unit.

Writing prompt #2 is modeled on that of standardized tests.

Vocabulary in Context: Informational Text for Unit 9 is available online at **vocabularyworkshop.com**.

9

Vocabulary in Context

Literary Text

The following excerpts are from Jane Austen's novel Pride and Prejudice. *Some of the words you have studied in this unit appear in* **boldface** *type. Complete each statement below the excerpt by circling the letter of the correct answer.*

1. "But to be **candid** without ostentation or design—to take the good of everybody's character and make it still better, and say nothing of the bad—belongs to you alone."

   If you are **candid** you are

   a. sweet   **c.** deceitful
   b. religious   **d.** straightforward

Jennifer Ehle portrayed Elizabeth Bennet in the 1995 TV miniseries *Pride and Prejudice*.

2. Lady Lucas began directly to calculate, with more interest than the matter had ever excited before, how many years longer Mr. Bennet was likely to live; and Sir William gave it as his decided opinion, that whenever Mr. Collins should be in possession of the Longbourn estate, it would be highly **expedient** that both he and his wife should make their appearance at St. James's.

   Something **expedient** is

   a. beneficial   **c.** preferable
   b. legal   **d.** obligatory

3. "These bitter accusations might have been suppressed, had I, with greater policy, concealed my struggles, and flattered you into the belief of my being **impelled** by unqualified, unalloyed inclination; by reason, by reflection, by everything."

   If you are **impelled** by something, you are

   a. disgusted   **c.** attacked
   b. motivated   **d.** hindered

4. The respect created by the conviction of his valuable qualities, though at first unwillingly admitted, had for some time ceased to be **repugnant** to her feeling; and it was now heightened into somewhat of a friendlier nature....

   If something is NOT **repugnant** it is

   a. disgusting   **c.** pleasing
   b. unsightly   **d.** unworthy

5. Though suspicion was very far from Miss Bennet's general habits, she was absolutely **incredulous** here.

   To be **incredulous** is to be

   a. unbelieving   **c.** relaxed
   b. unyielding   **d.** reflective

Snap the code, or go to **vocabularyworkshop.com**

Vocabulary for Comprehension

*Read the following selection in which some of the words you have studied in Units 7–9 appear in **boldface** type. Then answer the questions on page 119.*

The state of Louisiana has an abundance of nutrias. The following passage explains why.

(Line)

A nutria is not a vitamin, a Japanese car, a cancer-preventing vegetable, or even a subatomic particle. No, no, no. Nutrias are

(5) **pugnacious** twenty-pound semiaquatic rodents with webbed feet. Their whiskered faces resemble those of a beaver, while the **sparse** hair on their tails is more reminiscent

(10) of a rat's.

Nutrias are indigenous to South America but were introduced to the United States in the 1930s by fur traders looking for a cheap version

(15) of mink. In 1937, Tabasco® sauce tycoon E. A. McIlhenny imported thirteen pairs of nutrias to Avery Island, Louisiana, to start a fur farm. But nutria fur never caught on, and

(20) all the animals were released into the wild. With a reproductive rate of five to eight young per litter and up to three litters yearly, the North American nutria population did not

(25) **dwindle**. Before long, there were a million "giant rats" in Louisiana, and they spread to Mississippi, Alabama, Texas, and Florida. In addition,

nutrias were introduced throughout

(30) the Gulf of Mexico region to control specific types of aquatic vegetation in lakes and ponds; but since nutrias are consumers of all vegetation, this process failed. At their population

(35) **apex**, the **horde** of nutrias numbered about ten million nationwide.

Many North American ecosystems cannot **assimilate** nutrias, and they damage wetlands and beach dunes,

(40) compete with indigenous species such as muskrats and waterfowl for food, and eat farmers' crops. They make their nests out of plant materials in burrows dug into river

(45) banks and can eat up to twenty-five percent of their body weight per day. In Louisiana, people are being urged to "Save the Coast, Eat Nutrias"—as in nutria sausage, barbecued nutria,

(50) and nutria chili.

The nutria explosion is a reminder that with a global transportation network, it is becoming increasingly easy for people and animals to move

(55) from place to place—sometimes with unexpected results.

CCSS Vocabulary: 4.a.; Reading (Informational Text): 2, 4, 6. (See pp. T14–15.)

1. Which of the following titles best summarizes the content of the passage?
   a. The Nutria Explosion
   b. Save the Nutria
   c. The Meaning of Nutria
   d. Nutria Sausage
   e. Order Rodentia

2. In the first paragraph (lines 1–10), the nutria is described as a
   a. relative of a mink
   b. cross between a pug and a duck
   c. form of neutrino
   d. kind of waterfowl
   e. cross between a beaver and a rat

3. **Pugnacious** (line 5) most nearly means
   a. amicable
   b. combative
   c. active
   d. inquisitive
   e. adventurous

4. **Sparse** (line 8) is best defined as
   a. coarse
   b. thick
   c. scanty
   d. silky
   e. dense

5. Paragraph 2 (lines 11–36) focuses mainly on
   a. nutria control
   b. nutria biology
   c. wetland damage
   d. nutria history
   e. fur industry statistics

6. Apparently nutrias have overrun North America primarily because of their
   a. high reproductive capacity
   b. ability to nest in water
   c. popularity as a source of fur
   d. ravenous appetites
   e. ability to live on land

7. The meaning of **dwindle** (line 25) is
   a. stabilize
   b. shrink
   c. swell
   d. vanish
   e. explode

8. **Apex** (line 35) is best defined as
   a. plateau
   b. core
   c. nadir
   d. median
   e. peak

9. **Horde** (line 35) most nearly means
   a. group
   b. family
   c. multitude
   d. handful
   e. species

10. The evidence presented in the third paragraph (lines 37–50) suggests that
    a. there is a need to reduce the nutria population
    b. nutrias will become endangered
    c. nutrias cannot thrive in the Louisiana wetlands
    d. nutrias can comfortably coexist with muskrats and waterfowl
    e. there is more room for nutrias in the Gulf of Mexico than in Louisiana

11. The meaning of **assimilate** (line 38) is
    a. withstand
    b. adopt
    c. like
    d. incorporate
    e. segregate

12. According to the passage, all of the following statements are true EXCEPT
    a. Nutrias compete with native species for food.
    b. Nutrias have a negative impact on many South American ecosystems.
    c. Nutrias are a significant threat to the wetlands in Louisiana.
    d. Nutrias are not indigenous to North America.
    e. Nutrias have the ability to eat large quantities of aquatic vegetation.

CCSS Vocabulary: 4.a.; Reading (Informational Text): 2, 4, 6. (See pp. T14–15.)

Review Units 7–9 ■ **119**

Two-Word Completions

Select the pair of words that best complete the meaning of each of the following passages.

1. Does the old saying, "Nothing _____, nothing gained," mean that someone who expects to be _____ well for his or her efforts must be prepared to take some risks?
   a. scuttled . . . maligned
   b. feigned . . . impelled
   c. ventured . . . remunerated
   d. assimilated . . . inundated

2. After fighting my way all year along the noisy, crowded streets of a bustling modern _____ like Tokyo or New York, I find it quite a pleasure to _____ aimlessly along a winding country road.
   a. realm . . . dilate
   b. metropolis . . . meander
   c. asylum . . . impel
   d. cubicle . . . venture

3. As soon as the robins and the crocuses herald the _____ of spring, our personnel department is _____ with a veritable deluge of letters from college students asking about summer employment.
   a. interim. . . impelled
   b. advent . . . inundated
   c. prognosis . . . rejuvenated
   d. flair . . . consoled

4. "Over the years, consumer prices have soared, while the real purchasing power of the dollar has _____," the speaker said. "If the cost of living continues to _____, the value of our money must surely shrink even more."
   a. dwindled . . . dwindle
   b. escalated . . . dwindle
   c. escalated . . . escalate
   d. dwindled . . . escalate

5. "They're asking far too much for this _____ merchandise," I remarked. "I'd be a fool to pay such a(n) _____ price for goods that are so badly made."
   a. bogus . . . rasping
   b. sterling . . . expedient
   c. shoddy . . . exorbitant
   d. grievous . . . auxiliary

6. Roman governors had at their command both regular legionary troops and _____ units drawn from the native population to repel the _____ of savage barbarians that from time to time swarmed into the provinces of the Empire like an invasion of locusts.
   a. pugnacious . . . tirades
   b. heterogeneous . . . envoys
   c. vagrant . . . realms
   d. auxiliary . . . hordes

7. Some people really enjoy doing all the tiresome and time-consuming chores associated with housework, but to me such _____ is truly _____.
   a. drudgery . . . repugnant
   b. immunity . . . obstreperous
   c. liability . . . grievous
   d. assurance . . . pensive

Idioms

In the selection about pests in urban areas (see pages 88–89), the author says, "with so many pests to keep at bay, keeping our homes and cities clean remains a momentous task."

"Keep at bay" is an idiom that means "keep a safe distance away" or "stop something troublesome from getting too close." An **idiom** is an informal expression that cannot be translated literally; its actual meaning is often quite different from the literal meanings of its words. Idioms often rely on figures of speech, or imaginative comparisons, as in the phrase "the apple of my eye." The meaning of an idiom may not be obvious or self-evident, so idioms must be learned, just like any new or unfamiliar vocabulary.

Choosing the Right Idiom

*Read each sentence. Use context clues to figure out the meaning of each idiom in **boldface** print. Then write the letter of the definition for the idiom in the sentence.*

1. My sister, who is a real **goody two-shoes,** follows every rule to the letter. ___h___

2. It's **a blessing in disguise** that no one wanted to play ball, as there were strong thunderstorms today. ___i___

3. Diets that claim to help people lose weight quickly are **a dime a dozen**. ___f___

4. It's a **toss up** between who is a better soccer player, me or my brother. ___a___

5. I thought my friend was really hurt, but he was just **crying wolf**. ___d___

6. The lead part in the play was won by **a dark horse**—that quiet, shy new girl from Boston. ___g___

7. My real fear is that when my friends find out about my encounter with an angry duck, they will have **a field day** making fun of me. ___j___

8. If I **go out on a limb** and hire you, you will need to prove to me that I made a good choice. ___b___

9. Unfortunately, the gerbil we bought for my sister **kicked the bucket** only a week after we brought it home. ___c___

10. My cousin dragged me to a comic book convention, where I felt like a real **fish out of water**. ___e___

a. an even chance

b. take a risk

c. died

d. asking for help or attention without really needing it

e. someone who feels out of place

f. easily available; extremely common

g. an unexpected contender

h. person who is smugly obedient and zealously conforms to the rules

i. something that reveals itself to be a good thing after the fact

j. a really good time

CCSS Vocabulary: 5.a. (See pp. T14–15.)

Writing with Idioms

Find the meaning of each idiom. (Use an online or print dictionary if necessary.) Then write a sentence for each idiom. **Answers will vary.**

1. sick as a dog
<u>**Sample answer: I was sick as a dog after eating too much fried food at the fair.**</u>

2. the best of both worlds

3. under the weather

4. nest egg

5. when pigs fly

6. slip through the cracks

7. go to seed

8. thorn in your side

9. turn over a new leaf

10. fifth wheel

11. pitch in

12. run a tight ship

Denotation and Connotation

The literal meaning of a word is its **denotation**, the formal definition of the word that you find in a dictionary. A word's denotation is usually *neutral* in tone and does not stir either strongly positive or strongly negative associations.

Words that have similar dictionary definitions can, however, carry shades of meaning called **connotations**—suggested meanings that a reader or listener associates with the words. Connotations can be either *positive* or *negative*.

Consider these synonyms for the neutral word *group*:

> team   community   horde   mob

The words *team* and *community* describe harmonious groups united by a common interest. These words have positive connotations. *Horde* and *mob* describe large, disorderly groups. The word *mob*, in fact, suggests an out-of-control, potentially violent crowd. Both *horde* and *mob* have negative connotations.

> **Think:** A friendly classroom can become a team or a community, but an angry group of protesters can become a horde or a mob.

Look at these examples of words that are similar in denotation but have different connotations.

NEUTRAL	POSITIVE	NEGATIVE
speech	discourse	tirade
candid	sincere	blunt
confidence	assurance	audacity

We all learn to distinguish such shades of meaning through building experience with words, encountering them in different contexts through reading, speaking, writing, and listening. Considerate writers and speakers think about how a word's connotations may affect their audience, and they adjust their choice of words accordingly.

Shades of Meaning

Write a plus sign (+) in the box if the word has a positive connotation.
Write a minus sign (–) if the word has a negative connotation. Put a zero (0)
if the word is neutral.

1. auxiliary `0`   **2.** remunerate `+`   **3.** interim `0`   **4.** malign `–`

5. momentous `+`   **6.** repugnant `–`   **7.** sprightly `+`   **8.** rejuvenate `+`

9. apex `+`   **10.** prognosis `0`   **11.** liability `–`   **12.** obstreperous `–`

13. pugnacious `–`   **14.** dross `–`   **15.** console `+`   **16.** venture `0`

CCSS Vocabulary: 5.b. (See pp. T14–15.)

WORD STUDY

Expressing the Connotation

Read each sentence. Select the word in parentheses that expresses the connotation (positive, negative, or neutral) given at the beginning of the sentence.

negative
1. When I opened the package, I was shocked to discover that someone had given me a (**worn**, **shoddy**) leather purse as a birthday present.

neutral
2. The ticket prices for the football game were more (**expensive**, **exorbitant**) than we had anticipated.

positive
3. That auto repair shop has a (**sterling**, **decent**) reputation.

neutral
4. Because of her (**immunity**, **invulnerability**) to the new strain of flu, she was the only employee who did not call in sick that week.

positive
5. I hear that you have a (**flair**, **capacity**) for decorating rooms with secondhand and inexpensive items.

neutral
6. She assessed the clutter in her kitchen with a(n) (**pensive**, **appraising**) expression on her face.

negative
7. You have found a truly (**expedient**, **opportunistic**) way to chart a career path in your company.

positive
8. Everyone thought his impromptu speech was (**flippant**, **clever**).

Challenge: Using Connotation

Choose vocabulary words from Units 7–9 to replace the highlighted words in the sentences below. Then explain how the connotation of the replacement word changes the tone of the sentence. **Answers will vary.**

perilous	sprightly	venture
warp	malign	surly

1. To the waiter, the woman's **abrupt** _____ surly _____ tone of voice was a sign that she would be one of those impossible-to-please customers. **Sample response: The negative connotation of *surly* shows that the woman's tone is not just hurried and abrupt but also gruff and rude.**

2. All night long I worried that walking near those cliffs by yourself in the dark would be **unsafe** _____ perilous _____ for you.
Sample response: The negative connotation of *perilous* suggests a danger that is potentially life-threatening.

3. Don't **criticize** _____ malign _____ my brother; it hurts my feelings.
Sample response: The negative connotation of *malign* suggests that the brother is not merely being disapproved of but also slandered.

Classical Roots

pol—city, state
ly—to loosen, to set free

The root **pol** appears in **metropolis**, "a large city" (page 91). The root **ly** appears in **catalyst**, "any agent that causes change" (page 62). Some other words based on these roots are listed below.

acropolis	cosmopolitan	metropolitan	political
analysis	electrolysis	paralysis	psychoanalysis

From the list of words above, choose the one that corresponds to each of the brief definitions below. Write the word in the blank space in the illustrative sentence below the definition. Use an online or print dictionary if necessary.

1. partial or complete loss, or temporary interruption, of the ability to move or experience sensation in part or all of the body; any condition of helpless inactivity or powerlessness

   A serious spinal cord injury can result in permanent ____**paralysis**____.

2. relating to a major city; comprised of a central city and its adjacent suburbs

   Most ____**metropolitan**____ newspapers include extensive arts and entertainment listings.

3. decomposition of an electrolyte caused by electric current passing through it; removal of excess hair or other tissue by destroying it with a needlelike electrode

   The first practice of ____**electrolysis**____ took place in 1869, when St. Louis eye doctor Charles Michel sent a current through a gold needle to remove a swollen ingrown eyelash.

4. the breaking apart of a complex whole into its simpler parts for closer study; a statement of the results of this process; a brief summary or outline

   Chemical ____**analysis**____ of the debris can establish the fire's cause.

5. concerned with the affairs of government, politics, citizens, or the state; involving politicians, governmental organizations, or parties on distinct sides in an issue

   When I register to vote, I may align myself with a particular ____**political**____ party.

6. a therapeutic examination of the mind, developed by Freud, to discover the unconscious desires, fears, and anxieties that produce mental and emotional disorders; psychiatric treatment based on this theory and its methodology

   The man will undergo ____**psychoanalysis**____ to cure his depression.

7. the fortified upper part or citadel of an ancient Greek city

   While in Greece, we visited the "Sacred Rock of Athens" to see the ruins of the ancient ____**acropolis**____.

8. common to or representative of the whole world; not national or local; at home everywhere, widespread; conversant with many spheres of interest

   Music is truly a ____**cosmopolitan**____ art form.

UNIT 10

Note that not all of the 20 unit words are used in this passage. *Emancipate*, *extemporaneous*, *mire*, *obtrusive*, and *preamble* are not included in the passage.

*Read the following selection, taking note of the **boldface** words and their contexts. These words are among those you will be studying in Unit 10. As you complete the exercises in this unit, it may help to refer to the way the words are used below.*

C CCSS Vocabulary: 4; Reading (Informational Text): 4, 6. (See pp. T14–15.)

Remarkable Mixes

<Textbook Entry>

A zorse is a hybrid of a zebra and a horse.

Hybrid Animals

A hybrid animal is born of parents of related but different species. About ten percent of all animal species naturally engage in interbreeding that produces offspring. Sometimes these hybrid offspring fill a biological niche that is not in competition with its parent species for survival. As a result, a distinct third species evolves.

Man-made Hybrids

It is **erroneous** to regard hybrid animals solely as the outcome of natural pairings. Some hybrids develop when people **aspire** to "build a better mousetrap." The following animals are examples of species interbred for human use:

a) Beefalo are the offspring of domestic cattle and American bison.[1] Beefalo meat is lower in fat, calories, and cholesterol than lean beef.

b) The cama is a hybrid that blends the strength, size, and endurance of a camel[2] with the sure-footed and more **diminutive** llama.[3]

c) The mule is a hardy cross between a horse and a donkey. The mule is **adept** in **rugged** terrain. It will navigate narrow passages and steep trails at a **languid** but sure-footed pace.

Interbreeding for Survival

Because climate change and overdevelopment threaten animals' natural habitats, prospects are **bleak** for

---

[1] a large bovine with short horns and large shoulders that occurs naturally in North America
[2] a large mammal native to Asian and African deserts, frequently used as a mount and pack animal
[3] a relative of the camel, smaller and native to South America, used for its wool and as a pack animal

the long-term survival of some species. However, evidence of interbreeding gives scientists hope. One example of such interbreeding is the grolar—part polar bear,[4] part grizzly bear.[5] This blend occurs rarely but naturally, where polar bears have left the ice to roam the land with grizzlies. Grolars resemble both parents. The hairy feet of a polar bear are ideally suited for the landscape where it lives, **rendering** the stark, Arctic tundra habitable. The hairy soles of a grolar's feet, coupled with its grizzlylike claws and humped back, made **skeptical** observers wonder whether to call this creature a polar bear or a grizzly bear. DNA testing gave **invincible** proof that the grolar had one parent of each bear. The grolar may signal a new kind of bear. Its mixed traits can help it adapt to changes in climate and habitat.

Health

When a hybrid is an improvement over its parents, it is said to have the advantage of hybrid vigor. An example of hybrid vigor is Hercules—a 900-pound, 12-foot-long liger. This cat was naturally born to a female tiger and a male lion in an American wildlife sanctuary. Hercules is strong, healthy, playful, and intelligent, though the long-term effects of this hybridization have not been studied. Not all hybrids, including

A liger is a cross between a tiger and a lion.

other ligers, are as successful as Hercules, as interbreeding can **impair** health. Some hybrids are sickly, sterile, or short-lived.

Ethical Concerns

Critics regard the planned interbreeding of species as a **despicable** act of arrogance borne of **slipshod** ethics. They **chide** breeders for **exploiting** already vulnerable species. The critics' concern is that endangered species may disappear not by extinction, but by the misdirected experimentation of science.

Whether hybrids are natural or man-made, their attempts to survive have fascinated humans for centuries. As genetic testing becomes more widespread and sophisticated, it is likely that new hybrids will be discovered among animals previously thought to be a separate species.

The mule is one of the best-known hybrid animals.

iWords

Snap the code, or go to
vocabularyworkshop.com

---

[4] a large, white bear native to polar regions
[5] a large, brown bear native to the United States and Canadian Northwest

Definitions

Note the spelling, pronunciation, part(s) of speech, and definition(s) of each of the following words. Then write the word in the blank spaces in the illustrative sentence(s) following. Finally, study the lists of synonyms and antonyms.

1. adept
(*adj.*, ə dept';
n., a' dept)

(*adj.*) thoroughly skilled; (*n.*) an expert

Not only is the soloist an accomplished singer, but he is also **adept** at playing the saxophone.

An **adept** at chess, she hopes to compete in tournaments against top-rated players.

SYNONYMS: (*adj.*) masterful, proficient
ANTONYMS: (*adj.*) clumsy, unskilled, maladroit; (*n.*) novice

2. aspire
(ə spīr')

(*v.*) to have ambitious hopes or plans, strive toward a higher goal, desire earnestly; to ascend

An early fascination with ants led the young naturalist to **aspire** to a career as an entomologist.

SYNONYMS: yearn, aim for, soar

3. bleak
(blēk)

(*adj.*) bare, dreary, dismal

Urban renewal can turn a run-down city with **bleak** economic prospects into a flourishing metropolis.

SYNONYMS: grim, cheerless, gloomy, desolate, barren
ANTONYMS: rosy, cheerful, sunny, promising, encouraging

4. chide
(chīd)

(*v.*) to blame; scold

The teacher **chided** the student for truancy and tardiness.

SYNONYMS: upbraid, reprimand, rebuke, chastise
ANTONYMS: approve, praise, compliment, pat on the back

5. despicable
(di spik' ə bəl)

(*adj.*) worthy of scorn, contemptible

Whatever the provocation, there is no justification for such **despicable** behavior.

SYNONYMS: low, cheap, sordid, detestable
ANTONYMS: praiseworthy, commendable, meritorious

6. diminutive
(də min' yə tiv)

(*adj.*) small, smaller than most others of the same type

The **diminutive** lapdog was so small that it actually fit in its owner's purse.

SYNONYMS: undersized, miniature, tiny, compact
ANTONYMS: oversized, gigantic, huge, enormous

CCSS Vocabulary: 4.c., 4.d. (See pp. T14–15.)

7. emancipate
(ēman' sə pāt)

(v.) to free from slavery; to release or liberate

Scientific knowledge can _____emancipate_____ humanity from blind superstition.

SYNONYMS: set loose, unchain, unfetter
ANTONYMS: enslave, snare, chain, shackle

8. erroneous
(e rō' nē əs)

(adj.) incorrect, containing mistakes

An _____erroneous_____ first impression is not easily corrected.

SYNONYMS: mistaken, fallacious, all wrong
ANTONYMS: accurate, correct, exact, unerring

9. exploit
(v., ek sploit';
n., ek' sploit)

(v.) to make use of, develop; to make improper use of for personal profit; (n.) a feat, deed

A good debater knows how to _____exploit_____ weaknesses in an opponent's argument.

The _____exploits_____ of Robin Hood and his Merry Men are so well known that they have become a part of Western culture.

SYNONYMS: (v.) turn to advantage, misuse

10. extemporaneous
(ek stem pə rā' nē əs)

(adj.) made or delivered on the spur of the moment

The stand-up comedian's outrageous act included about twenty minutes of completely _____extemporaneous_____ banter.

SYNONYMS: spontaneous, off-the-cuff
ANTONYMS: planned, prepared, practiced

11. impair
(im pâr')

(v.) to make imperfect, damage, harm

I am fortunate that the scratch on my eye will not permanently _____impair_____ my vision.

SYNONYMS: injure, disable, cripple, enervate
ANTONYMS: improve, strengthen, promote, advance

12. invincible
(in vin' sə bəl)

(adj.) not able to be defeated, unbeatable

Napoleon I, emperor of France, was _____invincible_____ until he launched a disastrous invasion of Russia.

SYNONYMS: unconquerable, indomitable, insuperable
ANTONYMS: vulnerable, conquerable, surmountable

13. languid
(laŋ' gwid)

(adj.) drooping; without energy, sluggish

A big lunch makes me feel _____languid_____ for the rest of the day.

SYNONYMS: lazy, listless, slack, lethargic
ANTONYMS: lively, energetic, vigorous, enlivening

14. mire
(mīr)

(*n.*) mud; wet, swampy ground; a tough situation; (*v.*) to get stuck

The once verdant expanse of the soccer field has become a rectangle of muck and _____ **mire** _____.

Congress will never ratify that bill _____ **mired** _____ in controversy.

SYNONYMS: (*n.*) swamp, bog, slough

15. obtrusive
(əb trü′ siv)

(*adj.*) forward; undesirably prominent; thrust out

I don't blame you for being put off by his _____ **obtrusive** _____ attempt to dominate the conversation.

SYNONYMS: brash, conspicuous, protruding
ANTONYMS: reserved, deferential, recessed

16. preamble
(prē′ am bəl)

(*n.*) an introduction to a speech or piece of writing

The _____ **preamble** _____ to the Constitution describes the purpose of our national government.

SYNONYMS: opening, prologue, preliminary
ANTONYMS: ending, closing, epilogue

17. render
(ren′ dər)

(*v.*) to cause to become; to perform; to deliver officially; to process, extract

The freelance writer presented the managing editor with a bill for services _____ **rendered** _____.

SYNONYMS: present, furnish, submit, make, effect

18. rugged
(rəg′ əd)

(*adj.*) rough, irregular; severe, stern; strong; stormy

Settlers had a rough time crossing the _____ **rugged** _____ Appalachian Mountains.

SYNONYMS: rocky, blunt, harsh, hardy, tough
ANTONYMS: smooth, flat, soft, mild, tender, delicate

19. skeptical
(skep′ tə kəl)

(*adj.*) inclined to doubt; slow to accept something as true

I am _____ **skeptical** _____ of promises made by politicians when they are running for office.

SYNONYMS: suspicious, incredulous
ANTONYMS: believing, credulous, gullible, ingenuous

20. slipshod
(slip′ shäd)

(*adj.*) untidy in dress, personal habits, etc.; careless, sloppy

The commission attributed the unfortunate collapse of the apartment building to its _____ **slipshod** _____ construction.

SYNONYMS: messy, untidy, slovenly, slapdash, cursory
ANTONYMS: tidy, neat, orderly, careful, painstaking

C CCSS Vocabulary: 4.c. (See pp. T14–15.)

Choosing the Right Word

*Select the **boldface** word that better completes each sentence. You might refer to the selection on pages 126–127 to see how most of these words are used in context.*

1. In Jonathan Swift's fictional country of Lilliput, everyone and everything is pint-sized, or (**diminutive, erroneous**).

2. The visitor's huge bulk, combined with his (**extemporaneous, languid**) manner, made me think of a tired whale.

3. A good scientist will always be (**skeptical, despicable**) about any theory that is not backed by convincing evidence.

4. Passengers could not exit the bus without tripping over the (**invincible, obtrusive**) package in the aisle.

Gulliver meets the tiny Lilliputians in *Gulliver's Travels*

5. The artist, who had trained as an architect, (**rendered, impaired**) a realistic drawing of the hotel lobby that was nearly as detailed as a photograph.

6. I could see that the merchant's long, sad story about bad luck was only the (**adept, preamble**) to a request for a loan.

7. After four years as the President's press secretary, I have become a noted (**adept, exploit**) in the art of fielding questions.

8. The goalie's reflexes were as sharp as ever, but the knee injury had plainly (**impaired, aspired**) his ability to maneuver.

9. After enslaved African-Americans were (**mired, emancipated**), many emigrated to northern states in order to start new lives.

10. I am not accusing anyone of deliberately lying, but I can prove beyond doubt that the charges are (**rugged, erroneous**).

11. Rita, who until a year ago had never prepared anything more complicated than scrambled eggs, is now quite an (**adept, obtrusive**) cook.

12. When I asked the student why he wasn't going to the senior prom, he answered only with a(n) (**bleak, obtrusive**) smile.

13. It is worse than useless to (**render, chide**) children for misbehaving without giving them an opportunity to behave better.

14. That monologue about the young accountant on her very first day on the job (**rendered, emancipated**) me helpless with laughter.

15. The sculptor has done a superb job of representing the strong, rough planes of Lincoln's (**languid, rugged**) features.

16. When we tried to straighten out the mess, we found ourselves (**mired, chided**) in a mass of inaccurate, incomplete, and mixed-up records.

17. Sergeant Alvin York was awarded this nation's highest honor for his many daring (**preambles, exploits**) during World War I.

18. Just as in fairy tales, the way to Grandma's house was a long, winding, and (**slipshod, rugged**) path through dark woods.

19. I would never trust my funds to anyone who is so (**bleak, slipshod**) in managing his own affairs.

20. In the (**slipshod, extemporaneous**) give-and-take of a televised debate, it is easy for a nervous nominee to make a slip of the tongue.

21. When Emerson said, "Hitch your wagon to a star," he meant that we should (**aspire, mire**) to reach the very highest levels of which we are capable.

22. Our basketball team, with its well-planned attack, tight defense, and seven-foot center, proved all but (**invincible, skeptical**).

23. Far from admiring the way they got those letters of recommendation, I consider their deception utterly (**diminutive, despicable**).

24. It is up to all of us to (**impair, emancipate**) ourselves from prejudices and false ideas acquired early in life.

25. Sergei (**chided, exploited**) Natasha's love for him by asking for a favor.

Synonyms

*Choose the word from this unit that is the same or most nearly the same in meaning as the **boldface** word or expression in the phrase. Write that word on the line. Use a dictionary if necessary.*

1. a **vile** and cowardly act   despicable

2. wallow like an alligator in the **marsh**   mire

3. **dubious** about the chances of winning   skeptical

4. **mar** relations between nations   impair

5. **unshackle** a person from bondage   emancipate

6. **impromptu** speech on a humorous topic   extemporaneous

7. an **adroit** musician   adept

8. not just assertive, but **impudent**   obtrusive

9. **utilize** natural resources   exploit

10. the opening remarks, or **preface**   preamble

C CCSS Vocabulary: 5. (See pp. T14–15.)

The synonyms and antonyms here do not appear on the Definitions page.

10

Antonyms

*Choose the word from this unit that is most nearly opposite in meaning to the **boldface** word or expression in the phrase. Write that word on the line. Use a dictionary if necessary.*

1. **released** from legal proceedings _____ mired (in) _____

2. to **capture** a group of people _____ emancipate _____

3. a **meek** theater usher _____ obtrusive _____

4. a **conclusion** to the report _____ preamble _____

5. deliver a **rehearsed** speech _____ extemporaneous _____

Completing the Sentence

From the words in this unit, choose the one that best completes each of the following sentences. Write the word in the space provided.

1. The warmth of the June sun made me feel so _____ languid _____ that I scarcely had the energy to brush away the flies.

2. Since it had rained all night, the newly-plowed fields were now an impassable _____ mire _____.

3. The _____ diminutive _____ but powerful halfback from Syracuse was one of the lightest men ever to play professional football.

4. The honoree's after-dinner speech was so polished and sure that we never guessed that it was _____ extemporaneous _____.

5. To improve their standard of living, the people of an underdeveloped country must learn to _____ exploit _____ the resources of their land.

6. How can you _____ aspire _____ to work in the space program when you haven't even been able to pass your science and math courses?

7. I understand math very well, but, according to my teacher, my performance in class is, at best, _____ slipshod _____.

8. The master silversmith was extraordinarily _____ adept _____ in the use of simple hand tools.

9. Why do you take it on yourself to _____ chide _____ me whenever I say or do anything even slightly out of line?

10. Marching over the _____ rugged _____ terrain under a broiling sun, we were soon on the verge of exhaustion.

CCSS Vocabulary: 4.a. (See pp. T14–15.)

Unit 10 ▪ *133*

11. The inconsistencies in the suspect's story made the police highly
_____skeptical_____ of his alibi.

12. The Welsh mining village, with its rows of drab cottages, seemed terribly
_____bleak_____ and uninviting in the cold autumn rain.

13. Poor diet, lack of exercise, and insufficient rest have done a great deal to
_____impair_____ my health.

14. It is better to admit ignorance than to give _____erroneous_____ information.

15. We learned that the matchless discipline and superior leadership of the Roman
legions made them all but _____invincible_____.

16. Before we get into the specific details of our proposal, we should write a(n)
_____preamble_____ that will explain in general terms what we want to do.

17. There are many millions of people throughout the world still waiting to be
_____emancipated_____ from the bonds of grinding poverty.

18. Against the solemn hush of the memorial service, the boisterous laughter we heard
was _____obtrusive_____.

19. The fiddler _____rendered_____ the Virginia reel in a very lively fashion.

20. The social worker said with great emphasis that anyone who would take advantage
of an elderly person is utterly _____despicable_____.

Writing: Words in Action

Answers to both prompts will vary.

1. Look back at "Remarkable Mixes" (pages 126–127). Is it unethical to
interbreed species for human use? Should all animal hybrids be the result of
natural pairings? In a brief essay, explore the benefits and drawbacks of both
kinds of animal hybrids. Use at least two details from the passage and three
unit words to support your choice.

2. In "Remarkable Mixes," the author states, "Prospects are bleak for the long-
term survival of some species." How far should people go to ensure the
survival of animal species that are teetering on the brink of extinction? Do
some solutions, like genetic manipulation or cloning, go too far? Write a brief
editorial in which you present and support your views on protecting animals
from extinction. Support your views with specific examples of your observations,
studies, reading (refer to pages 126–127), or your own experience. Write at least
three paragraphs, and use three or more words from this unit.

Writing prompt #2 is modeled on that of standardized tests.

C CCSS Vocabulary: 6; Writing: 1.c., 2.d. (See pp. T14–15.)

Vocabulary in Context: Informational Text for Unit 10 is available online at **vocabularyworkshop.com**.

10

Vocabulary in Context

Literary Text

The following excerpts are from Wilkie Collins's famous mystery novel The Woman in White. *Some of the words you have studied in this unit appear in* **boldface** *type. Complete each statement below the excerpt by circling the letter of the correct answer.*

1. Not content with paying the nation in general the compliment of invariably carrying an umbrella, and invariably wearing gaiters and a white hat, the Professor further **aspired** to become an Englishman in his habits and amusements, as well as in his personal appearance.

    If you **aspire**, you

    a. avoid
    b. refuse
    c. mock
    d. strive ✓

2. The church, a dreary building of grey stone, was situated in a little valley, so as to be sheltered from the **bleak** winds blowing over the moorland all round it.

    Winds that are **bleak** are

    a. harsh ✓
    b. welcome
    c. warm
    d. moderate

3. So far, I did not feel called on to say anything to him about my own opinion, but when he proceeded, in his most aggravatingly **languid** manner, to suggest that the time for the marriage had better be settled next, in accordance with Sir Percival's wishes, I enjoyed the satisfaction of assailing Mr. Fairlie's nerves with as strong a protest against hurrying Laura's decision as I could put into words.

    Someone acting in a **languid** manner does NOT act

    a. slothfully
    b. forcefully ✓
    c. sluggishly
    d. weakly

Eleanor Parker plays Laura Fairlie in the 1948 film *The Woman in White.*

4. On the ground floor there are two hugely long galleries, with low ceilings lying parallel with each other, and **rendered** additionally dark and dismal by hideous family portraits—every one of which I should like to burn.

    Something that has been **rendered** has been

    a. torn to pieces
    b. used for display
    c. made a certain way ✓
    d. burned to the ground

5. It was the face of an elderly woman, brown, **rugged**, and healthy, with nothing dishonest or suspicious in the look of it.

    A **rugged** face is

    a. craggy ✓
    b. misshapen
    c. honest
    d. scrubbed

Interactive Quiz

Snap the code, or go to **vocabularyworkshop.com**

Note that not all of the 20 unit words are used in this passage. *Demure*, *garble*, and *staccato* are not included in the passage.

*Read the following selection, taking note of the **boldface** words and their contexts. These words are among those you will be studying in Unit 11. As you complete the exercises in this unit, it may help to refer to the way the words are used below.*

C CCSS Vocabulary: 4; Reading (Informational Text): 4, 6. (See pp. T14–15.)

Failing Infrastructure
<Newspaper Editorial>

Washington, D.C.—April 11

Yesterday, Concerned Citizens for Safe Infrastructure (CCSI), a national watchdog organization with headquarters in the nation's capital, released its annual report, "State of Our Infrastructure." The news was not encouraging. Petunia Hargraves, Executive Director of CCSI, did not mince words as she delivered a **concise** summary of the group's findings.

"Almost everywhere we look, public facilities have **deteriorated** badly," she said. "All levels of government must act urgently to **forestall** future damage and **depreciation** of these public assets. The costs will be substantial, but we must not **recoil** from our obligation to society."

Thirteen lives were lost when a bridge collapsed in Minneapolis.

Infrastructure, as every highway commuter inching past a construction site knows, is the basic cluster of facilities on which a city or state depends. Roads, airports, bridges, tunnels, railways, and ports: All are infrastructure.

CCSI was founded shortly after the collapse of a section of a major bridge along I-35 in Minneapolis in August 2007. That disaster claimed 13 lives and injured 145 people. Even before that incident, the Department of Transportation (DOT) **divulged** some unsettling facts about the maintenance of our nation's infrastructure.

Its numbers show that, due to neglect, millions of commuters' lives are put at risk every day. In 1971, Congress passed a **statute** requiring that all bridges be inspected every two years. Unfortunately, many states, using various loopholes in the law, have failed to **comport** with this federal regulation. Those with the worst rates of compliance are shown in the chart below.

Bridge Inspections Two or More Years Overdue	
Utah	60%
Alaska	45%
Delaware	38%
Maine	34%
Colorado	27%
California	23%

The National Transportation Safety Board diagnosed the probable cause of the Minneapolis bridge collapse with striking **brevity**: "inadequate load capacity."

Clearly, there are more cars on the road today than there were 40 years ago, but infrastructure has not kept pace.

"Obsolete public facilities need to be replaced," says CCSI's Hargraves. "With each incident like the I-35 bridge collapse, the public becomes more **enlightened** about the necessity for maintaining infrastructure. But people have short memories. What we have at present is a mere **rivulet** of corrective action. What we need is a torrent."

"The age of each asset is not the only risk factor," a DOT official pointed out to this reporter. "Quality, too, is important." The bridge that collapsed in Minneapolis was 40 years old, he notes, but at Charles de Gaulle Airport in Paris, the roof of a brand-new terminal caved in. That disaster, which occurred in May 2004 and killed four people, followed the terminal's grand opening by barely a year.

CCSI's Hargraves put forward an analogy from the ancient world. "It's a bad bridge that's narrower than the stream. The Romans did not ignore vital infrastructure and they did not cut corners when building," she asserted. "Their roads, bridges, theaters, and aqueducts are still with us. We should follow their example. Any other approach **reeks** of complacency."

As the world urbanizes, infrastructure needs grow at a **relentless** pace. In China, for example, **proponents** of high-speed train service have convinced the government to double the country's rail coverage by the year 2020. This ambitious goal is estimated to cost $300 billion. Some economists harbor doubts as to whether China's plan will work. The state, these critics claim, is **squandering** funds: It will not **recoup** its investment, because high-speed fares are too expensive for the average traveler.

To create an infrastructure that is truly modern, efficient, and safe, says the CCSI report, governments must not **quaver**: They should look to the values of the past while boldly building for the future.

Less than a year after it was built, a Parisian airport terminal collapsed.

iWords

Snap the code, or go to **vocabularyworkshop.com**

Definitions

Note the spelling, pronunciation, part(s) of speech, and definition(s) of each of the following words. Then write the word in the blank spaces in the illustrative sentence(s) following. Finally, study the lists of synonyms and antonyms.

1. brevity
(brev′ ə tē)

(*n.*) shortness

The speech was notable more for its _____ **brevity** _____ than for its clarity.

SYNONYMS: terseness, pithiness
ANTONYMS: verbosity, long-windedness, prolixity

2. comport
(kəm pôrt′)

(*v.*) to conduct or bear oneself, behave; to be in agreement

As the students started to leave, the principal reminded them to _____ **comport** _____ themselves as school emissaries.

SYNONYMS: agree, concur

3. concise
(kən sīs′)

(*adj.*) expressing much in a few words

As a rule of thumb, editors and readers appreciate writing that is _____ **concise** _____ and forceful.

SYNONYMS: brief, succinct, terse, pithy, to the point
ANTONYMS: wordy, verbose, long-winded, prolix

4. demure
(di myùr′)

(*adj.*) sober or serious in manner, modest

Despite her _____ **demure** _____ appearance, she is a competitive speed skater, always ready for a challenge on ice.

SYNONYMS: shy, sedate, seemly, decorous
ANTONYMS: forward, assertive, immodest

5. depreciation
(di prē shē ā′ shən)

(*n.*) a lessening in value; a belittling

The accountant calculated the _____ **depreciation** _____ of the computer over a period of five years.

SYNONYMS: cheapening, lowering
ANTONYMS: increase, appreciation, enhancement

6. deteriorate
(di tir′ ē ə rāt)

(*v.*) to lower in quality or value; to wear away

It is painful for anyone, particularly a doctor, to watch someone's health _____ **deteriorate** _____.

SYNONYMS: worsen, decline, degenerate, debase
ANTONYMS: fix up, enhance

7. divulge
(di vəlj′)

(*v.*) to tell, reveal; to make public

On some occasions, scrupulous reporters cannot _____ **divulge** _____ their sources of information.

SYNONYMS: disclose, impart, spill the beans, "leak"
ANTONYMS: hide, conceal, cover up, secrete, keep under wraps

Ⓒ CCSS Vocabulary: 4.c., 4.d. (See pp. T14–15.)

8. enlightened
(en līt' ənd)

(*adj.*) free from ignorance and false ideas; possessing sound understanding

An ____enlightened____ society is ruled by knowledge and reason rather than superstition and prejudice.

SYNONYMS: knowing, aware, cultivated
ANTONYMS: ignorant, unaware, untaught, benighted

9. forestall
(fôr stôl')

(*v.*) to prevent by acting first

Sometimes it is possible to ____forestall____ a cold by taking Vitamin C.

SYNONYMS: hinder, thwart, preclude, ward off
ANTONYMS: welcome, accept, allow, submit, abide by

10. garble
(gär' bəl)

(*v.*) to distort in such a way as to make unintelligible

If you've played "telephone," you know how easy it is to inadvertently ____garble____ a message.

SYNONYMS: jumble, confuse, misrepresent
ANTONYMS: elucidate, articulate

11. proponent
(prō pō' nənt)

(*n.*) one who puts forward a proposal; one who supports a cause or belief

Lucretia Coffin Mott and Elizabeth Cady Stanton were among the first ____proponents____ of women's suffrage in the United States.

SYNONYMS: supporter, advocate, exponent
ANTONYMS: opponent, critic, foe, adversary

12. quaver
(kwā' vər)

(*v.*) to shake, tremble; to trill

My voice ____quavers____ whenever I try to reach the high notes.

SYNONYMS: vibrate, shiver, quake, palpitate

13. recoil
(*v.*, ri koil';
n., rē' koil)

(*v.*) to spring back, shrink; (*n.*) the act of springing back

In "The Adventure of the Speckled Band," sleuth Sherlock Holmes points out that "violence does, in truth, ____recoil____ upon the violent."

When the engineer accidentally released the giant spring, its powerful ____recoil____ sent him sprawling.

SYNONYMS: (*v.*) flinch; (*n.*) kickback
ANTONYMS: (*v.*) advance, proceed, gain ground

14. recoup
(ri küp')

(*v.*) to make up for, regain

I plan to _____ recoup _____ my family's lost fortune by working hard, earning extra money, and investing wisely.

SYNONYMS: recover, retrieve
ANTONYMS: lose, default, forfeit, kiss good-bye

15. reek
(rēk)

(*n.*) an unpleasant smell; (*v.*) to give off unpleasant smells; to give a strong impression

The unmistakable _____ reek _____ of spoiled food greeted us as we entered the long-abandoned cabin.

In *How the Other Half Lives* (1890), Jacob Riis describes tenements in urban neighborhoods that _____ reek _____ of poverty.

SYNONYMS: (*n.*) stench; (*v.*) stink, smell
ANTONYMS: (*n.*) perfume, fragrance, bouquet

16. relentless
(ri lent' ləs)

(*adj.*) unyielding, harsh, without pity

The novel *Les Misérables* recounts ex-convict Jean Valjean's lifelong flight from a _____ relentless _____ police inspector.

SYNONYMS: stern, merciless, persistent
ANTONYMS: merciful, accommodating, indulgent

17. rivulet
(riv' yü lət)

(*n.*) a small stream

While we could hear the running water, dense vegetation hid the _____ rivulet _____ from view.

SYNONYMS: creek, rill

18. squander
(skwän' dər)

(*v.*) to spend foolishly, waste

I think that it is criminal to _____ squander _____ our natural resources.

SYNONYMS: misspend, dissipate
ANTONYMS: save, economize, hoard, squirrel away

19. staccato
(stə kät' ō)

(*adj.*) detached or disconnected in sound or style

We strained to listen, and we heard _____ staccato _____ hoofbeats striking the pavement.

SYNONYM: abrupt
ANTONYMS: continuous, flowing

20. statute
(stach' üt)

(*n.*) a law

The student body is governed by the _____ statutes _____ of the university.

SYNONYMS: rule, enactment

C CCSS Vocabulary: 4.c. (See pp. T14–15.)

Choosing the Right Word

*Select the **boldface** word that better completes each sentence. You might refer to the selection on pages 136–137 to see how most of these words are used in context.*

1. William Shakespeare expressed the tragic (**brevity, statute**) of life by comparing it to a candle that must soon go out.

2. In an attempt to mislead the enemy, the crafty prisoner of war deliberately (**divulged, garbled**) his account of how the attack had been planned.

3. The young woman's (**demure, staccato**) smile and flirtatious manner drew admiring glances.

4. (**Rivulets, Reeks**) of sweat ran down the faces of the men working in that terrible heat.

Poet and dramatist William Shakespeare is considered by many to be the greatest writer in the English language.

5. He was not surprised that the recession had affected the value of his comic book and action figure collections, resulting in their (**depreciation, deterioration**).

6. In spite of the vast number of details in the United States Constitution, the document is remarkably (**relentless, concise**).

7. I beseeched the employees at the florist's shop to (**divulge, enlighten**) the name of the person who had anonymously sent me flowers, but they refused.

8. She tried to appear calm, but her voice (**quavered, squandered**), revealing her agitation.

9. An old Chinese proverb suggests: "Make a candle to get light; read a book to get (**enlightened, concise**)."

10. After the huge fire burned down several houses in our area, the air was filled with ashes and the (**garble, reek**) of acrid smoke.

11. Once a political leader has lost the confidence of voters, it is almost impossible to (**comport, recoup**) it.

12. I wish there were a (**rivulet, statute**) that would prevent people from revealing the ending of a detective story!

13. In order to (**recoil, forestall**) criticism of my proposal, I prepared for the meeting by gathering relevant facts and figures beforehand.

14. (**Statutes, Proponents**) of the new youth soccer league met with the local parents to discuss by-laws, safety rules, uniforms, and other pressing issues.

15. I'm not saying that you shouldn't watch TV, but why (**recoup, squander**) so much of your time on those inane programs?

16. A person accused of a crime is not obliged to (**divulge**, **deteriorate**) anything that might be incriminating.

17. The charitable programs sponsored by this organization (**forestall**, **comport**) well with our conception of a just and compassionate society.

18. "Wear and tear" is the (**depreciation**, **proponent**) that results from ordinary use, not from misuse.

19. Early rifles had such a "kick" to them that inexperienced soldiers were often injured by the (**recoil**, **depreciation**) after pulling the trigger.

20. When I learned how the air and water were being polluted, I became a strong (**brevity**, **proponent**) of ecological reforms.

21. It's all very well to build new housing, but we should also rehabilitate neighborhoods that have (**deteriorated**, **garbled**) through neglect.

22. It's not surprising that the clothing of firefighters often (**quavers**, **reeks**) of smoke and sweat.

23. The speaker's (**enlightened**, **staccato**) delivery truly reminded us of a jackhammer breaking up concrete.

24. Seeing my childhood friend so gray and infirm, I became keenly aware of the (**relentless**, **demure**) passage of the years.

25. He (**recoiled**, **comported**) when he saw the rat scurry across the rug.

Synonyms

*Choose the word from this unit that is the same or most nearly the same in meaning as the **boldface** word or expression in the phrase. Write that word on the line. Use a dictionary if necessary.*

1. the **devaluation** of currency _____ depreciation

2. the **unremitting** persecution of Huguenots _____ relentless

3. a **runnel** of salt water _____ rivulet

4. a **disjointed** style of speech _____ staccato

5. an **ordinance** passed by the legislature _____ statute

6. a **diffident** and tentative reaction to strangers _____ demure

7. **deport oneself** with dignity _____ comport

8. **quiver** with emotion _____ quaver

9. **scramble** a radio message _____ garble

10. value **conciseness** in a short story _____ brevity

CCSS Vocabulary: 5. (See pp. T14–15.)

The synonyms and antonyms here do not appear on the Definitions page.

11

Antonyms

Choose the word from this unit that is most nearly opposite in meaning to the **boldface** word or expression in the phrase. Write that word on the line. Use a dictionary if necessary.

1. to **clarify** the message — garble
2. **steady** speech — quaver
3. a **fluid** melody — staccato
4. accompanied by an **aggressive** glance — demure
5. likely to **improve** with age — deteriorate

Completing the Sentence

From the words in this unit, choose the one that best completes each of the following sentences. Write the word in the space provided.

1. The child **recoiled** in fear and disgust as the harmless water snake slithered over the floor.

2. What we need is not a lot of new legislation, but tough enforcement of the **statutes** already on the books.

3. To the district attorney's dismay, the witness **garbled** all the facts and misled the jury.

4. Since you are charged for every word you use in a telegram, it pays to be as **concise** as possible.

5. The telltale **reek** of gas alerted us that someone had left a burner open on the stove.

6. It's up to us to work twice as hard to **recoup** our losses now that the storm has damaged the crops.

7. As it wound its way through the desert, the mighty river became a mere **rivulet** that travelers could easily wade across.

8. Despite the creature comforts we now enjoy, I feel that the quality of life has somehow **deteriorated** in recent years.

9. Leaders are judged by how well they **comport** themselves in times of crisis.

10. Since you worked so long and hard for the money you earned, it's doubly foolish to **squander** it on things you don't really want or need.

11. The witnesses have testified at great length, but how much really valuable information have they _____ **divulged** _____ to the investigating committee?

12. The assertive heroines portrayed in many TV programs are a far cry from the _____ **demure** _____ young ladies depicted in nineteenth-century novels.

13. The program featured a debate between _____ **proponents** _____ of gun control and critics of legislation restricting ownership of firearms.

14. "I'm not afraid of anyone!" the boy piped up bravely, but we noticed that his voice _____ **quavered** _____ as he said it.

15. Economists will tell you that inflation results in an increase in the supply of money and a(n) _____ **depreciation** _____ in its value.

16. In saying that "_____ **brevity** _____ is the soul of wit," Shakespeare was reminding comedians to keep their jokes short and snappy.

17. A(n) _____ **enlightened** _____ public opinion, said Jefferson, is essential to a democratic society.

18. In a passage that a composer has marked _____ **staccato** _____, every note should sound like the quick thrust of a knife.

19. How often have we heard candidates for public office promise that they will be tough and _____ **relentless** _____ in fighting organized crime!

20. A President will often try to _____ **forestall** _____ the defeat of a legislative program by appealing for the public's support on TV.

Writing: Words in Action

Answers to both prompts will vary.

1. Look back at "Failing Infrastructure" (pages 136–137). Write a letter to your state representative describing an infrastructure problem in your community and urging swift action. Thoroughly describe the problem and its solution, explaining why it is vital to take action immediately. Use at least two details from the passage and three unit words to support your appeal.

2. In the larger scheme of government responsibility, how important is maintaining infrastructure as compared to other priorities, such as education, defense, and health care? In a brief essay, support your point of view with specific examples from your observations, studies, reading (refer to pages 136–137), or your own experience. Write at least three paragraphs, and use three or more words from this unit.

Writing prompt #2 is modeled on that of standardized tests.

C CCSS Vocabulary: 6; Writing: 1.c., 2.d. (See pp. T14–15.)

Vocabulary in Context: Informational Text for Unit 11 is available online at **vocabularyworkshop.com**.

11

Vocabulary in Context

Literary Text

The following excerpts are from Nathaniel Hawthorne's novels The House of the Seven Gables *and* The Scarlet Letter. *Some of the words you have studied in this unit appear in* **boldface** *type. Complete each statement below the excerpt by circling the letter of the correct answer.*

1. Clifford's countenance glowed, as he **divulged** this theory; a youthful character shone out from within, converting the wrinkles and pallid duskiness of age into an almost transparent mask. (*The House of the Seven Gables*)

If you **divulge** something, you

a. read it aloud
b. conceal it
c. criticize it
(d.) reveal it

2. "A bank-robber, and what you call a murderer, likewise, has his rights, which men of **enlightened** humanity and conscience should regard in so much the more liberal spirit, because the bulk of society is prone to controvert their existence...." (*The House of the Seven Gables*)

Someone who is **enlightened**

(a.) shows wisdom
b. follows the rules
c. has rights
d. feels superior

3. He put into her hand a daguerreotype; the same that he had shown her at their first interview in the garden, and which so strikingly brought out the hard and **relentless** traits of the original. (*The House of the Seven Gables*)

A **relentless** person is

a. optimistic
(b.) uncompromising
c. unhappy
d. immoral

4. We linger too long, no doubt, beside this paltry **rivulet** of life that flowed through the garden of the Pyncheon House. (*The House of the Seven Gables*)

A **rivulet** is NOT a

a. bubbling creek
b. trickle of water
(c.) rushing river
d. slow-moving stream

Built in 1662, this seven-gabled house in Salem, Massachusetts, inspired Hawthorne's novel.

5. "Was not the secret told me, in the natural **recoil** of my heart, at the first sight of him, and as often as I have seen him since?" (*The Scarlet Letter*)

A **recoil** is

(a.) a drawing back
b. an inner chamber
c. an advancement
d. a strong blast

Interactive Quiz

Snap the code, or go to **vocabularyworkshop.com**

Note that not all of the 20 unit words are used in this passage. *Blasphemy*, *brawny*, *lithe*, and *wily* are not included in the passage.

*Read the following selection, taking note of the **boldface** words and their contexts. These words are among those you will be studying in Unit 12. As you complete the exercises in this unit, it may help to refer to the way the words are used below.*

C CCSS Vocabulary: 4; Reading (Informational Text): 4, 6. (See pp. T14–15.)

Social Networks and Virtual Communication

<Debate>

Today's debate question is this one: *Does social networking lead to real friendships and true communication?*

Monique: I don't think social networking leads to great friendships or communication, and frankly, I don't understand its appeal. Why should I spend an **appreciable** amount of time every day reading tiresome chit-chat? People bragging about themselves, putting others down, assuming everyone agrees with them on every issue—their posts can be unbearable! Social networking is a **synthetic** substitute for true, person-to-person interaction. If you have real friends, you don't need to sit at home and post notes to your cyber buddies. I sometimes worry that social networking has become a **subversive** force, turning us into a nation of loners, glued to computers and unable to deal with others face-to-face.

Rafael: Such a grim picture of social networking is biased and shortsighted. Rather than **contend** that social networking is synthetic, why not see it instead as the latest step in humankind's **concerted** effort to communicate better? Written language, the postal service, telephones—are these artificial too? No, these historic developments in communication bettered people's lives and, in my more **temperate** view, the same is true of social networking. The ability to keep in touch daily with friends and relatives—and to meet new people—is a great gift. Regular online contact with people we care about won't isolate us; instead, it will make us more connected, more **humane**.

Sharing our thoughts and feelings on social networks deepens our ties with others, both those we see all the time and even those we've never met. This is true at the international level, as well. In recent years, we have seen examples of **illustrious** people all around the world using social networks to organize. Digitally connected, strangers have come together *in person* to express their demands for a better society.

Monique: Isn't it ironic that we insist on the term *social* networking when so many online conversations seem *antisocial* in tone? Cyber-bullies, for example, use their computers to harass or **maltreat** their so-called friends, and their **venomous** posts can remain online indefinitely, doing lasting damage. I also **blanch** when I see some of the information that people choose to share on their own pages. What's so "social" about expressing private thoughts and experiences so publicly? I am also concerned that **autocratic** owners of some social networking Web sites might gather information about users of their sites. Such a development would be **intolerable**. Can we be sure that our privacy is safe?

Rafael: As I **ponder** such comments, I must advise that when judging social networks, don't throw the baby out with the bath water. Wading through the long list of risks attributed to social networking by its critics proves to be a **laborious** effort. Yet such critics should at least acknowledge some of its benefits. I believe that the social networking world is a mirror of the real world. In everyday life, we try to avoid bullies and decide who our true friends are, and we must do the same when networking. Just as people sometimes act objectionably in the real world, some users will post **irreverent** or even offensive comments online. Everyone feels the need to express him or herself, and social networking sites simply give people a ready audience— and instant feedback, pro or con. Social networking is still a relatively new phenomenon. As time passes, we're bound to become more savvy as users of this medium, maximizing its advantages and avoiding its pitfalls.

Snap the code, or go to
vocabularyworkshop.com

Definitions

Note the spelling, pronunciation, part(s) of speech, and definition(s) of each of the following words. Then write the word in the blank spaces in the illustrative sentence(s) following. Finally, study the lists of synonyms and antonyms.

1. appreciable
(ə prē′ shə bəl)

(*adj.*) sufficient to be noticed or measured

The injured woman lost an _____**appreciable**_____ amount of blood before the paramedics arrived.

SYNONYMS: detectable, considerable
ANTONYMS: slight, trivial, inconsequential, negligible

2. autocratic
(ô tə krat′ ik)

(*adj.*) absolute in power or authority

For many years, the island was under the _____**autocratic**_____ control of a dictator.

SYNONYMS: domineering, dictatorial, tyrannical, bossy
ANTONYMS: democratic, egalitarian, lenient, permissive, indulgent

3. blanch
(blanch)

(*v.*) to remove the color from; to make or turn pale; to parboil

Even the veteran rescue worker _____**blanched**_____ upon seeing the crash site.

SYNONYMS: bleach, drain, wash out, go white
ANTONYMS: color, dye, infuse, blush, flush

4. blasphemy
(blas′ fə mē)

(*n.*) an act, utterance, or writing showing contempt for something sacred

Galileo was accused of _____**blasphemy**_____ for asserting that the sun, and not the earth, is the center of the universe.

SYNONYMS: curse, profanity, imprecation
ANTONYMS: veneration, devotion, respect

5. brawny
(brô′ nē)

(*adj.*) strong, muscular

In Arthurian legend, one _____**brawny**_____ knight after another tries to pull the sword Excalibar from the stone, but none succeeds.

SYNONYMS: broad-shouldered, strapping, burly
ANTONYMS: slight, frail, puny

6. concerted
(kən sər′ tid)

(*adj.*) planned or performed in cooperation with others

Teenagers and adults, northerners and southerners alike, participated in a _____**concerted**_____ drive to register new voters.

SYNONYMS: cooperative, combined, consolidated
ANTONYMS: unorganized, unilateral, diffused

7. contend
(kən tend')

(*v.*) to fight, struggle; to compete; to argue

I enjoy watching the four major tennis tournaments in which brilliant players _____ contend _____ for the "grand slam" titles.

SYNONYMS: battle, vie, maintain, assert
ANTONYMS: yield, acquiesce, submit, relinquish

8. humane
(hyü mān')

(*adj.*) kind, merciful

The _____ humane _____ legal code of Hammurabi, king of Babylonia, was ahead of its time in seeking justice for the weak and the oppressed.

SYNONYMS: sympathetic, compassionate, kindhearted
ANTONYMS: cruel, merciless, unfeeling, brutal, heartless

9. illustrious
(i ləs' trē əs)

(*adj.*) very famous, distinguished

As a student of world politics, I would be thrilled to meet an _____ illustrious _____ member of Parliament.

SYNONYMS: eminent, renowned, prominent, celebrated
ANTONYMS: unknown, obscure, nameless, anonymous

10. intolerable
(in täl' ər ə bəl)

(*adj.*) unbearable

To a perfectionist, mediocrity is more than unacceptable; it is simply _____ intolerable _____.

SYNONYMS: insufferable, outrageous
ANTONYMS: pleasant, pleasing

11. irreverent
(i rev' ər ənt)

(*adj.*) disrespectful

The student's _____ irreverent _____ comments show a lack of respect for people in authority.

SYNONYMS: profane, impious, sacrilegious
ANTONYMS: awed, respectful, devout, pious, deferential

12. laborious
(lə bôr' ē əs)

(*adj.*) not easy, requiring hard work; hardworking

After cleaning the gutters, we moved on to the _____ laborious _____ task of raking and bagging the leaves.

SYNONYMS: arduous, difficult, strenuous, wearisome
ANTONYMS: easy, effortless, facile

13. lithe
(līth)

(*adj.*) bending easily, limber

The burly linebacker was as _____ lithe _____ and agile as a ballet dancer.

SYNONYMS: flexible, pliant, lissome; ANTONYMS: rigid, inflexible, taut

14. maltreat
(mal trēt′)

(v.) to abuse, use roughly or crudely

The candidate pledged to shut down any factory or manufacturing plant found to _____maltreat_____ workers.

SYNONYMS: misuse, mistreat, harm
ANTONYMS: coddle, pamper, indulge

15. ponder
(pän′ dər)

(v.) to consider carefully, reflect on

I need time to _____ponder_____ all of my options before deciding how to spend the summer.

SYNONYMS: ruminate, contemplate

16. subversive
(səb vər′ siv)

(adj.) intended to undermine or overthrow; (n.) one who advocates or attempts to undermine a political system

The underground movement circulated _____subversive_____ pamphlets that criticized the government.

The Alien and Sedition Acts enacted in 1798 gave the U.S. president the power to deport any noncitizen deemed a _____subversive_____.

SYNONYMS: (adj.) traitorous; (n.) a revolutionary
ANTONYMS: (adj.) patriotic, loyal, true-blue

17. synthetic
(sin thet′ ik)

(adj.) made or put together by people; (n.) something artificial

Sometimes only a jeweler can detect the difference between an expensive _____synthetic_____ gem and a natural stone.

Nylon, rayon, and polyester are all _____synthetics_____ that have revolutionized the textile industry.

SYNONYMS: (adj.) artificial, ersatz; ANTONYMS: (adj.) natural, genuine

18. temperate
(tem′ pər ət)

(adj.) mild, moderate

It's impossible to have a _____temperate_____ discussion with a hotheaded person.

SYNONYMS: composed, balanced, mellow, fair
ANTONYMS: immoderate, extreme, excessive, harsh

19. venomous
(ven′ ə məs)

(adj.) poisonous; spiteful, mean

Only after we had rushed the child to the emergency room did we learn that he'd been bitten by a _____venomous_____ spider.

SYNONYMS: nasty, malicious, virulent, malevolent
ANTONYMS: harmless, innocuous, benign

20. wily
(wī′ lē)

(adj.) sly, shrewd, cunning

The fur trappers of colonial North America were known to be _____wily_____ traders.

SYNONYMS: tricky, artful, foxy, cagey
ANTONYMS: dull-witted, dense, straightforward

C CCSS Vocabulary: 4.c. (See pp. T14–15.)

Choosing the Right Word

*Select the **boldface** word that better completes each sentence. You might refer to the selection on pages 146–147 to see how most of these words are used in context.*

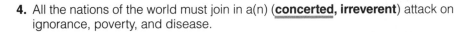

1. Is there any other creature in the entire world that is as graceful and (**subversive, lithe**) as the common house cat?

2. In days gone by, a dollar was a(n) (**concerted, appreciable**) sum, and was not to be spent lightly.

3. When the suspect (**pondered, blanched**) at the sudden accusation, her bloodless countenance as much as proclaimed her guilt.

4. All the nations of the world must join in a(n) (**concerted, irreverent**) attack on ignorance, poverty, and disease.

5. The librarian still (**ponders, contends**) that she was not the only person in the library at midnight, but no one seems to believe her.

6. In a country as rich as ours, it is simply (**illustrious, intolerable**) that so many people live below the poverty level.

7. He has the reputation of being a (**laborious, wily**) coach who can work with less experienced players and win.

8. Computer-generated synthesizers that produce (**humane, synthetic**) speech enable individuals who have lost their voices to disease to communicate.

9. Even those of us not philosophically inclined occasionally like to (**contend, ponder**) the meaning of life.

10. Many novels about football players or boxers are written in a style as (**brawny, venomous**) as the athletes they portray.

11. The (**laborious, venomous**) task the ditch-diggers undertook was not going to be finished before nightfall, in spite of their best efforts.

12. The official policy of the school is neither to pamper students nor to (**blanch, maltreat**) them.

13. Is it (**irreverent, appreciable**) of me to suggest that the "great man" may not be as great as he thinks he is?

14. To a skeptic, who doubts everything, the absolute belief in anything is (**blasphemy, synthetic**).

15. The (**venomous, intolerable**) snake's bite left her with a painful leg wound that took many weeks to completely heal.

16. We believe that a government can be strong, resourceful, and efficient without being (**wily, autocratic**).

17. After the potatoes have been (**temperate, blanched**) in hot water, they should be covered in the olive oil and herbs marinade.

18. Although the song had a cheerful tune, the authoritarian government decided that the lyrics were (**subversive, temperate**).

19. As a public official, I have learned to expect criticism of my ideas, but not (**venomous, temperate**) attacks on my character.

20. It's unusual to have an election in which two siblings (**maltreat, contend**) for the same office.

21. After completing the textbook, the writer faced the (**laborious, brawny**) job of compiling the index.

22. Isn't it amazing how the Adams family of Massachusetts produced so many (**illustrious, intolerable**) men and women throughout the years?

23. Advocates of American independence were regarded by Great Britain not as patriots, but as dangerous (**subversives, blasphemy**).

24. Some people criticized the judge as being "too lenient," but I thought she was simply being (**autocratic, humane**).

25. After months of counting calories, I learned to be (**temperate, lithe**) in eating.

Synonyms

*Choose the word from this unit that is the same or most nearly the same in meaning as the **boldface** word or expression in the phrase. Write that word on the line. Use a dictionary if necessary.*

1. exiled for **treasonous** acts — subversive

2. a **joint** effort to find a solution — concerted

3. a **perceptible** increase in temperature — appreciable

4. a comedian's **flippant** humor — irreverent

5. take time to **think over** the offer — ponder

6. prosecuted by the authorities for **sacrilege** — blasphemy

7. a **clever** and manipulative person — wily

8. the **husky** arms of the village blacksmith — brawny

9. a toothache that is **unendurable** — intolerable

10. a **supple** and graceful beech tree — lithe

CCSS Vocabulary: 5. (See pp. T14–15.)

Antonyms

*Choose the word from this unit that is most nearly opposite in meaning to the **boldface** word or expression in the phrase. Write that word on the line. Use a dictionary if necessary.*

1. **reverence** toward the holy book   <u>blasphemy</u>

2. a **delicate** build   <u>brawny</u>

3. an **enjoyable** performance   <u>intolerable</u>

4. **stiff** dance movements   <u>lithe</u>

5. a **guileless** person   <u>wily</u>

Completing the Sentence

From the words in this unit, choose the one that best completes each of the following sentences. Write the word in the space provided.

1. Some <u>synthetic</u> fibers are actually better than natural materials for certain purposes.

2. Despite his image as a "hard-boiled businessman," he is notably <u>humane</u> in his dealings with all of his employees.

3. The mountain climbers had to <u>contend</u> with unfavorable weather and with the fatigue brought on by high altitude.

4. I resented the <u>autocratic</u> manner in which he told us—without even asking for our opinion—what we should do to improve our situation.

5. Instead of trying to accomplish something worthwhile on her own, she spends her time boasting about her <u>illustrious</u> ancestors.

6. Mexico City is located deep in the tropics, but because of the altitude, its climate is <u>temperate</u>.

7. When I said that the famous rock star was singing off-key, his devoted fans seemed to think I was guilty of <u>blasphemy</u>.

8. While a weight lifter generally has a muscular build, a gymnast typically is slim and <u>lithe</u>.

9. The years had <u>blanched</u> the auburn from her hair, which now resembled a crown of snowy white.

10. I needed the job badly, but the working conditions in that company were so <u>intolerable</u> that I finally had to quit.

11. The bite of the rattlesnake and the sarcastic words of a supposed friend can be equally ___venomous___.

12. Only when the new drug was administered did the patient begin to show ___appreciable___ signs of improvement.

13. Our climb up the mountain was so ___laborious___ that we had to take a long rest before starting back down.

14. The ___brawny___ scout leader hoisted the canoe on his shoulders and carried it up the steep hill.

15. Some people were amused and others were outraged by the speaker's lighthearted, ___irreverent___ attitude toward the institutions of government.

16. "Once upon a midnight dreary, while I ___pondered___ weak and weary, Over many a quaint and curious volume of forgotten lore..."

17. We learned too late that the ___wily___ fox had escaped our trap by doubling back on its own tracks.

18. The suspect was charged with writing and printing pamphlets that were considered ___subversive___ by the government.

19. Students joined with faculty in a(n) ___concerted___ effort to increase the school's involvement in community affairs.

20. In 1875 New York State instituted child protection laws that made it criminal to ___maltreat___ children.

Writing: Words in Action

Answers to both prompts will vary.

1. Look back at "Social Networks and Virtual Communication" (pages 146–147). Which position do you take on the issue of social networking? Write a brief letter to the speaker of your choice, Monique or Rafael, explaining whether you agreed or disagreed with his or her position. Add an example or anecdote of your own to support your views on social networking. Use at least two details from the passage and three unit words to support your observations.

2. A strong area of debate concerning Internet access is the issue of the "digital divide," the idea that some people in the world have full access to the rich information technology available today while others, due to social, economic, and educational barriers, do not have such access. In a brief essay, explore an inequity that might occur because of the "digital divide," and suggest one or two solutions to the problem. Support your views with examples of your observations, studies, reading, or your own experience. Write at least three paragraphs, and use three or more words from this unit.

Writing prompt #2 is modeled on that of standardized tests.

Vocabulary in Context: Informational Text for Unit 12 is available online at **vocabularyworkshop.com**.

12

Vocabulary in Context

The following excerpts are from Henry Fielding's novel Joseph Andrews. *Some of the words you have studied in this unit appear in* **boldface** *type. Complete each statement below the excerpt by circling the letter of the correct answer.*

1. Matters being now composed, the company retired to their several apartments; the two gentlemen congratulating each other on the success of their good offices in procuring a perfect reconciliation between the **contending** parties....

   Individuals who are **contending** are
   a. compromising   **c.** conspiring
   b. conquering   **d.** competing

2. "Not so fast," says the player: "the modern actors are as good at least as their authors, nay, they come nearer their **illustrious** predecessors; and I expect a Booth on the stage again, sooner than a Shakespeare or an Otway; and indeed I may turn your observation against you, and with truth say, that the reason no authors are encouraged is because we have no good new plays."

   An **illustrious** predecessor is NOT
   a. forgotten   **c.** respected
   b. talented   **d.** well-known

3. "Your virtue!" said the lady, recovering after a silence of two minutes; "I shall never survive it. Your virtue!—**intolerable** confidence!"

   Something that is **intolerable** is
   a. agreeable   **c.** remarkable
   b. unendurable   **d.** inexplicable

4. Mr. Joseph Andrews...was of the highest degree of middle stature; his limbs were put together with great elegance, and no less strength; his legs and thighs were formed in the exactest proportion; his shoulders were broad and **brawny**, but yet his arm hung so easily, that he had all the symptoms of strength without the least clumsiness.

   Brawny shoulders are
   a. unsightly   **c.** powerful
   b. twisted   **d.** stiff

Portrait of eighteenth-century English author Henry Fielding

5. Adams rebuked her for disputing his commands, and quoted many texts of Scripture to prove "That the husband is the head of the wife, and she is to submit and obey." The wife answered, "It was **blasphemy** to talk Scripture out of church."

   Blasphemy is
   a. irreverence   **c.** arrogance
   b. gossip   **d.** faithfulness

Interactive Quiz

Snap the code, or go to **vocabularyworkshop.com**

Vocabulary for Comprehension

*Read the following selection in which some of the words you have studied in Units 10–12 appear in **boldface** type. Then answer the questions on page 157.*

The following passage discusses a unique life experience that is shared by many.

(Line)

The A.T., as its admirers call it, is America's most **illustrious** long-distance hiking path, the Appalachian Trail. Conservationist
(5) Benton MacKaye first envisioned the trail in 1921. When its many sections were linked in 1948, the A.T. was an impressive 2,158 miles long, winding through green hills and **rugged**
(10) mountains in 14 states.

Three kinds of hikers are found on the trail. Day hikers go on short, scenic jaunts. Section hikers tackle specific parts of the trail on
(15) extended outings. Thru-hikers set out to hike the entire trail, starting from either the northern terminus (Mount Katahdin, Maine) or the southern terminus (Springer
(20) Mountain, Georgia).

Thru-hikers are women, men, and young adults from around the world. They differ widely from one another but are united in their fierce desire to
(25) complete the A.T. despite having to **contend** with hardship and danger.

Before setting out, they need to be well equipped with packs, cooking gear, water bottles, and much more.
(30) Durable boots that fit are essential, since nothing can **impair** a hiker's stride faster than badly blistered feet. Once on the A.T., a typical hiker can expect to travel at about one
(35) mile per hour. As he or she grows accustomed to the **laborious** nature of thru-hiking, two (or even three) miles per hour can be achieved.

But don't get the **erroneous**
(40) impression that life on the trail is dull. The Appalachian terrain is varied and beautiful, and hikers must be ever vigilant to avoid a host of ills, such as dehydration, hypothermia,
(45) leg injury, and bad water. It generally takes five or six months to complete the trail. Those who finish will tell you that the adventure, the friendships made, and the exultation at the end
(50) of the hike are worth every second of hardship.

CCSS Vocabulary: 4.a.; Reading (Informational Text): 2, 4, 6. (See pp. T14–15.)

1. The passage is primarily concerned with
   a. A.T. conditions
   (b.) thru-hiking on the A.T.
   c. the history of the A.T.
   d. the beauty of the A.T.
   e. planning an A.T. hike

2. The author uses the first paragraph (lines 1–10) to do all of the following EXCEPT
   (a.) present the main idea
   b. set the scene
   c. provide background information
   d. introduce the passage
   e. create interest

3. **Illustrious** (line 2) most nearly means
   a. discussed
   b. noticeable
   c. difficult
   d. scenic
   (e.) celebrated

4. **Rugged** (line 9) is best defined as
   a. tedious
   b. well-traveled
   c. shaggy
   (d.) rocky
   e. steep

5. In the second paragraph (lines 11–20), the author discusses
   a. preparing for hiking
   (b.) choices for hiking
   c. hardships of hiking
   d. hiker conduct
   e. principles of hiking

6. The meaning of **contend** (line 26) is
   a. coexist
   b. argue
   c. yield
   d. endure
   (e.) battle

7. **Impair** (line 31) most nearly means
   a. double
   (b.) disable
   c. attack
   d. quicken
   e. strengthen

8. At the end of the third paragraph (lines 33–38), the author cites the speed of a typical hiker to show that the hike is
   a. impossible
   b. easy
   c. fast
   (d.) grueling
   e. boring

9. **Laborious** (line 36) is best defined as
   a. repetitive
   b. tedious
   (c.) arduous
   d. time-consuming
   e. effortless

10. The meaning of **erroneous** (line 39) is
    a. doubtful
    (b.) fallacious
    c. errorless
    d. imaginary
    e. thoughtless

11. Based on the passage, all of the following words can be used to describe life on the A.T. EXCEPT
    (a.) isolating
    b. exhausting
    c. exciting
    d. dangerous
    e. challenging

12. The author of the passage would probably agree with which of the following statements?
    a. Only world-class backpackers should attempt the A.T.
    (b.) Ultimately attitude is what allows a thru-hiker to finish the trail.
    c. Enthusiasm is all you need to make it from Springer Mountain to Katahdin.
    d. There are no valid reasons for quitting the A.T.
    e. A thru-hiker is, by definition, a little crazy.

C CCSS Vocabulary: 4.a.; Reading (Informational Text): 2, 4, 6. (See pp. T14–15.)

Review Units 10–12 ■ *157*

Two-Word Completions

Select the pair of words that best complete the meaning of each of the following passages.

1. A ballerina's _____ and graceful figure contrasts sharply with a weight lifter's massively _____ physique.
a. demure . . . languid
b. lithe . . . brawny
c. diminutive . . . concise
d. slipshod . . . rugged

2. When Shakespeare's Polonius says that _____ is the soul of wit, he extols the virtues of a _____ and succinct phrase.
a. brevity. . . concise
b. blasphemy . . . wily
c. depreciation . . . staccato
d. brawn . . . venomous

3. Though a(n) _____ master might deal kindly and generously with his or her animals, a cruel one would _____ and abuse them.
a. autocratic . . . impair
b. enlightened . . . emancipate
c. humane . . . maltreat
d. relentless . . . exploit

4. Her talents are just average, but she has _____ them to the fullest. On the other hand, he was given great natural abilities, but he has _____ them on trifles.
a. exploited . . . squandered
b. pondered . . . impaired
c. divulged . . . recouped
d. contended . . . forestalled

5. The _____ statistics cited in the magazine article certainly _____ its effectiveness. If the author had made sure that his figures were correct, his argument might have been more convincing.
a. bleak . . . quavered
b. laborious . . . enlightened
c. slipshod . . . rendered
d. erroneous . . . impaired

6. I did everything I could to _____ his cunning attempts to undermine my authority in the company; unfortunately, he proved too _____ and persistent for me to anticipate all his moves all the time.
a. chide . . . impair
b. forestall . . . wily
c. divulge . . . slipshod
d. subvert . . . demure

7. She has always been a strong _____ of organic, natural ingredients in foods, so I wonder why she tolerates the _____ sweeteners and food colorings in diet sodas.
a. statute . . . subversive
b. temperate . . . venomous
c. proponent . . . synthetic
d. adept . . . languid

Idioms

In the essay about hybrid animals (see pages 126–127), the author says that in creating hybrids, people are attempting to "build a better mousetrap."

"Build a better mousetrap" is an idiom that means "improve something with design." An **idiom** is a common saying, an informal expression that conveys its meaning in non-literal terms. A reader cannot usually "decode" an idiom by looking at the meaning of each of the words that form it, since idioms, like figures of speech, express one idea in terms of another. To understand the meaning of an idiom, readers often have to simply learn what it means, similar to learning the meaning of a new vocabulary word.

Choosing the Right Idiom

Read each sentence. Use context clues to figure out the meaning of each idiom in **boldface** *print. Then write the letter of the definition for the idiom in the sentence.*

1. We need to **strike a balance** between the opposing parties. ___j___

2. I will be the **devil's advocate** and suggest that the reason you didn't get the job is that the manager didn't like you. ___d___

3. Do not **shoot yourself in the foot** by dressing sloppily on the day of your big interview. ___c___

4. To find a solution to this unusual problem, we have to **think outside the box**. ___g___

5. The prodigy could play Mozart **by ear**. ___h___

6. I am almost done—don't **breathe down my neck**! ___e___

7. When it is my turn to plan a party, I will **call the shots** and choose the music myself. ___f___

8. When I asked why she was late, that really opened up a **can of worms**. ___a___

9. If no one wants this last orange, I guess it is **fair game**. ___b___

10. She was **hands down** the most talented singer in the contest. ___i___

a. something that is troublesome and problematic

b. available to anyone who wants it

c. undermine yourself

d. someone who states the less popular viewpoint for the sake of argument

e. monitor someone closely in an unpleasant way

f. be in charge; direct the action

g. go beyond traditional ideas

h. after listening to something, and without a written guide

i. without a doubt

j. make things more equal

Writing with Idioms

Find the meaning of each idiom. (Use an online or print dictionary if necessary.) Then write a sentence for each idiom. **Answers will vary.**

1. fight tooth and nail **Sample answer:**
   I wonder why my cousin and I fight tooth and nail over such trivial things?

2. keep your cool

_____

3. bide your time

_____

4. keep tabs on

_____

_____

5. make a splash

_____

_____

6. knuckle under

_____

_____

7. mean business

_____

8. beat around the bush

_____

9. rough it

_____

10. ring hollow

_____

11. catch my drift

_____

12. run ragged

_____

Denotation and Connotation

The dictionary definition of a word is its **denotation**. The denotation is what the word actually means. A word's denotation has a literal, *neutral* meaning, without positive or negative implied meanings.

Words that have similar denotations can have different **connotations**—suggested, or implied, meanings that readers or listeners associate with the word. For example, the word *tense* has a relatively neutral connotation, while the words *anxious* and *apprehensive*, which share a similar denotation, have a more negative connotation.

Consider these synonyms for the neutral word *spend*:

> *purchase   acquire   splurge   squander*

Purchase and *acquire* have neutral or mildly positive connotations, while *splurge* and *squander* have negative connotations.

> **Think:** People who are careful with money purchase or acquire the things they need, but spendthrifts splurge or squander money on trivial things they don't need.

Look at these examples of words that are similar in denotation but have different connotations.

NEUTRAL	POSITIVE	NEGATIVE
brevity	succinctness	terseness
quiet	temperate	diffident
smell	scent	reek

Recognizing connotations can help you to evaluate what you read and hear, since the words writers and speakers choose can reveal bias, or prejudice.

Shades of Meaning

Write a plus sign (+) in the box if the word has a positive connotation.
Write a minus sign (–) if the word has a negative connotation. Put a zero (0)
if the word is neutral.

1. humane $\boxed{+}$ **2.** despicable $\boxed{-}$ **3.** laborious $\boxed{-}$ **4.** invincible $\boxed{+}$

5. bleak $\boxed{-}$ **6.** illustrious $\boxed{+}$ **7.** subversive $\boxed{-}$ **8.** preamble $\boxed{0}$

9. enlightened $\boxed{+}$ **10.** emancipate $\boxed{+}$ **11.** lithe $\boxed{+}$ **12.** deteriorated $\boxed{-}$

13. rivulet $\boxed{0}$ **14.** obtrusive $\boxed{-}$ **15.** blasphemy $\boxed{-}$ **16.** proponent $\boxed{+}$

WORD STUDY

Expressing the Connotation

Read each sentence. Select the word in parentheses that expresses the connotation (positive, negative, or neutral) given at the beginning of the sentence.

positive
1. Our (**hardworking, relentless**) boss made us stay late to finish the project.

negative
2. The editorial offended some readers, who found the tone too (**lighthearted, irreverent**) for such a serious subject.

positive
3. The chairperson's speeches were often witty, engaging, and insightful, in spite of the fact that they were (**unplanned, extemporaneous**).

neutral
4. The black kitten, (**diminutive, small**) but lively and alert, quickly won my heart.

negative
5. Since he seldom gave me a direct answer, I was (**skeptical, unsure**) of his intentions.

negative
6. The salesperson explained the rules of the sweepstakes in a (**slipshod, concise**) manner.

positive
7. I tried to (**hinder, forestall**) any ideas he had about inviting me to the school dance on Friday by mentioning my intention to stay at home.

neutral
8. If you are in a hurry to get going, Andrew's (**unhurried, languid**) manner can be frustrating.

Challenge: Using Connotation

Choose vocabulary words from Units 10–12 to replace the highlighted words in the sentences below. Then explain how the connotation of the replacement word changes the tone of the sentence. **Answers will vary.**

divulge	wily	autocratic
laborious	recoup	bleak

1. Because of the prime minister's **controlling** _____autocratic_____ nature, no one, including his family, dared to disagree with him.
Sample response: The negative connotation of *autocratic* suggests a nature that insists on absolutes and is so controlling as to be dictatorial and tyrannical.

2. I have worked with her for over three years, but my coworker still will not **reveal** _____divulge_____ anything personal about herself. **Sample response:** The connotation of *divulge* suggests a stronger, more deliberate, and more public disclosure of information than *reveal*.

3. It is unlikely that they will be able to **recover** _____recoup_____ their losses after those bad investments. **Sample response:** To *recoup* something rather than just *recover* it suggests getting back an equivalent amount to make up for what was lost.

Classical Roots

spec, spic—to look

This root appears in **despicable** (page 128), which means "that which is to be looked down at." Some other words based on this root are listed below.

aspect	introspection	prospective	respective
conspicuous	perspicacious	retrospect	specter

From the list of words above, choose the one that corresponds to each of the brief definitions below. Write the word in the blank space in the illustrative sentence below the definition. Use an online or print dictionary if necessary.

1. keen in observing and understanding (*"able to see through"*)

Nineteenth-century writer Alexis de Tocqueville was a(n) ___perspicacious___ observer of American society, politics, and culture of the day.

2. belonging to each; individual (*"looking back and forth"*)

Mother sent the children to their ___respective___ rooms to cool off after the argument.

3. with reference to the past; a survey of the past (*"a looking back"*)

"In ___retrospect___," he mused, "my college years were probably some of the happiest times of my life, though I certainly didn't realize it at the time."

4. looked forward to, expected

I plan to invite my ___prospective___ sister-in-law out to lunch next week.

5. a phantom, apparition; a fearful image or threatening possibility

The hooded figure was a frightening ___specter___ that Halloween night.

6. an examination of one's own thoughts and feelings (*"looking within"*)

The recluse was given to long hours of ___introspection___ and meditation.

7. an appearance; a side or view; the direction something faces

It's important to consider all ___aspects___ of an issue before coming to a conclusion.

8. noticeable, drawing attention

We never expected to enjoy living in such a large and ___conspicuous___ building.

Note that not all of the 20 unit words are used in this passage. *Buoyant*, *clique*, *congenial*, *rustic*, and *sever* are not included in the passage.

*Read the following selection, taking note of the **boldface** words and their contexts. These words are among those you will be studying in Unit 13. As you complete the exercises in this unit, it may help to refer to the way the words are used below.*

C CCSS Vocabulary: 4; Reading (Informational Text): 4, 6. (See pp. T14–15.)

From Trash to Tabletop

<Interview>

Interviewer: Sherlynia Singh, as the owner of Frank's Fish Shop on Washington Avenue, what do you think is the most interesting development in your business today?

Singh: My father, who was a fisherman, used to say, "Give a man a fish, and you feed him for a day. Teach a man to fish, and you feed him for a lifetime." I think it's ironic that overfishing, the depleting of our fish stocks, is now a great challenge to us all. The oceans cannot produce fish **ad infinitum**. I have become fascinated by the rising interest in trash fish, which might help us to solve this problem.

Interviewer: What are trash fish?

Singh: Trash fish are fish that consumers don't like—they're not popular food sources, and they don't fetch high prices in the marketplace. Most commercial fishing operations target high-value fish, like tuna, salmon, or cod. Such operations use huge nets or long lines with hundreds of hooks to catch thousands of fish at a time. In the

process, they pick up a lot of so-called trash fish. Once, these low-value fish were discarded, but now they are retained and processed for sale.

Interviewer: What changed people's minds about fish once considered trash?

Singh: Most experts would **concede** that the growth of fish-farming is a major factor. Since overfishing has caused wild populations of popular species to **wane**, more of the fish we eat comes from fish farms. Many fish farms raise high-value carnivorous species, like salmon and tuna, that require massive quantities of food. Increasingly, it's trash fish that are processed to make fish meal and fish oils used to feed farmed fish. Since fish-farming relies on wild-caught trash fish, overfishing our oceans is still a problem. But without trash fish, fish-farming would soon become **untenable**.

Interviewer: So, trash fish play an important role in fish-farming, but they aren't consumed by humans.

Singh: Actually, some trash fish does find its way to our dinner table. Small, family-run fishing enterprises are still common in developing countries, often operating in rather **sordid** conditions. Local fishermen **apportion** some of their catch—the low-value fish—for home consumption and sell the rest of their yield to others. In many countries, great quantities of fish we consider low-value are sold for human consumption. This is often a matter of local preferences. In much of East Asia, for example, a wide variety of low- and high-value fish are an important part of the traditional diet.

These fish are the by product of commercial shrimp-fishing.

Saltwater salmon pens on a fish farm in the United States

Interviewer: It sounds as if determining whether or not a fish species is a trash fish might be a matter of opinion.

Singh: To some extent, that's true, but our taste for fish has changed as supplies have changed. When popular species become less common due to overfishing, environmental changes, or **migration**, local fisheries find new species to satisfy demand. Tuna is a classic example. In the days before refrigeration and canning, tuna flesh would quickly become **rancid**, so tuna was unpopular and usually discarded. That changed early in the 20th century, when a sudden drop in sardine populations prompted fisheries to start catching tuna off the California coast. Before long, tuna had become one of the most popular and **versatile** fish consumed in America, and it's now one of the most highly valued fish in the world. A single bluefin tuna can fetch $150,000 in a Tokyo market today! That's quite a **lofty** sum.

Interviewer: So, sellers and buyers alike are learning that yesterday's trash fish can become tomorrow's food fish.

Singh: It sounds **perverse**, but it's true. The fishing industry is rapidly changing due to environmental problems, over-fishing, and innovations in fish-farming. People forget that many fish that are popular around the world today were **perceived** as "trash" not long ago: hake, tilapia, Chilean sea bass, pangasius, monkfish, and shark all fall into this category. For years, I predicted we would expand our seafood diet to include more overlooked species, and now that people have done so, I feel **vindicated**. It seems that, for many species, status as a trash fish is only a **prelude** to **bona fide** popularity.

iWords

Snap the code, or go to **vocabularyworkshop.com**

Definitions

Note the spelling, pronunciation, part(s) of speech, and definition(s) of each of the following words. Then write the word in the blank spaces in the illustrative sentence(s) following. Finally, study the lists of synonyms and antonyms.

1. ad infinitum
(ad in fə nī′ təm)

(*adv.*) endlessly

Children who hear a favorite story read over and over
_____**ad infinitum**_____ are learning about language.

SYNONYMS: forever, unceasingly, incessantly, ceaselessly
ANTONYMS: succinctly, concisely, tersely, briefly

2. apportion
(ə pôr′ shən)

(*v.*) to divide and give out in shares

The aging king decided to _____**apportion**_____ the
lands of his vast kingdom among his three daughters.

SYNONYMS: distribute, allot, parcel out, allocate

3. bona fide
(bō′ nə fīd)

(*adj.*) genuine; sincere

The appraiser studied the old book and declared it to be a
_____**bona fide**_____ first edition of *Moby-Dick*.

SYNONYMS: authentic, indisputable, legitimate, certified
ANTONYMS: false, fake, bogus, spurious, counterfeit

4. buoyant
(boi′ ənt)

(*adj.*) able to float easily; able to hold things up; cheerful, hopeful

We were weary and anxious to get home, but our friend's
_____**buoyant**_____ spirits kept us going.

SYNONYMS: jaunty, lighthearted, animated
ANTONYMS: downcast, gloomy, morose

5. clique
(klēk; klik)

(*n.*) a small, exclusive group of people

The queen was surrounded by a _____**clique**_____ of
powerful nobles who actually ran the country.

SYNONYM: inner circle

6. concede
(kən sēd′)

(*v.*) to admit as true; to yield, submit

Even though the votes were all in and counted, the losing
candidate refused to _____**concede**_____ the election.

SYNONYMS: acknowledge, grant, allow, assent
ANTONYMS: contest, dispute, gainsay, challenge

7. congenial
(kən jēn′ yəl)

(*adj.*) getting on well with others; agreeable, pleasant

I was relieved when my bunkmate at summer camp turned
out to be considerate and _____**congenial**_____.

SYNONYMS: sociable, amiable, compatible
ANTONYMS: disagreeable, cold, standoffish

CCSS Vocabulary: 4.c., 4.d. (See pp. T14–15.)

8. lofty
(lôf′ tē)

(*adj.*) very high; noble

My mentor maintains _____lofty_____ standards and works hard to adhere to them.

SYNONYMS: elevated, exalted, grand
ANTONYMS: base, petty, low, sordid, despicable

9. migration
(mī grā′ shən)

(*n.*) a movement from one country or region to another

_____Migration_____ from north to south has contributed to the political clout of the Sun Belt.

SYNONYMS: population shift, mass movement

10. perceive
(pər sēv′)

(*v.*) to be aware of through the senses, observe; to grasp mentally

I thought I _____perceived_____ a flicker of guilt on my brother's face when I asked who ate my slice of pie.

SYNONYMS: notice, discern, understand
ANTONYMS: miss, overlook, be blind to

11. perverse
(pər vərs′)

(*adj.*) inclined to go against what is expected; stubborn; turned away from what is good and proper

Some teenagers get _____perverse_____ pleasure from blasting music that their parents do not like.

SYNONYMS: obstinate, contrary, mulish
ANTONYMS: tractable, docile, amenable, yielding

12. prelude
(pre′ lüd)

(*n.*) an introduction; that which comes before or leads off

The orchestral _____prelude_____ to the new opera seemed more interesting to me than the opera itself.

SYNONYMS: preface, overture, prologue, "curtain-raiser"
ANTONYMS: epilogue, postlude, aftermath

13. rancid
(ran′ sid)

(*adj.*) stale, spoiled

When he opened the door, there poured forth the unmistakably _____rancid_____ odor of some ancient leftovers.

SYNONYMS: foul, rank, fetid, sour, rotten, putrid
ANTONYMS: wholesome, fresh

14. rustic
(rəs′ tik)

(*adj.*) country-like; simple, plain; awkward; (*n.*) one who lives in the country

We rented a _____rustic_____ cabin, with no electricity or running water, twenty miles from the town.

On the trail we met an amiable old _____rustic_____ carrying a fishing pole and a string of trout he'd caught.

SYNONYMS: (*adj.*) rough, unsophisticated, countrified
ANTONYMS: (*adj.*) urban, sophisticated

15. sever
(sev′ ər)

(v.) to separate, divide into parts

It was extreme of her to _____ **sever** _____ ties with her former best friend, but that is what she did.

SYNONYMS: cut off, amputate, dissolve
ANTONYMS: unite, weld together

16. sordid
(sôr′ did)

(adj.) wretchedly poor; run-down; mean or selfish

Nineteenth-century reformers made people aware of just how _____ **sordid** _____ conditions were in city slums.

SYNONYMS: filthy, squalid, base, vile, seedy, sleazy
ANTONYMS: pure, noble, opulent, lavish

17. untenable
(ən ten′ ə bəl)

(adj.) not capable of being held or defended; impossible to maintain

Minutes into the debate she had a sinking feeling that her position was completely _____ **untenable** _____.

SYNONYMS: indefensible, insupportable
ANTONYMS: irrefutable, impregnable, incontestable

18. versatile
(vər′ sə təl)

(adj.) able to do many things well; capable of many uses

By moving from comedy to drama to musicals, he has shown himself to be a truly _____ **versatile** _____ actor.

SYNONYMS: adaptable, all-around, many-sided
ANTONYMS: limited, specialized, restricted

19. vindicate
(vin′ də kāt)

(v.) to clear from hint or charge of wrongdoing; to defend successfully against opposition; to justify

Though the accused was _____ **vindicated** _____ in the end, his career was all but ruined by the allegations.

SYNONYMS: acquit, absolve, exonerate, advocate
ANTONYMS: implicate, incriminate, condemn, convict

20. wane
(wān)

(v.) to lose size, strength, or power

As the moon _____ **waned** _____, the nights grew darker; we could hardly see our way along the forest trails.

SYNONYMS: diminish, decline, subside
ANTONYMS: grow, wax, amplify, balloon, increase

C CCSS Vocabulary: 4.c. (See pp. T14–15.)

Choosing the Right Word

*Select the **boldface** word that better completes each sentence. You might refer to the selection on pages 164–165 to see how most of these words are used in context.*

1. Leonardo da Vinci was a (**versatile, buoyant**) genius who excelled in many different fields of art and science.

2. American society has been deeply affected by the steady (**migration, clique**) from the inner city to the suburbs.

3. Because our tank forces had been destroyed, the position of the ground troops proved (**congenial, untenable**).

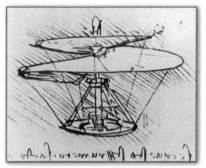

4. One of the aims of education is to enable us to (**perceive, sever**) the difference between what is truly excellent and what is second-rate.

Leonardo da Vinci conceived of a flying machine hundreds of years before the first airplane was invented.

5. The fatty layer beneath their skin not only enables seals to be naturally (**buoyant, versatile**), but it also helps them to store energy and conserve their body heat.

6. They will not be allowed to vote in the election because they are not considered (**ad infinitum, bona fide**) residents of the community.

7. The psychologist said that troubled young people often have a (**perverse, rancid**) impulse to do exactly what will be most injurious to them.

8. The atmosphere in the tiny, airless cell soon grew as (**buoyant, rancid**) as the foul-smelling soup that the prisoner was fed every night.

9. The long range of (**buoyant, lofty**) mountains was dramatically silhouetted against the glowing purple, red, and pink sunset.

10. He talks a great game of tennis, but I (**wane, concede**) nothing to him until he has shown that he can beat me on the court.

11. When he came home from college for Thanksgiving break, he treated us "high school kids" with (**sordid, lofty**) scorn.

12. They claimed to be unselfish patriots, but we knew that, in reality, they were acting from the most (**untenable, sordid**) motives.

13. Our team was more than just (**sordid, congenial**); our friendships were meaningful and deep, and we were very involved in one another's lives.

14. This (**versatile, untenable**) new kitchen tool can chop, slice, and blend. I wish it could do the cooking, too!

15. I appreciate her interest in me, but I am annoyed by her tendency to offer criticism and advice (**bona fide, ad infinitum**).

16. I could tell from his animated expression and his sprightly step that he was in a (**buoyant**, **versatile**) mood.

17. You are at a stage of life when you should begin to (**wane**, **sever**) the apron strings that tie you to your mother.

18. Our problem now is not to (**sever**, **apportion**) blame for our failures, but to find a way to achieve success.

19. There are more than 100 members in the state legislature, but the real power is held by a small (**clique**, **prelude**) of insiders.

20. The general's army was in full retreat, and he was forced to (**vindicate**, **concede**) that his nation had lost the war.

21. The successful invasion of France in June 1944 was only a (**prelude**, **migration**) to the great Allied victories that ended the war in Europe.

22. Good citizens should not sit idly by while the vitality of their community (**wanes**, **concedes**).

23. A good politician must appear (**sordid**, **congenial**) even when he or she is feeling cross and unsociable.

24. Shakespeare's clowns are often simple (**cliques**, **rustics**) who are trying to behave like sophisticated men of the world.

25. My faith in that seemingly ordinary young girl was entirely (**vindicated**, **perceived**).

Synonyms

*Choose the word from this unit that is the same or most nearly the same in meaning as the **boldface** word or expression in the phrase. Write that word on the line. Use a dictionary if necessary.*

1. the **towering** mountain peaks _____lofty_____

2. a kind and **friendly** host _____congenial_____

3. her elevated mood and **blithe** spirit _____buoyant_____

4. a **coterie** of influential donors _____clique_____

5. shocked by their **wayward** behavior _____perverse_____

6. watched the initial enthusiasm **dwindle** _____wane_____

7. ridiculously **groundless** reasons _____untenable_____

8. a **handy** gadget with many uses _____versatile_____

9. a charming **rural** scene _____rustic_____

10. a move to **break off** relations with that country _____sever_____

Antonyms

*Choose the word from this unit that is most nearly opposite in meaning to the **boldface** word or expression in the phrase. Write that word on the line. Use a dictionary if necessary.*

1. a **depressed** mood   _____buoyant_____

2. an **inclusive organization** in the community   _____clique_____

3. able to **join** the two   _____sever_____

4. a **citified** gentleman   _____rustic_____

5. a **surly** answer   _____congenial_____

Completing the Sentence

From the words in this unit, choose the one that best completes each of the following sentences. Write the word in the space provided.

1. I realize that I made a bad mistake, but at least I possess the strength of character to _____concede_____ that I was wrong and apologize.

2. In 1776 the Continental Congress moved to _____sever_____ all political connections between the colonies and Great Britain.

3. Isn't it boring when people go on and on about their looks, their clothes, and their popularity _____ad infinitum_____?

4. She's not really hungry; she's just being _____perverse_____ in insisting on eating now.

5. The oil, which had been inadvertently stored in a heated room, soon began to exude a rank odor that told us it had turned _____rancid_____.

6. The early cold spell proved to be a fitting _____prelude_____ to one of the most severe winters of modern times.

7. It takes a really _____versatile_____ athlete to win varsity letters in three different sports.

8. Although many of my friends seem to like him, I've never found him to be a particularly _____congenial_____ companion.

9. Dismissing all his rivals as impostors, the undefeated heavyweight boxer pronounced himself the only _____bona fide_____ contender for the crown.

10. We found it easy to float in the lake because the high salt content makes the water extremely _____buoyant_____.

11. When the mayor failed to carry out his campaign promises, his popularity quickly _____ waned _____, and he failed to win reelection.

12. New employees are assigned their duties by the office manager, who is responsible for _____ apportioning _____ work among the staff.

13. The Declaration of Independence first set forth the _____ lofty _____ standards to which we as a nation have ever since aspired.

14. The accused clerk _____ vindicated _____ himself by producing signed receipts for all the questioned items.

15. I am convinced that the Drama Club is run by a(n) _____ clique _____ of students who reserve all the best roles for themselves.

16. The seasonal _____ migration _____ of birds southward reminds us that we have come to the end of the summer vacation.

17. Who would believe that this peaceful, _____ rustic _____ hideaway is only twenty-five miles from the city?

18. We began to _____ perceive _____ the impact of the tornado only after viewing the flattened neighborhood and interviewing residents.

19. Since the theory is based on inaccurate and out-of-date information, it is clearly _____ untenable _____.

20. It is a regrettable fact of our history that several presidential administrations have been tainted by _____ sordid _____ scandals.

Writing: Words in Action

Answers to both prompts will vary.

1. Look back at "From Trash to Tabletop" (pages 164–165). Why are certain fish formerly considered "trash" now being considered suitable for people to eat? Write an essay describing this transition. Use at least two details from the passage and three unit words to support your points.

2. As the world's population grows, so do concerns about Earth's ability to supply enough food to sustain billions of people. In addition to overfishing, what are some other problems that affect the global food supply? Think of one problem that needs to be addressed to assure that people have enough safe and nutritious food to eat. In a brief essay, describe this problem and explore one possible solution to the problem, citing specific examples from your observations, studies, reading (refer to pages 164–165), or personal experience. Write at least three paragraphs, and use three or more words from this unit.

Writing prompt #2 is modeled on that of standardized tests.

C CCSS Vocabulary: 6; Writing: 1.c., 2.d. (See pp. T14–15.)

Vocabulary in Context: Informational Text for Unit 13 is available online at **vocabularyworkshop.com**.

13

Vocabulary in Context

Literary Text

The following excerpts are from Thomas Hardy's novel The Woodlanders. *Some of the words you have studied in this unit appear in **boldface** type. Complete each statement below the excerpt by circling the letter of the correct answer.*

1. There was no doubt that he had lost his houses by an accident which might easily have been circumvented if he had known the true conditions of his holding. The time for performance had now lapsed in strict law; but might not the intention be considered by the landholder when she became aware of the circumstances, and his moral right to retain the holdings for the term of his life be **conceded**?

If one's right to something has been **conceded**, it has been
a. revised   **c.** ignored
b. disagreed with   (**d.**) agreed to

2. Their way homeward ran along the crest of a **lofty** hill, whence on the right they beheld a wide valley....

A **lofty** hill is NOT
(**a.**) squat   **c.** towering
b. high   **d.** tall

3. "Nobody except our household knows that you have left home. Then why should you, by a piece of **perverseness**, bring down my gray hairs with sorrow to the grave?"

Someone who is acting with **perverseness** is acting in a way that is
(**a.**) contrary   **c.** well-meaning
b. careless   **d.** cooperative

Emily Woof plays Grace Melbury in the 1997 film *The Woodlanders*.

4. ...Dr. Jones went home and wrote to Mr. Melbury at the London address he had obtained from his wife. The gist of his communication was that Mrs. Fitzpiers should be assured as soon as possible that steps were being taken to **sever** the bond which was becoming a torture to her; that she would soon be free....

To **sever** is to
a. speak   **c.** abuse
(**b.**) break   **d.** give up

5. Day after day waxed and **waned**; the one or two woodmen who sawed, shaped, spokeshaved on her father's premises at this inactive season of the year, regularly came and unlocked the doors in the morning, locked them in the evening, supped, leaned over their garden-gates for a whiff of evening air....

Something that has **waned** has
a. echoed   **c.** amplified
b. silenced   (**d.**) lessened

Interactive Quiz

Snap the code, or go to **vocabularyworkshop.com**

Note that not all of the 20 unit words are used in this passage.
Exonerate, *glib*, and *haphazard* are not included in the passage.

*Read the following selection, taking note of the **boldface** words and their contexts. These words are among those you will be studying in Unit 14. As you complete the exercises in this unit, it may help to refer to the way the words are used below.*

C CCSS Vocabulary: 4; Reading (Informational Text): 4, 6. (See pp. T14–15.)

ASIA MINOR

Temple of Artemis in Ephesus

Tomb of Mausolus in Halicarnassus

SYRIA

Statue of Zeus in Olympia

Colossus of Rhodes

MEDITERRANEAN

Hanging Gardens of Babylon

Great Pyramid of Giza

Lighthouse of Alexandria

Seven Wonders
<Magazine Article>

The conquests of Alexander the Great broadened the horizons of the ancient Greek world. Many territories **annexed** by Alexander were home to civilizations with longer **pedigrees** than the Greeks', such as Babylon and Egypt. Each of these civilizations had its own culture, its own style of architecture, art, music, and cuisine. Each had its own traditions and history. Commerce and curiosity **incited** interest in travel. A steady **influx** of travelers was drawn to major cities and famous landmarks. Moved by the **profuse** interest in travel, Greek authors compiled lists of spectacular sites. **Cleaving** to custom, these ancient travel writers normally included seven locations in their lists. In ancient times, the sites listed varied from one author to another. But today the landmarks mentioned in these ancient travel guides are remembered as the Seven Wonders of the World.

Statues of the Gods

The Statue of Zeus soared more than 40 feet high. Built in 432 BCE, it sat in a temple in Olympia, on mainland Greece. Across the Aegean, on the island of Rhodes, a bronze statue of the sun god

Colossus of Rhodes

Helios guarded the harbor from atop a massive stone pillar, which served as its **cornerstone**. The giant statue of Helios was known as the Colossus of Rhodes.

Temple and Tomb

The Temple of Artemis was located in the town of Ephesus on the Anatolian coast, which is in modern-day Turkey. The temple was destroyed and rebuilt twice before the **debacle** of its final destruction at the hands of a rioting mob in 401 CE.

Also on the Anatolian coast was the Tomb of Mausolus, which stood nearly 150 feet high. A provincial governor of the Persian Empire, Mausolus had his capital in Halicarnassus. When he died in 353 BCE, his wife could hardly **reconcile** herself to his death. As a tribute to her husband, she had the great tomb built.

The Lighthouse and the Pyramid

For centuries, the Lighthouse of Alexandria guided Mediterranean navigators into the busy Egyptian port. An engineering marvel that rose to a height of 400 feet above the water, it could be seen 29 miles away by approaching sailors.

The Great Pyramid of Giza is the oldest of the Seven Wonders and the only one that remains standing today. Its endurance is recalled in the old Arabic saying, "Man fears time, but time fears the Pyramids." The builders **improvised** the pyramid's bricks from the local limestone. Its **precipitous** stone walls extended nearly 500 feet in height and reflected the golden **pallor** of the desert sun. Contrary to many accounts, the laborers who built the pyramid were

Hanging Gardens of Babylon

not slaves in **shackles** and **threadbare** clothing, but rather teams of villagers who took pride in their work.

A Garden for a Homesick Queen

The Babylonian king Nebuchadnezzar was extremely active during his long reign. He spent much of his time **embroiled** in wars and engaged in massive building projects. He is credited with constructing the Hanging Gardens of Babylon. According to legend, the king's wife, Amytis of Media, deeply missed her homeland. Media was a land rich in forests and greenery, and Amytis felt **devitalized** in the plains of Babylon. To enliven Amytis's mood, the king ordered the construction of the Hanging Gardens, a lush expanse of trees and plants.

Though nobody can be sure the king's **cordial** gesture had its desired effect, the gardens, like the other wonders, were a marvel of ancient ingenuity, and they attracted sightseers from across the known world.

Great Pyramid of Giza

Snap the code, or go to **vocabulary workshop.com**

Definitions

Note the spelling, pronunciation, part(s) of speech, and definition(s) of each of the following words. Then write the word in the blank spaces in the illustrative sentence(s) following. Finally, study the lists of synonyms and antonyms.

1. annex
(*v.* ə neks′;
n. an′ eks)

(*v.*) to add to, attach; to incorporate; (*n.*) an attachment or addition

The two nations protested when their militant neighbor
_____**annexed**_____ the disputed territory.

All back issues of magazines are kept next door on the
second floor of the new library _____**annex**_____.

SYNONYMS: (*v.*) join, acquire, procure

2. cleave
(klēv)

(*v.*) to cut or split open; to cling to

It is possible to _____**cleave**_____ a ripe coconut
neatly in two with just one swing of a machete.

SYNONYMS: sever, halve, adhere, clasp

3. cordial
(kôr′ jəl)

(*adj.*) in a friendly manner, hearty; cheery; (*n.*) a liqueur

Our aunt's _____**cordial**_____ welcome made us all
feel right at home in her huge, drafty Victorian house.

Grasshopper pie is made not with grasshoppers but with
crème de menthe, a _____**cordial**_____.

SYNONYMS: (*adj.*) hospitable, affable, warm, convivial
ANTONYMS: (*adj.*) gruff, unfriendly, unsociable

4. cornerstone
(kôr′ nər stōn)

(*n.*) the starting point of a building; a fundamental principle or element

The _____**cornerstone**_____ of the American judicial system
is the presumption of innocence.

SYNONYMS: base, underpinning, support

5. debacle
(di bäk′ əl)

(*n.*) an overwhelming defeat, rout; a complete collapse or failure

After the _____**debacle**_____ of their crushing loss in
the World Series, the team vowed to return next year.

SYNONYMS: disaster, calamity
ANTONYMS: success, victory, coup

6. devitalize
(dē vīt′ ə līz)

(*v.*) to make weak or lifeless

The long, dark winter, with its cold rain and gloomy skies,
_____**devitalized**_____ her usually buoyant spirit.

SYNONYMS: sap, enervate
ANTONYMS: enliven, stimulate, excite

Ⓒ CCSS Vocabulary: 4.c., 4.d. (See pp. T14–15.)

7. embroil
(em broil')

(*v.*) to involve in a conflict or difficulty; to throw into confusion

The last thing I want is to _____ **embroil** _____ myself in a dispute between two of my best friends.

SYNONYMS: entangle, ensnarl
ANTONYMS: disentangle, separate, disconnect

8. exonerate
(eg zän' ə rāt)

(*v.*) to clear from a charge or accusation

The prisoner was set free after ten years, thanks to new evidence that _____ **exonerated** _____ him of all charges.

SYNONYMS: absolve, acquit, vindicate
ANTONYMS: incriminate, inculpate

9. glib
(glib)

(*adj.*) ready and fluent in speech; thoughtless, insincere

The salesman had such _____ **glib** _____ answers to every objection that I grew extremely skeptical of his claims.

SYNONYMS: superficial, pat, oily, unctuous
ANTONYMS: halting, tongue-tied, speechless

10. haphazard
(hap haz' ərd)

(*adj.*) by chance, not planned; lacking order

The _____ **haphazard** _____ arrangement of facts in his presentation left his listeners completely confused.

SYNONYMS: random, slapdash
ANTONYMS: deliberate, purposeful, orderly

11. improvise
(im' prə vīz)

(*v.*) to compose or perform without preparation; to construct from available materials

After the earthquake, stunned villagers were forced to _____ **improvise** _____ shelters from the debris.

SYNONYMS: ad-lib, play it by ear, wing it, extemporize
ANTONYMS: plan, rehearse

12. incite
(in sīt')

(*v.*) to rouse, stir up, urge on

Company agents were hired to _____ **incite** _____ a riot at the steelworkers' protest demonstration.

SYNONYMS: spur, kindle, provoke, instigate, prompt
ANTONYMS: check, curb, impede, restrain, smother

13. influx
(in' fləks)

(*n.*) a coming in, inflow

An _____ **influx** _____ of arctic air has brought unseasonably cold weather to half the country.

SYNONYMS: inpouring, inrush
ANTONYMS: outpouring, exodus, departure

14. pallor
(pal' ər)

(*n.*) an extreme or unnatural paleness

"A ghost!" the girl gasped, her _____pallor_____ making her look much like a ghost herself as she ran away.

SYNONYMS: wanness, lividness, bloodlessness
ANTONYMS: flush, blush, rosiness, bloom

15. pedigree
(ped' ə grē)

(*n.*) a list of ancestors, family tree; the history or origins of something

Despite his impressive _____pedigree_____, the colt showed little enthusiasm for racing.

SYNONYMS: lineage, ancestry, genealogy

16. precipitous
(pri sip' ət əs)

(*adj.*) very steep

The novice hikers were very nervous as they carefully negotiated the _____precipitous_____ mountain trail.

SYNONYMS: abrupt, sharp
ANTONYMS: shallow, graded, incremental

17. profuse
(prō fyüs')

(*adj.*) very abundant; given or flowing freely

How can I stay upset with him when he is so sincere and _____profuse_____ with his apologies?

SYNONYMS: extravagant, lavish, bounteous, plenteous
ANTONYMS: sparse, scanty, meager, insufficient

18. reconcile
(rek' ən sīl)

(*v.*) to restore to friendship; to settle; to resign (oneself)

After so many years of feuding, it will be difficult for the brothers to _____reconcile_____ and begin anew.

SYNONYMS: conciliate, mend fences
ANTONYMS: antagonize, alienate, drive a wedge between

19. shackle
(shak' əl)

(*v.*) to put into chains; (*n., usually pl.*) a chain, fetter

The guards attempted to _____shackle_____ the prisoner before allowing him to board the waiting airplane.

His wicked plot discovered, the prince was bound in _____shackles_____ and taken to the dank dungeon.

SYNONYMS: (*v.*) manacle, enslave; (*n.*) handcuffs, bonds, irons
ANTONYMS: (*v.*) free, unfetter, emancipate, liberate

20. threadbare
(thred' bâr)

(*adj.*) shabby, old and worn

My brother has carefully collected a closetful of faded, _____threadbare_____ jeans, sweatshirts, and sneakers.

SYNONYMS: frayed, seedy, ragged, shopworn
ANTONYMS: luxurious, costly, sumptuous

CCSS Vocabulary: 4.c. (See pp. T14–15.)

Choosing the Right Word

Select the **boldface** word that better completes each sentence. You might refer to the selection on pages 174–175 to see how most of these words are used in context.

1. Separation of powers is one of the (**cornerstones, shackles**) upon which the American form of government is built.

2. We learned from the film that Spartacus was a Roman gladiator who (**reconciled, incited**) his fellow slaves to armed rebellion.

3. The President said in his inaugural address that he firmly believes that we must not (**embroil, devitalize**) ourselves in the quarrels of other nations.

4. The couple thanked me so (**profusely, haphazardly**) for the small favor I had done them that I was almost embarrassed.

The U.S. Supreme Court in Washington, D.C.

5. My campaign for the class presidency ended in an utter (**influx, debacle**) when I forgot my speech as I was about to address the assembly.

6. Some people think that, because she wears mismatched clothing, her approach to dressing herself is (**glib, haphazard**), but I think she plans her outfits very carefully.

7. Although I had never even met her, the emails she wrote to me were so (**cordial, threadbare**) that I felt we were old friends.

8. The (**pedigree, debacle**) of that dog cannot be in question; the breeder has extensive documentation to prove that he is from a line of award-winning collies.

9. After he was brought in by the police, he remained (**shackled, embroiled**) to a chair for about half an hour.

10. What we need is not *talkers* with (**glib, cordial**) solutions for all our problems, but *doers* who are prepared to pitch in and help.

11. How can he (**cleave, reconcile**) his claim that he is a "good citizen" with the fact that he doesn't even bother to vote?

12. The famous actor applied a layer of ashen makeup to simulate the ghastly (**pallor, pedigree**) of a ghost.

13. Let's (**improvise, reconcile**) a shelter from these fallen branches before it gets too dark to see in these woods.

14. We are tired of listening to those (**cordial, threadbare**) old excuses for your failure to keep your promises.

15. The story of his unhappy childhood aroused our sympathy but did not (**exonerate, improvise**) him from the charge of criminal assault.

16. The disaster was so great that the overcrowded hospital was forced to house some patients in a makeshift (**annex, debacle**).

17. With such a (**precipitous, haphazard**) way of keeping accounts, is it any wonder that your budget is a disaster?

18. True, he comes from an aristocratic family, but he won that promotion on the basis of merit, not because of his (**pedigree, cornerstone**).

19. Runaway inflation can cause a (**glib, precipitous**) decline in the value of a nation's currency.

20. Modern processing methods (**devitalize, annex**) many foodstuffs sold today, resulting in a loss of both taste and nutritional value.

21. In spite of all the progress made in recent years, we are still not entirely free from the (**shackles, debacles**) of prejudice and superstition.

22. To seaside resorts, the annual (**influx, pallor**) of tourists marks the true beginning of the summer season.

23. In a time of unrest and bewildering change, it is more important than ever to (**incite, cleave**) to the basic principles that give meaning to our lives.

24. He is the kind of speaker who is more effective when he (**improvises, exonerates**) his remarks than when he reads from a prepared script.

25. The glade was resplendent with (**profuse, glib**) flowers.

Synonyms

*Choose the word from this unit that is the same or most nearly the same in meaning as the **boldface** word or expression in the phrase. Write that word on the line. Use a dictionary if necessary.*

1. the team became **enfeebled** due to the hot sun   devitalized

2. a **sheer** drop of 300 feet into the old quarry   precipitous

3. an **invasion** of deer stripping the foliage   influx

4. **exculpated** by last-minute eyewitness testimony   exonerated

5. able to **sunder** a knight's shield with one blow   cleave

6. pleasing design resulting from **accidental** paint drippings   haphazard

7. conversation that revealed a **facile** wit   glib

8. an **unpracticed** comic skit   improvised

9. bored by the driver's **trite** jokes   threadbare

10. the embarrassing **fiasco** of her mother's party   debacle

(C) CCSS Vocabulary: 5. (See pp. T14–15.)

The synonyms and antonyms here do not appear on the Definitions page.

14

Antonyms

*Choose the word from this unit that is most nearly opposite in meaning to the **boldface** word or expression in the phrase. Write that word on the line. Use a dictionary if necessary.*

1. a prisoner **implicated** by the evidence   exonerated

2. an **awkward** explanation for his tardiness   glib

3. the **meticulous** arrangement of her collection   haphazard

4. the **prepared** statement of the representative   improvised

5. removed the **plush** winter coat from storage   threadbare

Completing the Sentence

From the words in this unit, choose the one that best completes each of the following sentences. Write the word in the space provided.

1. With one flashing stroke of his mighty axe, the skilled woodsman was able to _____ cleave _____ the heavy branch from the tree trunk.

2. Our dress rehearsal was a disaster: Actors blew their lines, and doors on the set got stuck shut; it was a complete _____ debacle _____!

3. We certainly did not expect to receive such a(n) _____ cordial _____ greeting from someone who had been described to us as cold and unsociable.

4. The heavy rains of June brought a(n) _____ influx _____ of mosquitoes into the neighborhoods bordering the marshland.

5. Her deathly _____ pallor _____ and distraught expression told us she had already received the tragic news.

6. In the untended garden the weeds were so _____ profuse _____ that they all but smothered the few flowers that managed to blossom.

7. With the Louisiana Purchase of 1803, Jefferson _____ annexed _____ a vast territory that doubled the size of the nation.

8. Millions of immigrants willingly came to America from all over the world, but many Africans arrived here in _____ shackles _____.

9. As we grow older and perhaps wiser, we _____ reconcile _____ ourselves to the fact that we will never achieve all that we had hoped for in life.

10. Rebels would find it difficult to _____ incite _____ people who are reasonably well satisfied with their government to rise up against it.

11. His books are scattered around in such a(n) _____**haphazard**_____ manner that it is a mystery to me how he can find the ones he wants.

12. I saw nothing but peril in the prospect of trying to scale a cliff so sheer and _____**precipitous**_____ that even expert climbers shied away from it.

13. He is certainly a(n) _____**glib**_____ talker, but does he have a firm grasp of the subject he is discussing?

14. Three customers fought noisily over the last sale-priced sweater until they finally _____**embroiled**_____ the store manager in their dispute.

15. My dog Rover may look like a mutt at first glance, but in fact he has a distinguished _____**pedigree**_____.

16. The illness so _____**devitalized**_____ her that it was several weeks before she could return to her job.

17. By proving that his eighteenth birthday came one day before the election, the student was _____**exonerated**_____ of the charge of unlawful voting.

18. The Roman numeral MCMXCVI is inscribed on the commemorative plaque that adorns the _____**cornerstone**_____ of the building.

19. His old-fashioned clothes were patched and _____**threadbare**_____, but we could see that he had made every effort to keep them spotlessly clean.

20. The entertainer cleverly _____**improvised**_____ limericks and other comic rhymes on subjects suggested by the audience.

Writing: Words in Action

Answers to both prompts will vary.

1. Look back at "Seven Wonders" (pages 174–175). Imagine that remnants of all seven wonders, not just the Great Pyramid of Giza, still exist as tourist destinations. Choose the wonder you think is most interesting or impressive, and write a brief article about it for a travel magazine or Web site. Describe what the wonder looks like today and why people should travel to see it. Use at least two details from the passage and three unit words to support your claim.

2. The Seven Wonders were human creations of the ancient world. What are some wonders—either natural or human-made—that exist in the world today? Choose one amazing place, construction, or invention that you think should be considered one of the Seven Wonders of the World. Write a persuasive essay explaining and supporting your choice. Support your ideas with specific examples of your observations, studies, reading (refer to pages 174–175), or personal experience. Write at least three paragraphs, and use three or more words from this unit.

Writing prompt #2 is modeled on that of standardized tests.

C CCSS Vocabulary: 6; Writing: 1.c., 2.d. (See pp. T14–15.)

Vocabulary in Context: Informational Text for Unit 14 is available online at **vocabularyworkshop.com**.

14

Vocabulary in Context

Literary Text

The following excerpts are from Stephen Crane's novel The Red Badge of Courage, *his story "The Blue Hotel," and his novella* The Monster. *Some of the words you have studied in this unit appear in* **boldface** *type. Complete each statement below the excerpt by circling the letter of the correct answer.*

1. "Who yeh talkin' to, Wilson?" he demanded. His voice was anger-toned. "Who yeh talkin' to? Yeh th' derndest sentinel—why—hello, Henry, you here? Why, I thought you was dead four hours ago!... Where was yeh?"

   "Over on th' right. I got separated"—began the youth with considerable **glibness**. (*The Red Badge of Courage*)

   To express something with **glibness** is to say it
   a. with great weariness
   b. in a shy, hesitant way
   c. in a loud, frightened voice
   (d.) with smoothness and conviction

2. Sometimes he would achieve a position half erect, battle with the air for a moment, and then fall again, grabbing at the grass. His face was of a clammy **pallor**. (*The Red Badge of Courage*)

   A face that has a **pallor** is
   a. covered with sweat
   b. frozen in fear
   (c.) drained of blood
   d. yellowish and dry

3. He had no rifle; he could not fight with his hands.... Well, rifles could be had for the picking. They were extraordinarily **profuse**. (*The Red Badge of Courage*)

   Something **profuse** is NOT
   a. widespread   c. common
   (b.) scarce   d. everywhere

Audie Murphy stars as The Youth in the 1951 film *The Red Badge of Courage*.

4. Each time that he held superior cards he whanged them, one by one, with exceeding force, down upon the **improvised** table.... ("The Blue Hotel")

   Something that has been **improvised** has been
   a. made by a blacksmith
   b. reinforced with strong materials
   c. worn away from overuse
   (d.) put together from what is available

5. Trescott looked gravely at the other boys, and asked them to please go home. They proceeded to the street much in the manner of frustrated and revealed assassins. The crime of trespass on another boy's place was still a crime when they had only accepted the other boy's **cordial** invitation.... (*The Monster*)

   A **cordial** invitation is
   (a.) amiable   c. angry
   b. saccharine   d. commanding

Interactive Quiz

Snap the code, or go to **vocabularyworkshop.com**

Note that not all of the 20 unit words are used in this passage. *Harry*, *plaintiff*, *probe*, *quarry*, and *subterfuge* are not included in the passage.

*Read the following selection, taking note of the **boldface** words and their contexts. These words are among those you will be studying in Unit 15. As you complete the exercises in this unit, it may help to refer to the way the words are used below.*

CCSS Vocabulary: 4; Reading (Informational Text): 4, 6. (See pp. T14–15.)

Jesse Owens: 1913–1980
<Obituary>

April 1, 1980
by Mindy K. Valentine

Olympic hero Jesse Owens died yesterday in Tucson, Arizona. The cause was cancer.

Jesse Owens's story and his **legion** of achievements is compelling. The African-American track-and-field luminary captured four gold medals and set three records at the 1936 Olympics in Berlin, Germany, and his astounding achievements shattered the Nazi ideology of a so-called master race.

James Cleveland Owens was born in the segregated South, in Oakville, Alabama, in 1913. His grandparents had been enslaved, and his parents were sharecroppers who struggled to feed their children. Hoping to improve its prospects, the family resettled in Cleveland, Ohio, when J.C. was nine years old. At this time "J.C." became "Jesse"—a teacher misunderstood his strong Southern drawl when taking attendance, and the nickname stuck.

A coach in junior high recognized young Jesse's **dormant** talents and launched his track-and-field career. As a teenager, Jesse set or tied national high school records, and as a student at Ohio State University, the "Buckeye Bullet" was invincible, breaking and setting world records.

In 1936, Jesse Owens and his teammates journeyed to Berlin, Germany, to compete against the world in the Summer Olympics. Adolf Hitler was using the Games to showcase Nazi propaganda and advance his theories of racial superiority. His intentions were clear, but despite the official line, some Germans embraced Owens. One in particular, fellow Olympian Luz Long, demonstrated that not all Germans were **knaves** and villains. Owens had stepped over the start line, a fault, while trying to qualify for the finals in the long jump. This mistake **actuated** Long's helpful intervention. Following Long's advice, Owens placed a towel in front of the start line and jumped from there, keeping a safe distance from the line, and **averting** another fault and disqualification. Later, Long died a **combatant** in the German army during World War II.

Jesse Owens won four gold medals and the admiration of the world.

Legend has it that Hitler openly **spurned** Owens at the medal ceremony, but according to some historians, this part of the story is **dubious**. Owens denied that Hitler's **boorish** behavior was directed solely at him, as other African-American athletes were also present, and six of the 10 black athletes won individual gold. But news accounts said Owens bore the **brunt** of the snub, and the legend endured. Despite the achievements of Owens and his teammates, Hitler was **impenitent**; his belief in Aryan supremacy never wavered. Newsreels show him **haranguing** huge crowds about German superiority.

Owens returned home in triumph to great acclaim and a ticker-tape parade in his honor, but reality threatened to negate his achievements. In the United States, he was still a second-class citizen whom many wanted to bring down or **abase**.

Only after a **protracted** delay of several decades did he get his due. Despite setbacks, Owens was known for his grace and **liberality**, and also for his generosity to and support of young people. He started a successful national program to involve young people in track and field that enhanced his own stellar reputation.

Belatedly, Jesse Owens's own country officially recognized the significance of his achievements. He was named a Presidential Goodwill Ambassador, and he received the Medal of Freedom and Living Legend Award.

Owens is survived by his wife, Ruth, and his three daughters. His body will lie in state at the Capitol Rotunda tomorrow before his burial in Cleveland, Ohio. No further details are available.

iWords

Snap the code, or go to **vocabularyworkshop.com**

Jesse Owens and Luz Long at the Berlin Olympics.

Jessie Owens traveled the country for public speaking engagements.

Definitions

Note the spelling, pronunciation, part(s) of speech, and definition(s) of each of the following words. Then write the word in the blank spaces in the illustrative sentence(s) following. Finally, study the lists of synonyms and antonyms.

1. abase
(ə bās')

(v.) to lower in esteem, degrade; to humble

My friend refused to _____ **abase** _____ herself by admitting to something she had not done.

SYNONYMS: lower, humiliate, prostrate, demean
ANTONYMS: elevate, ennoble, exalt

2. actuate
(ak' chü āt)

(v.) to move to action; to impel

A third bad accident at the notorious intersection finally _____ **actuated** _____ an angry community protest.

SYNONYMS: incite, instigate

3. avert
(ə vərt')

(v.) to turn aside, turn away; to prevent, avoid

Rigorous training of the new lifeguards will quite probably _____ **avert** _____ several tragedies each summer.

SYNONYMS: stop, deflect, ward off
ANTONYMS: invite, induce, provoke

4. boorish
(bür' ish)

(adj.) rude, unrefined; clumsy

Her musical genius was rivaled only by her legendary _____ **boorish** _____ behavior in public.

SYNONYMS: vulgar, crude, uncouth, ill-mannered, gauche
ANTONYMS: suave, urbane, polished, courtly, well-bred

5. brunt
(brənt)

(n.) the main impact, force, or burden

Fortunately, a sparsely populated area bore the _____ **brunt** _____ of the hurricane.

SYNONYMS: blow, shock
ANTONYMS: aftershock, aftermath, repercussion

6. combatant
(kəm bat' ənt)

(n.) a fighter; (adj.) engaged in fighting

Several times the referee had to step in and separate the two _____ **combatants** _____ after the bell rang.

The _____ **combatant** _____ forces from France and England met on the fields near Agincourt.

SYNONYMS: (n.) soldier, disputant, warrior; (adj.) hostile, battling
ANTONYMS: (n.) civilian; (adj.) peaceful, neutral

CCSS Vocabulary: 4.c., 4.d. (See pp. T14–15.)

7. dormant
(dôr′ mənt)

(*adj.*) inactive; in a state of suspension; sleeping

The warm spring sun stirred the _____dormant_____ daffodil bulbs we planted in the park last fall.

SYNONYMS: resting, still, quiescent
ANTONYMS: awake, active, lively, productive

8. dubious
(dü′ bē əs)

(*adj.*) causing uncertainty or suspicion; in a doubtful or uncertain state of mind, hesitant

Experts have said that the manuscript first attributed to Mark Twain was of _____dubious_____ authenticity.

SYNONYMS: questionable, suspect, unsettled, undecided
ANTONYMS: certain, positive, indubitable, reliable

9. harangue
(hə raŋ′)

(*v.*) to deliver a loud, ranting speech; (*n.*) a loud speech

From the moment we walked in, our math teacher began to _____harangue_____ us about our midterm exam scores.

The speaker was supposed to discuss the criminal justice system, but delivered a _____harangue_____ against lawyers.

SYNONYMS: (*v.*) rant, lecture; (*n.*) diatribe
ANTONYMS: (*n.*) whisper, murmur, undertone

10. harry
(har′ ē)

(*v.*) to make a destructive raid on; to torment, harass

My parents are forever _____harrying_____ me about cleaning up my room and playing music too loudly.

SYNONYMS: hound, pillage, ravage

11. impenitent
(im pen′ ə tənt)

(*adj.*) not feeling remorse or sorrow for errors or offenses

His _____impenitent_____ demeanor during the trial probably encouraged the judge to impose a harsh sentence.

SYNONYMS: remorseless, unrepentant, incorrigible
ANTONYMS: ashamed, remorseful, contrite, apologetic

12. knave
(nāv)

(*n.*) a tricky, unprincipled, or deceitful fellow

Her friends always knew that _____knave_____ of a first husband was only after her inheritance.

SYNONYMS: rascal, rogue, miscreant

13. legion
(lē′ jən)

(*n.*) a large military force; any large group or number; (*adj.*) many, numerous

It would undoubtedly take a _____legion_____ of skilled mechanics to repair an old rattletrap like my car.

Her reasons for not attending the Community Gourmet Club's "Cooking with Beets Night" were _____legion_____.

SYNONYMS: (*n.*) multitude, host, throng, division, regiment
ANTONYMS: (*n.*) squad, platoon; (*adj.*) few, sparse

14. liberality
(lib ə ral′ ə tē)

(*n.*) generosity, generous act; breadth of mind or outlook

The dean's well-known _____liberality_____ allowed an atmosphere of spirited debate to flourish at the college.

SYNONYMS: magnanimity, broad-mindedness
ANTONYMS: stinginess, miserliness, narrow-mindedness

15. plaintiff
(plān′ tif)

(*n.*) one who begins a lawsuit

His lawyers objected that the _____plaintiff_____ rather than the defendant was being put on trial.

SYNONYM: complainant; ANTONYM: defendant

16. probe
(prōb)

(*v.*) to examine, investigate thoroughly; (*n.*) an investigation; a device used to explore or examine

An auditor was brought in to _____probe_____ the company's financial irregularities.

An unmanned _____probe_____ was sent to examine the geology of the Martian surface.

SYNONYMS: (*v.*) explore; (*n.*) inquiry, detector
ANTONYMS: (*v.*) hide; (*n.*) cover-up, whitewash

17. protract
(prō trakt′)

(*v.*) to draw out or lengthen in space or time

Militants opposed to the peace treaty attempted to _____protract_____ the negotiations.

SYNONYMS: elongate, spin out
ANTONYMS: contract, compress, concentrate

18. quarry
(kwär′ ē)

(*v.*) to cut or take from (or as if from) a quarry; (*n.*) a place from which stone is taken; something that is hunted or pursued

The Internet makes it easier to _____quarry_____ information from the world's vast supply.

Bargain hunters armed with sale ads raced through the store, urgently seeking their _____quarry_____.

SYNONYMS: (*n.*) prey, game, victim, excavation, mine
ANTONYMS: (*n.*) hunter, predator

19. spurn
(spərn)

(*v.*) to refuse with scorn, disdain

He _____spurned_____ a full scholarship offered by a small college to go to a big state university instead.

SYNONYMS: turn down, decline, snub, repudiate
ANTONYMS: accept, welcome, greet

20. subterfuge
(səb′ tər fyüj)

(*n.*) an excuse or trick for escaping or hiding something

The accused embezzler's "heart attack" could be a clever _____subterfuge_____ to avoid his upcoming trial.

SYNONYMS: dodge, blind, deception, artifice

C CCSS Vocabulary: 4.c. (See pp. T14–15.)

Choosing the Right Word

Select the **boldface** word that better completes each sentence. You might refer to the selection on pages 184–185 to see how most of these words are used in context.

1. During the Great Depression millions of Americans were out of work, as much of the nation's productive capacity lay (**dormant**, **impenitent**).

2. When the referee called back a touchdown by the home team, he had to bear the (**probe**, **brunt**) of the crowd's anger.

3. Whenever I even suspect that a gory scene is about to start in a movie, I (**avert**, **actuate**) my eyes or even cover them with my hands.

4. After World War II, the United States and the Soviet Union became locked in a(n) (**protracted**, **actuated**) struggle known as the Cold War.

Soup kitchens and bread lines were the only source of food for countless unemployed people during the Great Depression of the 1930s.

5. Your (**liberality**, **subterfuge**) is to be admired, but it must be controlled so that it is not out of proportion to your means.

6. At a time when we need good will and cooperation, nothing will be gained by an emotional (**quarry**, **harangue**) about old abuses and mistakes.

7. People who think only of themselves, with no concern for the feelings of others, are bound to be (**brunt**, **boorish**).

8. The applicant's list of accomplishments, which went on for two pages, was (**dubious**, **impenitent**) at best.

9. I think that we can settle this dispute in a friendly way, without either of us becoming a defendant or a (**quarry**, **plaintiff**).

10. The dinner to celebrate the 50th anniversary of Mrs. Roth's teaching career was attended by a (**legion**, **probe**) of her former students.

11. For many years after the Civil War, thousands of (**combatants**, **legions**) in the great battle of Gettysburg met in annual reunions.

12. We'll need to (**quarry**, **probe**) for the large stones necessary for securing the foundation.

13. He pretended to be speechless with anger, but we recognized this as a (**subterfuge**, **harangue**) to avoid answering the charges against him.

14. Although we were fairly certain that the ice would be thick enough to hold us, we used a long stick as a (**subterfuge**, **probe**) to see if any part of the ice was too thin.

15. A new popular singing idol will often (**actuate**, **abase**) changes in clothing fashions.

16. I was ashamed of my poor behavior at the debate and hope I did not (**dormant, abase**) myself in the eyes of the moderator.

17. In the school library, all activity seemed to have become (**dormant, spurned**) as students napped with their heads and arms draped across desks.

18. The detective story was so cleverly constructed that the character whom we took to be the pursuer turned out to be the (**quarry, brunt**).

19. We began with confidence in his success in the election, but as he made one mistake after another, we grew more and more (**dubious, abased**).

20. Let us not (**spurn, avert**) our attention from the sufferings of the people living in the slums of our community.

21. Since his absurd scheme was never really intended to harm us, we regard him as more of a fool than a (**quarry, knave**).

22. We demand that the committee be made up of legislators who will (**actuate, probe**) fearlessly into the causes of the energy crisis.

23. Since the prisoner remained defiantly (**impenitent, boorish**), the review panel saw no reason for granting him parole.

24. A pack of reporters (**averted, harried**) the senator with pointed and persistent questions even as he was being whisked into his limousine.

25. How can that heartless beauty (**combat, spurn**) my offers of devotion!

Synonyms

*Choose the word from this unit that is the same or most nearly the same in meaning as the **boldface** word or expression in the phrase. Write that word on the line. Use a dictionary if necessary.*

1. the **accuser** took the stand to testify — plaintiff

2. a conflict **extended** by cease-fire violations — protracted

3. escape by means of a **ruse** involving false noses — subterfuge

4. a **tirade** prompted by a messy room — harangue

5. an attempt to **trigger** impeachment proceedings — actuate

6. an arts foundation famous for its **largesse** — liberality

7. a new contract that **precluded** a labor dispute — averted

8. mined limestone from a large **pit** near the site — quarry

9. investigators who will **scrutinize** their files — probe

10. tried to **pester** her mother into changing her mind — harry

The synonyms and antonyms here do not appear on the Definitions page.

15

Antonyms

*Choose the word from this unit that is most nearly opposite in meaning to the **boldface** word or expression in the phrase. Write that word on the line. Use a dictionary if necessary.*

1. will **appease** the pompous politician _____ harry _____
2. maintained **transparency** during the audit _____ subterfuge _____
3. **conceal** the evidence _____ probe _____
4. interviewed the **accused** after the verdict _____ plaintiff _____
5. the determination and stamina of the **pursuer** _____ quarry _____

Completing the Sentence

From the words in this unit, choose the one that best completes each of the following sentences. Write the word in the space provided.

1. Divers from the salvage ship will try to _____ probe _____ the ocean floor where the Confederate warship sank in 1863.

2. In A.D. 79, the sudden and violent eruption of a volcano that had been _____ dormant _____ for many years destroyed Pompeii in two days.

3. The entire boardwalk at the beach was smashed to bits when the full _____ brunt _____ of the hurricane struck it.

4. Because his feelings were hurt, he _____ spurned _____ any attempts on my part to provide help.

5. We learned that the bizarre sequence of events was _____ actuated _____ by an accidental tug on the switching device.

6. On the surface she seemed stubbornly _____ impenitent _____, but secretly she regretted the damage her thoughtlessness had caused.

7. The soldiers of the mighty Roman _____ legions _____ were organized in battle units called cohorts and maniples.

8. Why should you _____ abase _____ yourself by begging to be admitted to a club made up of snobs and phonies?

9. As a lawyer for the _____ plaintiff _____, you will have full opportunity to cross-examine the witnesses for the defendant.

10. The police were quickly ordered to the scene as a precautionary measure to _____ avert _____ a threatened riot.

11. The two _____**combatants**_____ fought it out with words rather than with fists.

12. The bloodhounds pursued their human _____**quarry**_____ through the swamps.

13. Bands of guerillas _____**harried**_____ the straggling soldiers as they retreated in disarray.

14. The "Speakers' Corner" in London's Hyde Park is home to soapbox orators who _____**harangue**_____ idlers and passersby.

15. His many donations of large sums of money to organizations dedicated to relieving world hunger are evidence of his _____**liberality**_____.

16. The Mississippi riverboats were home to crooks and _____**knaves**_____ of every description, from cardsharps to confidence men.

17. Our planned stopover in Denver was unexpectedly _____**protracted**_____ when a blizzard prevented us from leaving the city for days.

18. Fortunately, the loud and generally _____**boorish**_____ behavior of a few of the guests did not spoil the party for the rest of us.

19. Isn't friendship with a person who mistrusts you of _____**dubious**_____ value?

20. His illness was a(n) _____**subterfuge**_____ to get out of taking me to the dance!

Writing: Words in Action

Answers to both prompts will vary.

1. Look back at "Jesse Owens: 1913–1980" (pages 184–185). Which of Jesse Owens's accomplishments most likely brought him national fame and accolades? Which of his characteristics do you think are most deserving of admiration? Write a brief character sketch of Jesse Owens in which you focus on the dominant traits that make him an admired figure. Use at least two details from the passage and three unit words to support your claim.

2. *Hero* is a word that is used in many contexts. There are sports heroes and celebrity heroes, fictional heroes and historical heroes. What is a true hero, though? Is it someone who shows courage, someone who is exceptionally talented at something, or someone who accomplishes something great? In a brief essay, present your definition of a hero, and support your definition with several examples from your observations, studies, reading (refer to pages 184–185), or personal experience. Write at least three paragraphs, and use three or more words from this unit.

Writing prompt #2 is modeled on that of standardized tests.

　　CCSS Vocabulary: 6; Writing: 1.c., 2.d. (See pp. T14–15.)

Vocabulary in Context: Informational Text for Unit 15 is available online at **vocabularyworkshop.com**.

15

Vocabulary in Context

Literary Text

The following excerpts are from Mary Wollstonecraft Shelley's novel Frankenstein. *Some of the words you have studied in this unit appear in **boldface** type. Complete each statement below the excerpt by circling the letter of the correct answer.*

1. "Miserable himself that he may render no other wretched, he ought to die. The task of his destruction was mine, but I have failed. When **actuated** by selfish and vicious motives, I asked you to undertake my unfinished work, and I renew this request now, when I am only induced by reason and virtue."

To be **actuated** is to be

a. assisted   **c.** driven
b. obvious   **d.** hidden

2. The idea of renewing my labors did not for one instant occur to me; the threat I had heard weighed on my thoughts, but I did not reflect that a voluntary act of mine could **avert** it.

If you **avert** something, you

a. preclude it   **c.** conquer it
b. weather it   **d.** approach it

3. "The light became more and more oppressive to me, and the heat wearying me as I walked, I sought a place where I could receive shade.... I lay by the side of a brook resting from my fatigue, until I felt tormented by hunger and thirst. This roused me from my nearly **dormant** state, and I ate some berries which I found hanging on the trees or lying on the ground."

Boris Karloff plays the monster in the 1931 film *Frankenstein*.

Someone who is in a **dormant** state is NOT

a. sleepy   **c.** still
b. quiet   **d.** alert

4. ...[M]y residence there being no longer conducive to my improvements, I thought of returning to my friends and my native town, when an incident happened that **protracted** my stay.

Something that has been **protracted** has been

a. confused   **c.** shortened
b. prolonged   **d.** enlivened

5. "All men hate the wretched; how, then, must I be hated, who am miserable beyond all living things! Yet you, my creator, detest and **spurn** me, thy creature, to whom thou art bound by ties only dissoluble by the annihilation of one of us."

To **spurn** is to

a. strike   **c.** reject
b. comfort   **d.** forget

Interactive Quiz

Snap the code, or go to **vocabularyworkshop.com**

Vocabulary for Comprehension

*Read the following selection in which some of the words you have studied in Units 13–15 appear in **boldface** type. Then answer the questions on page 195.*

The museum that is described in the following passage features "art too bad to be ignored."

(Line)

One of New York's many superb art museums is the Museum of Modern Art (MOMA). MOMA showcases art and design of notable
(5) originality and excellence from the twentieth and twenty-first centuries.

Meanwhile, to the north, in Boston, lurks a lesser-known yet formidable institution. This rising star vying for
(10) admission to the small **clique** of the world's leading museums goes, not by MOMA, but by MOBA. It is the Museum of Bad Art.

According to its statement of
(15) purpose, the mission of MOBA is to "bring the worst art to the widest of audiences" by being dedicated to "the collection, preservation, exhibition, and celebration of bad
(20) art in all its glory." And what, you might ask, constitutes bad art? What **perverse** criteria do MOBA staffers apply when judging a submitted work?
(25) For MOBA, museum-quality bad art must be compelling. It must be so bad that the viewer can't stop looking at it, yet somehow **congenial** at the same time. In the words of the
(30) administrators, works must have "a special quality that sets them apart

from the merely incompetent." Highly prized qualities include no artistic control, courage and enthusiasm,
(35) and an inappropriate frame.

The MOBA permanent collection (housed in the basement of a community theater) exemplifies these standards. Many of the works
(40) have an unrivaled **pedigree**, having been rescued from Boston-area dumpsters. "Lucy in the Field with Flowers" (a scene of **rustic** strangeness), "Peter the Kitty," and
(45) "Two Trees in Love" are just a few of MOBA's worst.

In addition, the museum has mounted many unusual exhibitions since its 1993 founding, including
(50) "Awash with Bad Art: The World's First Drive Thru Art Gallery and Car Wash." And recent acquisitions are described as "the worst yet in the museum's long, proud tradition of
(55) ever-dropping standards."

The Museum of Bad Art offers a refreshing, funny alternative to the world's collections of "ordinary" masterpieces, which are **profuse** in
(60) number.

CCSS Vocabulary: 4.a.; Reading (Informational Text): 2, 4, 6. (See pp. T14–15.)

1. Which of the following titles best describes the content of the passage?
   a. Drive Thru Art
   b. Twentieth-Century Art
   c. Ordinary Masterpieces
   d. Ever-Dropping Standards
   e. Gloriously Bad Art

2. Which word best describes the tone of the passage?
   a. scornful
   b. nostalgic
   c. pretentious
   d. lighthearted
   e. sarcastic

3. The meaning of **clique** (line 10) is
   a. coterie
   b. union
   c. claque
   d. number
   e. organization

4. **Perverse** (line 22) is best defined as
   a. imaginative
   b. strange
   c. rude
   d. persistent
   e. contrary

5. The author uses the word **perverse** in line 22 to describe MOBA criteria because it is
   a. inappropriate to spoof MOMA
   b. unusual to have standards for badness
   c. rude to make fun of artists
   d. impossible to have compelling bad art
   e. wrong to have standards for judging art

6. The meaning of **congenial** (line 28) is
   a. ridiculous
   b. understandable
   c. pleasant
   d. laughable
   e. sociable

7. MOBA will have achieved its mission if upon viewing a picture a visitor says
   a. "I'm glad I didn't pay to see this."
   b. "There's nothing wrong with that picture."
   c. "That picture's not worth looking at."
   d. "This is a waste of time."
   e. "That piece is seriously bad."

8. **Pedigree** (line 40) most nearly means
   a. history
   b. title
   c. receipt
   d. education
   e. appearance

9. The meaning of **rustic** (line 43) is
   a. rube
   b. countrified
   c. corroded
   d. autumnal
   e. natural

10. The following places are all likely sources for works in MOBA EXCEPT
    a. a flea market
    b. a trash bin
    c. MOMA
    d. a thrift shop
    e. a garage sale

11. **Profuse** (line 59) most nearly means
    a. serious
    b. abundant
    c. scanty
    d. redundant
    e. profound

12. Evidently the founders of MOBA
    a. cannot get jobs in the fine art world
    b. have all produced bad art
    c. know how to showcase fine art
    d. cannot recognize fine art
    e. enjoy lampooning the fine art world

Two-Word Completions

Select the pair of words that best complete the meaning of each of the following passages.

1. Most dictators don't just address their audiences; they _____ them. Their words are not meant to soothe or enlighten; they are designed to _____ the listener to violence and hatred.
   - **a.** harangue . . . incite
   - **b.** probe . . . harry
   - **c.** apportion . . . reconcile
   - **d.** improvise . . . embroil

2. Before the curtain goes up on the first act, the orchestra plays a short _____ depicting in musical terms the _____ ideals of the high-minded knight who is the hero of the opera.
   - **a.** debacle . . . buoyant
   - **b.** prelude . . . lofty
   - **c.** brunt . . . glib
   - **d.** pedigree . . . threadbare

3. As Great Britain's power and prestige began to _____ and lose their luster, subjects all over the empire rose up to demand release from the onerous _____ that bound them so firmly to the motherland.
   - **a.** cleave . . . subterfuges
   - **b.** pall . . . cornerstones
   - **c.** wane . . . shackles
   - **d.** concede . . . cliques

4. Over the years, the _____ of our patrons and sponsors has kept the wolf from our door more than once. Without their generous support, I honestly don't know how our little theater company would have _____ disaster.
   - **a.** clique . . . reconciled
   - **b.** versatility . . . spurned
   - **c.** liberality . . . averted
   - **d.** migration . . . shackled

5. We can go ahead with this project just as soon as we know we have the money to finance it in the bank. Unfortunately, the plan must remain _____ as long as the necessary financial resources are _____.
   - **a.** untenable . . . profuse
   - **b.** dormant . . . dubious
   - **c.** sordid . . . haphazard
   - **d.** bona fide . . . perverse

6. "You'll usually win a debate if your arguments are valid and convincing," I observed. "But if your position is _____, you'll eventually be forced to _____ defeat."
   - **a.** untenable . . . concede
   - **b.** dubious . . . spurn
   - **c.** bona fide . . . avert
   - **d.** glib . . . improvise

7. Though urban life may suit some people to a tee, I have always found a _____ environment more _____.
   - **a.** lofty . . . protracted
   - **b.** sordid . . . perverse
   - **c.** cordial . . . haphazard
   - **d.** rustic . . . congenial

Adages

In the essay "Seven Wonders" (see pages 174–175), the author quotes an old Arabic saying: "Man fears time, but time fears the Pyramids."

"Man fears time, but time fears the Pyramids" is an adage that uses a few words to make its point: that human beings, being mortal, are at the mercy of time, while monuments like the pyramids have resisted time's ravages. An **adage** is a short saying that conveys a general truth in a figurative, rather than literal, way. Adages can be humorous, folksy, philosophical, or profound. Since their meanings are not always obvious or self-explanatory, they must be learned, just like new or unfamiliar words.

Choosing the Right Adage

Read each sentence. Use context clues to figure out the meaning of each adage in **boldface** *print. Then write the letter of the definition for the adage in the sentence.*

1. I always work on my math homework with a friend, since **two heads are better than one**. ___f___

2. When he told me that people often say he's rude, I responded, "Well, **if the shoe fits, wear it**." ___i___

3. **Where there's a will there's a way**, so I'm sure you'll come up with tickets to that sold-out concert. ___c___

4. Those who don't realize that some things are **too good to be true** often fall for financial scams. ___b___

5. If **practice makes perfect**, I don't understand why I still belly-flop every time I jump off the high dive. ___h___

6. It must be true that **birds of a feather flock together**, since Alex and Maria, who share a love for blues music and poetry, are inseparable. ___a___

7. When you leave that job, do it on good terms; **don't burn your bridges behind you**. ___e___

8. Since **no news is good news**, it's a good sign when we don't hear from my troublemaking cousin. ___j___

9. I should have started cleaning out the garage months ago. Well, it's **better late than never**. ___g___

10. My brother checks his phone incessantly for text messages from his girlfriend. I guess he's never learned that **a watched pot never boils**. ___d___

a. People who enjoy the same sorts of things enjoy spending time together.

b. Be wary of offers that seem too perfect.

c. If you want something bad enough, you can find a way to do it.

d. If you impatiently wait for something, it will seem to take forever.

e. Don't leave bad feelings behind when you move on.

f. Teamwork can make it easier to get things done.

g. Starting late is better than never starting at all.

h. By practicing something over and over again, you are bound to improve.

i. If a criticism applies to you, admit it.

j. The absence of bad news means that things are okay for now.

Writing with Adages

Find the meaning of each adage. (Use an online or print dictionary if necessary.) Then write a sentence for each adage. **Answers will vary.**

1. Don't bite the hand that feeds you. **Sample response:**
Don't bite the hand that feeds you by insulting your staunchest supporters.

2. There's no such thing as a free lunch.

3. It will all come out in the wash.

4. An ounce of prevention is worth a pound of cure.

5. One bad apple spoils the whole barrel.

6. Don't count your chickens before they've hatched.

7. Two wrongs don't make a right.

8. It's like looking for a needle in a haystack.

9. There's no time like the present.

10. Nothing ventured, nothing gained.

11. Beauty is only skin deep.

12. Actions speak louder than words.

Denotation and Connotation

A **denotation** is the literal but *neutral* meaning of a word—the formal way it is defined in a dictionary. However, words often mean more than their dictionary definitions would suggest.

As users of language, we make emotional associations to certain words. We are pleased to be called *clever* but not so pleased to be called *wily*. That is because each word, though it shares a similar denotation, has a very different **connotation**—an implied meaning that we associate with the word. That connotation can be either positive (*clever*) or negative (*wily*).

Consider these synonyms for the neutral word *friendly*:

> *cordial* *congenial* *ingratiating* *obsequious*

Cordial and *congenial* have positive connotations, while *ingratiating* and *obsequious* have negative connotations, suggesting an exaggerated and insincere friendliness.

> **Think:** If you greet the new principal in a polite and friendly way, you are being cordial or congenial; if you greet her in an exaggeratedly friendly and flattering way, you are being ingratiating or obsequious.

Look at these examples of words that are similar in denotation but have different connotations.

NEUTRAL	POSITIVE	NEGATIVE
start	activate	incite
persuasive	convincing	glib
strategy	stratagem	subterfuge

Understanding the sometimes subtle connotations of words allows you to write and speak more precisely and accurately so that you can get your point across with the assurance that you are saying exactly what you mean and will be understood.

Shades of Meaning

Write a plus sign (+) in the box if the word has a positive connotation.
Write a minus sign (–) if the word has a negative connotation. Put a zero (0)
if the word is neutral.

1. migration `0`   **2.** bona fide `+`   **3.** buoyant `+`   **4.** perverse `–`

5. rancid `–`   **6.** prelude `0`   **7.** sordid `–`   **8.** untenable `–`

9. versatile `+`   **10.** vindicate `+`   **11.** annex `0`   **12.** cordial `+`

13. pallor `–`   **14.** cornerstone `+`   **15.** exonerate `+`   **16.** devitalize `–`

Expressing the Connotation

Read each sentence. Select the word in parentheses that expresses the connotation (positive, negative, or neutral) given at the beginning of the sentence.

neutral
1. She used to have a beautiful wardrobe of designer clothing, so you can imagine my shock when I saw that the clothes she was wearing were (**threadbare, worn**).

negative
2. The (**unplanned, haphazard**) presentation turned out to be informative and worthwhile.

positive
3. If we can (**reconcile, settle**) our differences tonight over a nice meal, I will be very relieved.

negative
4. The (**precipitous, sheer**) side of that cliff inspires some rock climbers, but I am just as happy to stay away from it.

neutral
5. When I came out of my dressing room, I was met by a (**group, legion**) of screaming fans.

negative
6. Our organization's fund-raiser was more than a disappointment: it was a complete (**failure, debacle**).

positive
7. The new novelist has a very impressive (**pedigree, lineage**) that includes successful writers on both her mother's and father's sides of the family.

positive
8. The queen's (**liberality, munificence**), demonstrated by the way she reaches out to people of all classes, is her most admirable quality.

Challenge: Using Connotation

Choose vocabulary words from Units 13–15 to replace the highlighted words in the sentences below. Then explain how the connotation of the replacement word changes the tone of the sentence. **Answers will vary.**

ad infinitum	spurned	apportioned
boorish	improvised	quarry

1. The assassin observed her **target** _____quarry_____ for hours, standing patiently behind the curtain until he went to sleep. **Sample response:** *Quarry,* **which implies the idea of a hunt, gives the sentence a suspenseful, dramatic tone.**

2. He **rejected** _____spurned_____ our offer of a job, so you can cross him off our list of candidates forever, as far as I am concerned. **Sample response: If someone has not merely *rejected* a job offer but *spurned* it, he has rejected it in a contemptuous way that is insulting to the person who has offered the job.**

3. That opera star is often **unmannered** _____boorish_____ during meet-and-greet sessions prior to his performances, so be forewarned. **Sample response:** *Unmannered,* **while not complimentary, is less harshly critical than *boorish,* which implies that a person is very unpleasant and rude.**

Classical Roots

vert, vers—to turn

This root appears in **versatile** (page 168). The literal meaning of this word is "able to be turned." In modern usage it now refers to the ability to turn from one task to another with ease. Some other words based on the same root are listed below.

adversity	conversion	divert	reversion
aversion	diversion	invert	version

From the list of words above, choose the one that corresponds to each of the brief definitions below. Write the word in the blank space in the illustrative sentence below the definition. Use an online or print dictionary if necessary.

1. a change in condition or belief (*"turning toward"*)

The physical _____conversion_____ of solid ice into liquid water is known as melting.

2. to turn upside down; to change direction

The trick required them to _____invert_____ a glass of water without spilling any of its contents.

3. a turning aside; any distraction of attention; amusement, entertainment; pastime

Many students find athletics to be an excellent _____diversion_____ from the academic pressures of school.

4. a strong dislike; a thing disliked (*"turning against"*)

I'm not really sure why I've developed such a strong _____aversion_____ to country music.

5. distress, misfortune, hardship

It is said that _____adversity_____ can make victory sweeter.

6. a return to a former state, belief, or condition; a reversal

After some false starts, the coach made a(n) _____reversion_____ to a more traditional practice routine.

7. to turn aside; to entertain, amuse

A magician's most important task is to _____divert_____ the attention of an audience from the sleight of hand that makes the trick work.

8. a particular form of something; an account of an incident

After much gossip and speculation, we were eager to hear the official _____version_____ of the story.

Synonyms

Select the two words or expressions that are most nearly the same in meaning.

1. **a.** rancid **(b.)** garbled **(c.)** confused **d.** arbitrary

2. **(a.)** rugged **b.** rustic **(c.)** rough **d.** pliant

3. **(a.)** increase **(b.)** escalate **c.** venture **d.** sever

4. **(a.)** hew **b.** hamper **c.** educate **(d.)** cling

5. **a.** scream **(b.)** draw back **c.** adjourn **(d.)** recoil

6. **(a.)** destroy **b.** build up **(c.)** annihilate **d.** torture

7. **a.** expulsion **(b.)** advent **(c.)** arrival **d.** opposition

8. **(a.)** institute **b.** end **c.** improve **(d.)** begin

9. **a.** liability **(b.)** conciseness **(c.)** brevity **d.** prelude

10. **(a.)** introduction **b.** adherent **c.** semblance **(d.)** preamble

11. **a.** protest **b.** quaver **(c.)** behave **(d.)** comport

12. **a.** sweet **(b.)** candid **(c.)** outspoken **d.** alert

13. **(a.)** profuse **b.** scarce **c.** sincere **(d.)** plentiful

14. **(a.)** supporter **(b.)** proponent **c.** opponent **d.** plaintiff

15. **a.** awkward **(b.)** skilled **c.** concerted **(d.)** adept

Antonyms

Select the two words that are most nearly opposite in meaning.

16. **a.** apportion **(b.)** rejuvenate **c.** incite **(d.)** devitalize

17. **(a.)** emancipate **b.** fortify **(c.)** shackle **d.** tantalize

18. **a.** versatile **(b.)** bona fide **(c.)** bogus **d.** erratic

19. **(a.)** embroil **(b.)** disentangle **c.** defray **d.** abscond

20. **a.** annex **b.** usurp **(c.)** surmount **(d.)** succumb

21. **(a.)** lucid **(b.)** opaque **c.** lithe **d.** militant

22. **a.** commandeer **(b.)** actuate **c.** hoodwink **(d.)** terminate

23. **a.** languid **b.** illustrious **(c.)** haphazard **(d.)** circumspect

24. **a.** glib **(b.)** lofty **(c.)** abased **d.** alien

25. **a.** tenacious **(b.)** repugnant **(c.)** comely **d.** cumbersome

Analogies

Select the item that best completes the comparison.

26. feint is to **deception** as
a. muddle is to disorder
b. deadlock is to security
c. dilemma is to solution
d. altercation is to agreement

27. brigand is to **robbery** as
a. alien is to travel
b. adherent is to trophy
c. vagrant is to settle
d. marauder is to pillage

28. affluent is to **pauper** as
a. mediocre is to worker
b. cherubic is to angel
c. eminent is to nonentity
d. spurious is to imposter

29. wood is to **hew** as
a. hammer is to nail
b. shovel is to hole
c. banana is to fruit
d. bread is to slice

30. hoodwink is to **deception** as
a. revile is to encouragement
b. reprimand is to approval
c. taunt is to praise
d. supplant is to replacement

31. pompous is to **self-importance** as
a. diligent is to unconcern
b. boorish is to insensitivity
c. arbitrary is to reason
d. impoverished is to wealth

32. brawny is to **muscle** as
a. lithe is to speed
b. languid is to vigor
c. skeptical is to assurance
d. wily is to cunning

33. fated is to **destiny** as
a. posthumous is to status
b. superfluous is to necessity
c. accidental is to planning
d. random is to chance

Two-Word Completions

Select the word pair from among the choices given.

34. The child kept up a steady _____ as she described to her stuffed toys the _____ over which she was Queen.
a. prototype . . . gluttony
b. altercation . . . rift
c. monologue . . . realm
d. catalyst . . . exodus

35. Although Scott inherited a great deal of money, he lived as a(n) _____ and never _____ a cent.
a. vagrant . . . condoned
b. accomplice . . . impoverished
c. envoy . . . relinquished
d. pauper . . . squandered

36. My dog Fitz is small, but he has a(n) _____ attitude and gets into scuffles that he could have easily _____.
a. pugnacious . . . averted
b. boorish . . . actuated
c. cherubic . . . forestalled
d. preposterous . . . facilitated

37. Though he gained fame _____, nobody thought he was an _____ artist while he was alive.
a. posthumously . . . eminent
b. incorrigibly . . . lucrative
c. superfluously . . . intrepid
d. illegibly . . . sprightly

Supplying Words in Context

To complete each sentence, select the best word from among the choices given. Not all words in the word bank will be used. You may modify the word form as necessary.

abridge	wily	untenable	terse
recoup	immunity	sardonic	fodder
pilfer	malign	stagnant	impair
taunt	depreciation	exorcise	pensive

38. He who begins by _____**pilfering**_____ pennies may end by stealing millions.

39. All that we heard from my mysterious aunt was the _____**terse**_____ message, "I have arrived."

40. His job for the next year was to _____**abridge**_____ the two-volume biography into a single book.

41. The suspect agreed to testify against the other conspirators in exchange for _____**immunity**_____ from prosecution.

42. Lack of practice will certainly _____**impair**_____ your tennis game.

43. As he presented his explanation of the causes of inflation, his position seemed to me weak and _____**untenable**_____.

interim	bleak	obstreperous	impel
despicable	access	flippant	trite
assimilate	wane	alien	debris
staccato	intricate	apex	predispose

44. His _____**flippant**_____ wisecracks were clever but in bad taste.

45. As night came on and it became much colder, the courage of the runaways _____**waned**_____.

46. We felt rather gloomy as we looked out on the _____**bleak**_____ winter scene under the weak light of the moon.

47. In the _____**interim**_____ between the two semesters, we will enjoy a brief vacation at the seashore.

48. Scattered all over the beach was _____**debris**_____ from the wrecked ship.

49. Do you realize how _____**intricate**_____ a job it is to reschedule so many programs on the spur of the moment?

Word Associations

*Select the word or expression that best completes the meaning of the sentence or answers the question, with particular reference to the meaning of the word in **boldface** type.*

50. An **invincible** team is one that has never known
a. the joy of victory
b. the agony of defeat
c. the fear of flying
d. injury or illness

51. Which description would NOT apply to a typical **metropolis**?
a. bustling
b. crowded
c. large
d. rustic

52. Which of the following might apply to a person who is **mediocre**?
a. illustrious
b. immortal
c. undistinguished
d. sterling

53. You might say **adieu**
a. when someone sneezes
b. when you arrive
c. when you leave
d. when you step on someone's toes

54. A mistake that is **grievous** is
a. unnoticed
b. simple
c. serious
d. widespread

55. We may apply the word **dormant** to
a. a poem and a song
b. a talent and a volcano
c. the moon and the stars
d. shackles and freedom

56. A person who seeks **asylum** is looking for
a. an orphan to adopt
b. an easy job
c. public office
d. protection

57. Which nickname would a **doleful** person be most likely to have?
a. Sad Sam
b. Big John
c. Little Mo
d. Broadway Joe

58. The word **horde** might be used to describe
a. an efficient group of workers
b. an individual working alone
c. an invading army
d. a symphony orchestra

59. A country in a state of **anarchy** does NOT have
a. arts and sciences
b. law and order
c. education and medicine
d. food and water

60. We can apply the word **meander** to
a. rivers and arguments
b. victories and defeats
c. sellers and buyers
d. plaintiffs and defendants

61. A word closely associated with **altercation** is
a. revision
b. adherent
c. sensible
d. argument

Choosing the Right Meaning

Read each sentence carefully. Then select the item that best completes the statement below the sentence.

62. The computer **console** was so small that I strained my eyes using it.

In line 1 the word **console** most nearly means

a. monitor   **b.** comfort   **c.** keyboard   **d.** cost

63. During the heat wave, power was **erratic** and the electricity frequently went out for 15 minutes or more.

The word **erratic** in line 1 most nearly means

a. undependable   **b.** strong   **c.** unbearable   **d.** expensive

64. When I was a child, my worried mother frequently **admonished** me against riding my bike without a helmet.

The word **admonished** in line 1 most nearly means

a. rewarded   **b.** reminded   **c.** cautioned   **d.** prevented

65. Although the price we paid for the tickets seemed **exorbitant**, the experience of seeing the musicians in a live performance was well worth the money.

In line 1 the word **exorbitant** most nearly means

a. reasonable   **b.** unproven   **c.** excessive   **d.** modest

66. Security officers never found out how the thieves were able to **access** the vaults in the basement of the bank.

The best definition for the word **access** in line 1 is

a. approach   **b.** gain entry to   **c.** visualize   **d.** locate

67. The lottery winner's flashy car, designer clothes, elaborate hairdo and entourage of newly acquired friends **reeked** of new money.

The word **reeked** in line 2 most nearly means

a. was invulnerable to   **c.** gave the impression
b. smelled unpleasant   **d.** was the opposite

68. My grandmother gave me a set of antique **cordial** glasses that had been in the family for generations.

In line 1 the word **cordial** most nearly means

a. crystal   **b.** liqueur   **c.** water   **d.** friendship

69. At the end of the long, hard trip out West, the pioneers appeared as only a **semblance** of their former selves.

In line 2 the word **semblance** most nearly means

a. fraction   **b.** relative   **c.** enemy   **d.** likeness

70. The young potatoes must be **blanched** before they are roasted in the oven.

In line 1 the word **blanched** is best defined as

a. mashed   **b.** discolored   **c.** seasoned   **d.** boiled briefly

WORD LIST

The following is a list of all the words taught in the Units of this book. The number after each entry indicates the page on which the word is defined.

abase, 186
abridge, 34
abscond, 52
access, 52
accomplice, 62
actuate, 186
ad infinitum, 166
adept, 128
adherent, 34
adieu, 90
adjourn, 24
admonish, 14
advent, 90
alien, 24
altercation, 34
anarchy, 52
annex, 176
annihilate, 62
apex, 90
apportion, 166
appreciable, 148
arbitrary, 62
arduous, 52
aspire, 128
assimilate, 90
assurance, 100
asylum, 100
atone, 72
auspicious, 52
autocratic, 148
auxiliary, 110
avert, 186

blanch, 148
blasphemy, 148
bleak, 128
bogus, 90
bona fide, 166
bondage, 72
boorish, 186
brawny, 148
brazen, 62
breach, 14
brevity, 138
brigand, 14
brunt, 186
buoyant, 166

candid, 110
catalyst, 62
cherubic, 34
chide, 128
circumspect, 14
cleave, 176
clique, 166
combatant, 186
comely, 24
commandeer, 14
compensate, 24
comport, 138
concede, 166
concerted, 148
concise, 138
condone, 34
congenial, 166
console, 100
contend, 149
cordial, 176
cornerstone, 176
credible, 72
cubicle, 110
cumbersome, 14

daunt, 52
deadlock, 14
debacle, 176
debris, 15
defray, 72
demure, 138
depreciation, 138
despicable, 128
deteriorate, 138
devitalize, 176
diffuse, 15
dilate, 100
dilemma, 15
diligent, 72
diminutive, 128
disentangle, 53
dissent, 34
dissolute, 24
divulge, 138
doleful, 72
dormant, 187
dross, 100

drudgery, 110
dubious, 187
dwindle, 100

efface, 15
emancipate, 129
embroil, 177
eminent, 35
enlightened, 139
envoy, 110
erratic, 24
erroneous, 129
escalate, 110
exodus, 62
exonerate, 177
exorbitant, 90
exorcise, 35
expedient, 111
exploit, 129
expulsion, 25
extemporaneous, 129

fabricate, 35
facilitate, 63
fated, 53
feign, 111
feint, 25
flair, 111
flippant, 101
fodder, 25
forestall, 139
fortify, 25
garble, 139
ghastly, 72
glib, 177
gluttony, 35
grievous, 111

hamper, 73
haphazard, 177
harangue, 187
harry, 187
heterogeneous, 111
hew, 73
hoodwink, 53
horde, 111
humane, 149

illegible, 25
illustrious, 149
immunity, 101
impair, 129
impel, 111
impenitent, 187
impoverished, 73
improvise, 177
inanimate, 53
incessant, 73
incinerate, 53
incite, 177
incorrigible, 63
incredulous, 112
influx, 177
inscribe, 112
institute, 101
interim, 90
intolerable, 149
intrepid, 53
intricate, 73
inundate, 91
invincible, 129
irate, 35
irreverent, 149

jeer, 25

knave, 187

laborious, 149
languid, 129
larceny, 53
latent, 63
legion, 187
liability, 101
liberality, 188
lithe, 149
lofty, 167
lucid, 73
lucrative, 25

malign, 91
maltreat, 150
marauder, 35
meander, 91
mediocre, 26

INDEX